Copyright © 2017-2021 JANUS Research Group, Inc.
600 Ponder Place Dr
Evans, GA 30809
(706) 364-9100

All rights reserved. No part of this publication may be reproduced, distributed, or transmitted in any form or by any means, including photocopying, recording, or other electronic or mechanical methods, without the prior written permission of the publisher.

Linux is the registered trademark of Linus Torvalds in the U.S. and other countries.
Red Hat, **Red Hat Enterprise Linux**, **Enterprise Linux**, **Ansible**, **CentOS**, and **Fedora** are trademarks or registered trademarks of Red Hat, Inc. or its subsidiaries in the United States and other countries.
Oracle, **Oracle Linux**, and **Unbreakable Enterprise Kernel** are trademarks of Oracle and/or its affiliates
UNIX is a registered trademark of The Open Group.
The **Filesystem Hierarchy Standard** is a Copyright of The Filesystem Hierarchy Standard Group, and Daniel Quinlan, Paul Russel, and Christopher Yeoh. http://www.pathname.com/fhs/pub/fhs-2.3.html
The **OpenSCAP scap-security-guide** is an unlicensed, public domain work of the US Government.
AWS, **Amazon Linux**, **Amazon Machine Image (AMI)**, and **EC2** are trademarks of Amazon.

XFS is a trademark of Silicon Graphics International Corp. or its subsidiaries in the United States and/or other countries.

The systemd flow charts are from https://www.freedesktop.org and no assertion of ownership or creation is made.

Any other trade names or trademarks are the property of their respective owners. Neither the authors or JANUS Research Group assert any claim, affiliation, or endorsement with or by any of the above corporations or their intellectual property.

version 2.0 – March 2021

We want to thank all those who helped us make this book possible:
- Janus Research Group who employed us while we wrote
- The Army National Guard Professional Education Center Information Technology Training Center who gave us a reason to write the book in the first place
- Our friends and co-workers who put up with us
- Our wives, who encouraged us to keep writing
- The staff of Reno's Argenta Café, who fed us

This book is designed to be used either as a self-study guide, or as a basis for classroom instruction. If you use it to teach a class, please let us know. All errors and mis-edits are entirely our own; if you have suggestions or corrections, don't hesitate to contact us.

John Timaeus &

Russell C. Overton

academy@janusresearch.com

Module 1: Introduction 1

    Logging In 3
    Users and Groups 4
    Paths 5
    Standard Directories 7
    Command Syntax 8
    Typing at bash 9
    Redirection 10
    --help, man, info 14

Module 2: Files and Directories 15

    ls 15
    file, stat 16
    which 18
    whereis 18
    locate 19
    find 20
    cat, head, tail 25
    touch, echo 26
    mkdir, rm, rmdir 26
    cp, mv 27
    sort, wc, tr, uniq, diff 28

Module 3: vi 31

    Basics 32
    Cool Tricks, Pretty Colors 33
    Config files 38

Module 4: Users and Groups 39

    /etc/group, passwd, shadow 39
    useradd 40
    /etc/default/useradd, /etc/login.defs 40
    passwd, usermod, userdel 41
    vipw, vigr 42
    groupadd, groupmod, groupdel, groupmems, id 42
    su, wheel 42
    sudo, sudoers 43
    who, w, lastlog, last, lastb 44
    loginctl 44

Module 5: Permissions and Ownership 45
Ownership 45
Permissions 45
chmod 46
Special Purpose Access Modes 47
umask 48
Access Control Lists 48

Module 6: Regular Expressions 50
grep 50
Character Sets 51
Anchors 53
Modifiers and Alternation 54
Backreferences 55
Another Look 57
sed 58
awk 62
awk substitutions 63
awk programs 64

Module 7: Booting 66
Boot Sequence 66
grub.cfg, grub2-mkconfig, grub2-setpassword 67
Recovering the root Password 69
systemd 70
systemctl 72
Unit Files 73

Module 8: Processes and Services 76
ps, pgrep, kill, pkill, killall 76
jobs, bg, fg, disown 78
top, uptime, free, vmstat 79
nice, renice, ionice, taskset 81
cgroups: slices, scopes, services 82
limits.conf, ulimit 86

Module 9: Filesystems 87
Inodes 87
ln 90
parted, mkfs 92
mount, umount 96
systemd.mount 98
systemd.automount 101
/etc/fstab 102
swap 103
systemd.swap 104
Logical Volume Manager (LVM) 105
LUKS 109
LUKS on a Device 109
LUKS and LVM 111
Keys 112

Module 10: Scheduling Events 113
systemd.timer 114
systemd.time 115
systemd-run .timers 117
anacron 117
cron, crontab 118
at, atq, atrm, batch, atd 119

Module 11: Networking 120
nmcli, nmtui, ip 120
hostnamectl 122
nsswitch.conf, /etc/hosts 123
firewall-cmd 124
network tools 126

Module 12: Remote Access 129
ssh 129
ssh-keygen, ssh-copy-id 130
scp 130
sftp 131
cockpit 131
vsftpd, lftp 132
httpd, apachectl 133
curl, wget, lynx, elinks 134
NFS 135
x2go 138
vnc 139

Module 13: SELinux 141
- Enforcement 142
- User Classes and Roles 144
- Types and Policy 146
- Security Context Labels 149
- Booleans 152
- audit2allow 155
- Moving and Copying Files 156

Module 14: Logs 157
- rsyslogd, logrotate 157
- journald, journalctl 160
- auditd 162
- audisp-remote 164
- aureport, ausearch 165
- timedatectl, chronyc, hwclock 166

Module 15: Installing Software 167
- yum 167
- packagekit 170
- rpm 170
- Linux Installation 172

Module 16: Kernel Modules and Parameters 174
- lsmod, modinfo, modprobe 174
- Blacklisting 177
- sysctl 178

Module 17: Backups 179
- tar 179
- rsync 180
- dd 181
- ReaR 182

Module 18: Security 183
- aide 185
- oscap, scap-workbench 186
- ansible 187
- clam 188
- Securing the network stack 189

Command Summary 191
Labs 210

Module 1: Introduction

The Linux operating system is defined by the use of the Linux kernel, the core process. There are hundreds of variations of Linux – known as distributions or distros – that all share the same basic kernel. The kernel is the core of the operating system. It is tasked with directly manipulating hardware such as processors, memory, and disks.

The kernel **is** the operating system, and will be loaded at boot time into a special, protected area of system memory. Users do not interact directly with the kernel. User programs (binaries) run in separate 'user space memory', and interact with the kernel through system calls.

Linux in one form or another is present in everything from High Performance Computing clusters to cell phones. It is Unix-like but is not UNIX™. If you have used other Unix-like systems you will see many similarities, but be aware that many things, from the initialization process to the filesystem hierarchy, are different.

We will be focusing on operating systems from the Red Hat Enterprise Linux (RHEL) family. The primary distributions in this family are:

- **Fedora** – the free version of Red Hat. Owned by the Red Hat corporation, but not supported by them. It has a very quick release cycle and is often more cutting edge than the other versions. Each release is maintained for only a year or two. It is generally considered a good distro for desktop usage.
- **CentOS** – another free version. A direct recompilation of the RHEL source code (which they must release under the terms of the GNU license). Some small options may be changed during the compilation, and the Red Hat branding is removed. Support is provided by the community, rather than subscription.
  There are now two versions of CentOS: CentOS Linux and CentOS Stream. Stream is a more forward-leaning version for those who wish to help develop the next version. For purposes of this book, you should use CentOS Linux, not Stream.
- **Red Hat Enterprise Linux** – the not-free version. Owned and supported by the Red Hat corporation. You do have to pay for the support. The maintenance life cycle is guaranteed to be at least 10 years from release, and the release cycle is slower as the point of RHEL is stability. RHEL and Oracle Linux are currently the only EL distros approved for use on systems requiring Secure Technical Implementation Guide (STIG) compliance.
- **Oracle Linux** – a recompilation of RHEL with an option to use an alternative kernel, optimized for reliabiltiy and compatability with Oracle software.
- **Amazon Linux** – offered as an Amazon Machine Image on their EC2 cloud offering and based on the RHEL upstream offering. It is optimized for performance in the Amazon Cloud. The version numbering is different (current version is 2.3), and updates tend to lead the main RHEL release.

From this point on we will simply refer to the operating system as Enterprise Linux (EL). There are currently three major versions of EL under support:

- EL6, released 2010. To be retired November 2020; extended support ends 2024.
- EL7, released 2014 and supported until 2024.
- EL8, released 2019 and supported until 2029.

The labs and exercises for this book are valid for Red Hat Enterprise Linux and CentOS Linux, versions 7 and 8. There will be some slight deviation when using Amazon Linux. In particular, networking and firewall configuration is still performed as it was in EL6. Some software packages, such as `cockpit` will also not be available.

While many of the techniques taught are valid for EL6 and for other families of Linux, there are substantial differences. The introduction of `systemd` introduced in EL7 changed the way the system is administered dramatically. EL8 was, from an administrator's viewpoint, a much more incremental release. On the few occasions of divergence between EL7 and EL8, it will be noted in the book. For those still on EL6, we recommend our previous book.

There is a possible, but not recommended, direct upgrade path from EL6 to EL7. Reports of problems outnumber the reports of success. Instead, it is better to perform a fresh installation and migrate the data and running loads. There is a direct upgrade path from EL7 to EL8 using the `leapp` utility. You can determine your version of EL with the following command:

`# cat /etc/redhat-release` or `# cat /etc/os-release`

This book was written for administrators of systems owned by or operated on behalf of the US Government, particularly DoD systems. These systems are required to adhere to the DISA STIG, the security standard use for compliance in the DoD.

While we have tried to incorporate as much of the relevant portions of the DISA STIG and general best practices as possible, this book should not be considered authoratitive on regulations, practices, or procedures. The applicable regulations as interpreted by your security officers should be consulted instead.

For those outside the US Government, the STIG is not required. However it makes a good starting point for securing systems. Most of the techniques and standards referenced in this book also apply to the following security standards:

- Australian Cyber Security Center Essential Eight
- US Government Commercial Cloud Services (C2S)
- Criminal Jusitice Information Services (FBI-CJIS)
- ANSSI (France)
- Health Insurance Portability and Accountability (HIPPA)
- PCI-DSS (Payment Card Industry)
- Red Hat Corporate Profile for Certified Cloud Providers
- National Institute of Standards and Technology (NIST) Checklists, including CNSSI 1253, NIST 800-171 & 800-53, USGCB, and DISA's Security Requirements Guide
- NIAP (NSA & NIST) Protection Profile for General Purpose Operating Systems (OSPP)

The majority of these are either subsets of, or closely related to the STIG. If any of these standards apply to your environment, this book will build the skills needed to implement them. For more information on the standards consult the Security Guides at https://static.open-scap.org/ and at the source documentation referenced there.

The best way to learn is by doing. Have a working installation or two of EL ready to hand when reading this book. Customization scripts and the lab guide are available at https://github.com/janustechacademy/EL7

Before we dive into the details of the operating system we first need an acclimatization to the environment. While there is an optional graphical user interface (GUI) for EL, most servers will not have the GUI installed. Even if it is installed, the chances of it being missing or broken increase in direct proportion to the lateness of the hour, the criticality current task, and the presence of the boss looking over your shoulder. Thus, this book is based on the command line. While it isn't as slick as the GUI, it is dependable.

Logging In

The first thing you must do is log in. To do this you will need an account. All Unix-like systems have a default account called `root`. The root user is a built-in superuser, with full permission for all commands and files on the system. Under normal circumstances you should never log in as root. Instead you should log in as an unprivileged user then elevate your privilege level as needed. Initially you will need to log in as root. We will create other users and learn to switch between them later. Be aware that most security and sanity checks don't apply to root – issuing the wrong command can have catastrophic effects. Use caution.

Once logged in you will be in a command line shell called `bash` (Bourne Again SHell). You should have a prompt that looks like this:
`[root@localhost ~]#`

This prompt presents the username, the hostname, and the directory currently occupied by the user (the Present Working Directory, which can be displayed with the command `pwd`). The tilde ~ is a shorthand way of saying 'my home directory'. The prompt ends with a pound sign (or hash) #, this is a reminder that you are logged in as root. A normal, unprivileged, non-root prompt ends in a dollar sign like this:
`[user@localhost ~]$`

To end a bash session: # `exit` or press `CTL-d` at a blank prompt.

Users and Groups

User accounts are assigned to people and services who will interact with the Linux environment. For security, each user should have a unique account and only login using those credentials. By default, these accounts will exist in a system-local database, but they may be stored on a centralized authorization server (LDAP or Active Directory for example). When a user account is created, a few basic pieces of information will be recorded. These are:

- A **username** – also called "login name", "logname", or "login". It is the unique account name which identifies a user to the system during login. It might be as simple as a lowercase alphabetic string (`jsmith`), or it might incorporate other characters (`john.smith34`). As with most things on Linux, usernames are case sensitive.
- A **User ID** – abbreviated as UID, the User ID is a number that is used internally by the system for the purposes of identification. The root account, for example, always has a UID of zero 0. On most modern Linux systems, User IDs will be automatically assigned at the time of account creation, and will begin at 1000.
- A **password** – a password is a secret character string or phrase known only to an individual user, and are designed to provide a form of proof of identity. Various rules can be implemented to control the complexity, security, and longevity of passwords. Although accounts can be created without passwords (this is the default behavior), users cannot login without a password or similar mechanism. Accounts without passwords are used for other purposes, such as starting services or owning files.
- A **primary group** – user accounts can be associated together into groups based on factors such as shared function (`sales`, `accounting`) or by location (`office`, `headquarters`), or any other factors an administrator feels are appropriate. As with users, groups also have unique numerical identifiers, the Group ID, or GID.
    - Users will always be assigned to at least one group at account creation – a **primary group** which is created for them. In EL the default primary group for a user will be a unique group, with the same name as the username. Membership in other secondary groups is also possible.
    - Groups are an additional point to which permissions may be assigned. Without groups, we would have difficulty controlling which individuals should have access to files and resources on the system. Imagine trying to control access to every file, process, and device on a system using only user names. The access controls would quickly become impossible to maintain. Groups provide a way to identify sets of users with similar needs and access requirements. With them we can greatly simplify administration.
- A **home directory** – a directory designed to hold user specific files. Among these, are the configuration files which control certain parts of a user's environment such as `.bash_profile` and `.bashrc`. It is the directory into which a user will be deposited on login. By default users have full control over their home directory and its contents.
- A **shell** – we will cover shell – bash – more thoroughly in a moment. For now, understand that these are the programs that receive input from users and allow them to manipulate the operating system. The simplest way to explain a shell is to say that it is "the thing that you are typing at."

Paths

Enterprise Linux is, at its heart, a command line driven operating system. This means that, from a user's perspective, the operating system looks something like this:

```
# ls /var
account  cache   db     ftp       gopher  lib   lock  mail  opt      run    tmp   adm
crash    empty   games  kerberos  local   log   nis   preserve      spool  yp
```

For new users, this sort of environment can be difficult to comprehend. The output above is showing us a list (`ls`) of the contents of the directory `/var`. Directories are:

- A series of named containers
- Organized hierarchically
- Capable of containing files and other directories

Administrators are free to create any directory structure they like, but there are certain directories which will that will be present by default. We begin with the root directory (also called slash) indicated by a forward slash /. The root directory is similar in function to the root of a tree. All other directories grow up and out from the root.

```
/
  /var
    /var/log
      /var/log/audit
    /var/run
  /etc
    /etc/audit
```

When other filesystems are mounted, they will be mounted to a directory in the root filesystem. To describe the location of any file, we use the path to it, starting from slash /.

The path to any file can be described either from slash (the "absolute path") or from the present working directory (the "relative path"). Using the directory layout above, the path to the subdirectory `audit` under `/var` can be described as:

- Absolute path from anywhere: `/var/log/audit`
- Relative path from `/var`: `log/audit`
- Relative path from `/var/log`: `audit`

Note that the two relative paths in the examples above were **not** preceded by /. That is because a slash at the start of a path indicates that the path begins at the root directory. Consider the following command string using `cd` to change directories:

```
# cd audit
```

The effects of this command depend entirely on the user's Present Working Directory (`PWD`). The above command could:

- Go to `/etc/audit` (if `PWD` = `/etc`)
- Go to `/var/log/audit` (if `PWD` = `/var/log`)
- Fail (if `PWD` does not contain a directory called `audit`)

Prepending the slash would make the path look like this: **/audit**. This tells the system to start looking in slash **/** for a directory called **audit**. We can see in the earlier structure diagram that such a directory does not exist. This path is an absolute path, in that it begins from root, but the directions are wrong. This is cd with an absolute path:
cd /var/log/audit

This path will always take us to the **audit** directory in **/var/log**, regardless of **PWD**.

There are three special statements for directory manipulation:
- **.**   one dot, this directory.
- **..** two dots, the directory above this one (the parent).
- **~**   tilde, the user's home directory

We can better demonstrate this with a quick example. The **pwd** command will return a user's present working directory. Let's make use of it to explore the concept further:
pwd
/var/log/audit

cd .
pwd
/var/log/audit

Here we have invoked **cd** in order to change directories to **.** Since **.** is a surrogate for wherever we are, the **cd** command simply succeeds in putting us where we already were.
cd ..
pwd
/var/log/

cd ../../
pwd
/

Here we used **cd ..** to move from **/var/log/audit** to the parent directory **/var/log**. We then used **cd ../../** to move from **/var/log** up *two* directories to **/**.

Standard Directories

The Filesystem Hierarchy Standard (FHS) defines a standard set of names, locations, and permissions for many file types and directories in Unix and Linux. This provides a reasonably consistent environment across distributions. One would expect, for example, to find configuration files in **/etc** and device files in **/dev** regardless of distribution. The FHS lists the following top level directories:

- **/bin** – Essential command binaries.
- **/boot** – Static files of the boot loader
- **/dev** – Device files
- **/etc** – Host-specific system configuration
- **/lib** – Essential shared libraries and kernel modules
- **/media** – Mount point for removeable media
- **/mnt** – Mount point for mounting a filesystem temporarily
- **/opt** – Add-on application software packages
- **/sbin** – Essential system binaries
- **/srv** – Data for services provided by this system
- **/tmp** – Temporary files
- **/usr** – Secondary hierarchy
- **/var** – Variable data

Beginning with EL8 **/bin**, **/lib**, **/lib64**, and **/sbin** are mapped via a symbolic link to **/usr/bin**, **/usr/lib**, etcetera. This is a first step toward simplifying the hierarchy by eliminating duplication.

There are several special directories. These do not contain files, but they expose kernel level information to the user as if they did. These include:

- **/proc** – Contains running processes
- **/cgroup** – Control groups which limit resource usage
- **/dev** – Physical and virtual devices

Command Syntax

The command line environment requires operators to issue syntactically correct instructions. Linux is unforgiving of improperly formatted instructions, generally resulting in a failure to perform. More worrisome is the when a badly formatted command succeeds, doing unintended things. If you find a command is failing, check the command syntax. Often the failure results from simple misplacement of elements.

Command strings in Linux can be broken into three major parts:

- **Command** – The program we are calling
- **Options** – Modifiers to the default behavior of the called program. They take several forms:
    - Unix style switches: `-ef`, `-la`, `-v`
    - GNU style options: `--line-numbers`, `--name`
    - Sub-commands: `install`, `reload`, `mask`
- **Argument** – The target of the command

These will be separated by whitespace. In other words, when the shell sees a space in a command string, it assumes that we have finished with one statement and moved on to another.

If we call the `ls` command without options or arguments, it does this:
```
# ls
bin  dev  lab  lib64  misc  opt  sbin  sys  var  boot  etc  lab.tar
```
Here `ls` has returned a listing of files in the user's present working directory. We can alter the behavior of commands by supplying options. Using `-l` (long listing) and `-a` (all files):
```
# ls -l -a
total 136
dr-xr-xr-x.  28 root root  4096 Nov  7 14:58 .
dr-xr-xr-x.  28 root root  4096 Nov  7 14:58 ..
-rw-r--r--.   1 root root     0 Nov  7 08:21 .autofsck
dr-xr-xr-x.   2 root root  4096 Nov  7 14:58 bin
dr-xr-xr-x.   5 root root  4096 Sep  7 09:58 boot
drwxr-xr-x.   2 root root  4096 Oct  3 23:52 cgroup
drwx------.   3 root root  4096 Sep  7 08:47 .dbus
```
Notice that the format of the listing changed, and that new files are listed (specifically, filenames starting with a dot **.** are hidden from casual viewing).

We can also supply an argument, or target, for the command:
```
# ls -la /home
total 36
drwxr-xr-x.  6 root   root    4096 Sep 13 10:39 .
dr-xr-xr-x. 28 root   root    4096 Nov  7 14:58 ..
drwxrwxr-x.  5 grace  grace   4096 Nov  7 14:35 grace
drwx------.  4 harry  harry   4096 Sep 13 14:14 harry
drwx------.  2 root   root   16384 Sep  7 08:07 lost+found
```
Above, we instructed `ls` to retrieve a listing for the `/home` directory, even though we were not presently in that directory. We also combined two options into a single set, rather than specifying each individually. This is not always possible, but where it is, it simplifies command strings significantly.

Some commands which will take sub-commands, which may be mixed with other style options. For instance the command to control software packages, **yum**:

- # **yum provides */nslookup** – ask which package provides **nslookup**
- # **yum install bind-utils** – install the **bind-utils** package
- # **yum -y -q upgrade --security** – perform security upgrades, quitely, assume yes is the answer for confirmation questions

Typing at bash

There are lots of tricks you can do at the bash prompt. Many are covered later; there are a few you should know about now.

Capitalization matters: **File**, **file**, **FILE**, and **filE** are four separate things as far as Linux is concerned. As a general convention all lower case is preferred.

You can use the up and down arrows to access previous commands. You can edit the command by simply arrowing back to the appropriate place and typing.

You can jump to the beginning or end of a line by hitting **CTL-a** or **CTL-e**.

You can stop a running command by typing **CTL-c**. This will also abort the current input line.

Two exclamation points (bangs) **!!** will reissue the last command.

A bang dollar **!$** will reissue the last argument of the last command, usually the target. Below we ran a **ping** to test connectivity to a server, terminated the ping with **CTL-c**, then used **ssh** to establish a terminal session to the remote server.

```
# ping 192.168.1.155
PING 192.168.1.155 (192.168.1.155) 56(84) bytes of data.
64 bytes from 192.168.1.155: icmp_seq=1 ttl=64 time=0.964 ms
64 bytes from 192.168.1.155: icmp_seq=2 ttl=64 time=0.205 ms

# ssh !$
ssh 192.168.1.155
FIPS mode initialized
```

A reverse search of the history file can be executed using **CTL-r** and typing part of a previous command:
(reverse-i-search)`**pi**': ping 192.168.1.155

The command **history** which will display current shell's history with numbers prepended. You can reissue any command in the history by simply typing an exclamation point (called a bang **!**) followed by the number (no spaces). Note that each bash session will carry its own history in memory.

Enterprise Linux versions 7 & 8

Each user has a history file, `~/.bash_history`. By default this is only written to on graceful logout. This means that each shell will have a separate history, and that history will be lost if a session terminates unexpectedly. To make the history file update in real time add the following lines to the user's `.bashrc`:

```
##ensure that the history file appends not overwrites
shopt -s histappend
##append the history each time before getting a prompt
PROMPT_COMMAND="history -a;$PROMPT_COMMAND"
```

If you find yourself executing the same command string often, you can create an **alias** for it:
`# alias connect='ssh -i /home/bob/.ssh/7-key.pub bob@192.168.123.7'`

This allows you to simply type `# connect` rather than the long `ssh` string. Currently assigned aliases can be displayed with `# alias`. To make the alias persistent, add the command to `.bashrc` in your home directory. This file is read and executed on every login. To remove an alias for the duration of the current session `# unalias`

Redirection

By default most commands will send all output to the console. Often a command produces more output than will fit on a single screen, or produces output which we want to use as input to another command or which we want to save to a file. For this we use **redirection**.

The pipe – the vertical bar | – takes the output of one command and uses it as the input of the next. For instance, listing the contents of the `/etc/` directory using
`# ls -la /etc/` produces more text than a screen hold.

The command `less` allows us to view text one page at a time. Placed on the same line and joined by a pipe, the output of `ls` is piped into less: `# ls /etc/ | less`

Another common use of the pipe is "piping through **grep**". **grep** is a command which can find lines containing a regular expression — much more on that later. For now let's just look at the output of the `ip a` command, which will show our IP configuration. If we only wanted to see the lines containing `inet` (where the actual addresses are displayed), we could
`# ip a | grep inet`

If we wish to save the output of a command to a file we can redirect it using greater than >. This will place the output into a file, creating it if it doesn't exist, and **overwriting** any contents if it does. For instance, if you wanted to save the output of the `ip a` command to a file, you would
`# ip a > file`

You could then view the contents of that file using
`# less file`   or
`# cat file`   which will simply display it to the screen.

Note that `bash` opens all files and commands on a line at the beginning of command execution, thus `# cat file > file` opens and empties `file` before beginning to `cat file`. The result is `file` will be empty.

To **append** use two greater thans **>>** . To add the output from `ip route` to a file:
`# ip route >> file` Had you used a single greater here, it would have overwritten the file.

Using a single greater with no command before it:
`# > file` erases the contents of the file by overwriting it with the output of nothing. This is often used to empty a file (such as a log), without changing permissions or ownership.

You can string multiple redirections together to produce the desired results. To create a file containing the output of `ip a` and `ip route`, but only the lines containing `192` addresses in it:
`# ip a | grep 192 > file ; ip route | grep 192 >> file`
In this example the semicolon **;** separates two commands, which are run as if they were on separate lines.

If a line is too long for the display you can either simply continue typing and let it autowrap, or you can use the backslash **** followed by **RETURN**, which will extend the command input.

We might also wish to create a file to hold the output of a command or script. In these cases, we would typically use command line redirectors like **>** or **>>**. This will redirect all output which would have gone to **STDOUT**, which may not be desired. To send output to both **STDOUT** and a specified file, use **tee**. The **tee** command sends output to both **STDOUT** and to a file. It can be called from a script (for simple logging) or directly from the command line when we want to both view the output of a command and save a copy of it for later.
```
# ls /usr | column | tee outfile
bin       games      lib       libexec  sbin      src
etc       include    lib64     local    share     tmp

# cat outfile
bin       games      lib       libexec  sbin      src
etc       include    lib64     local    share     tmp
```

Unix style systems have a several special virtual files:
- **/dev/null** – A black hole, the bit bucket, a place where data goes and doesn't come back.
    - Unwanted output can be redirected here.
    - It can also be used as a source of "nothingness":
      # cat /dev/null > file1 will empty `file1`.
- **/dev/random** and **/dev/urandom** – raw sources of randomness.
- **/dev/zero** – an unending source of zeros.
    - Used to make an empty file.
    - These are binary zeros, they will not display as text.

In `bash` there are three "standard streams". These are the data streams flowing into and out of a command. Each has a designated number known as a file descriptor:
- **STDIN** – 0 The input to a command, either from the terminal, or a pipe
- **STDOUT** – 1 The result of a command
- **STDERR** – 2 Any error messages from a command

Under most conditions **STDOUT** is either displayed on a terminal, or passed to a redirection. **STDERR** is by default displayed on the terminal which invoked the command, not passed to a redirection. The standard streams can be redirected using the appropriate numeric descriptor:
- **# command 2> errorfile** – redirects **STDERR** of **command** to **errorfile**
- **# command 2> /dev/null** – sends **STDERR** of **command** to the void
- **# command 0< file** – use contents of file as **STDIN** to command
    - **# command < file** is equivalent
- **# command &> file** – redirects the **STDERR** of command to **STDOUT**, which will then be passed into the redirection to **file**.
    - **# command > file 2>&1** is equivalent

You can also make the execution of a second command dependent on the success of the first:
 # cmd1 && cmd2 – will run `cmd2` only if `cmd1` is successful
 # cmd1 || cmd2 – will only run `cmd2` if `cmd1` exits with an error code

All processes (and a command is just a process) exit with a code. By convention a code of **0** indicates success with no error, and all others indicate an error. The last exit code is stored in a special variable **$?** which is displayed using **# echo $?**

All processes have a Process ID (PID). Current running processes can be displayed using the **ps** command. The current shell's PID is stored in the special variable **$$**.

Many commands will take "glob" characters. These are special characters used for pattern matching. They follow the general pattern of regular expressions covered later. The most basic globbing patterns are the asterisk or splat * which matches anything; and the question mark ? which matches a single character. So:
`ls /etc/*.conf` – lists everything from /etc/ that ends in .conf
`ls /etc/*d*.conf` – everything that has a d followed and ends in .conf
`ls /etc/?d*.conf` – everything that has a d in the second position and ends in .conf

Command output can also be used as arguments to another command. This is done by piping the output of one command into **xargs** which will turn its input into the arguments for the next command. The **wc -l** command counts lines. If we do the following:
`ls /etc/?d*.conf` – returns the names of four files
/etc/idmapd.conf   /etc/kdump.conf   /etc/ld.so.conf   /etc/oddjobd.conf

`ls /etc/?d*.conf | wc -l` – counts the number of files returned
4

`ls /etc/?d*.conf | xargs wc -l` – counts the lines in each file returned
 137 /etc/idmapd.conf
 163 /etc/kdump.conf
   1 /etc/ld.so.conf
 131 /etc/oddjobd.conf
 432 total

Another way to accomplish the same thing is by using command expansion. To do this a command is placed in parenthesis, preceded by a dollar sign:
`wc -l $(ls /etc/?d*.conf)`

A command can be run in the background by appending an ampersand:
`tar -czpf backup.tar /etc/ &`

There are times you just want to get a good clean terminal to type at. This can be done with **CTL-l** or by issuing the **clear** command. It can also happen that you confuse your terminal by trying to print unprintable characters. This usually is the result of trying to display a binary encoded file, or having a program crash while updating the screen. To get everything straightened out
`reset`

Some commands will expect input until encountering and end-of-file (EOF) marker. This can be provided with **CTL-d**. Handing an **CTL-d** directly to a shell will end that shell.

Enterprise Linux versions 7 & 8

--help, man, info

If you know the name of a command and don't quite remember what goes after it, try tab completion. Sometimes that doesn't get the job done though so put `--help` after the command. In many cases this will bring up a brief help page, giving you the needed clues.

If you need more detail about a command you can use the built-in manual pages:
`# man` *command-name*

The page reader for `man` is `less`. Use `q` to exit the man page reader. To search within a man page, use `/`*pattern* (forward search), `n` (next pattern), `N` (previous pattern), and `?`*pattern* (reverse search). To go to the top or bottom use `gg` and `G`.

Many programs will also have separate man pages for configuration files or additional documentation in `/usr/share/doc/` or on the web. These are usually mentioned at the very bottom of the primary man page.

If you don't know what the name of the command you need is, you can try
`# man -k` *pattern*

The man page system (and the `-k` search feature) depends on a small built-in database. Under most circumstances this should be automatically updated as you install/remove software. Occasionally though, you will find that it did not update and a man page that should be available is not. If this occurs, you can update the database by running `# mandb`.

In EL7 `mandb` runs daily by default. In EL8, it does not. If you wish it to run daily, install `man-db-cron`.

The man pages are divided into numbered sections based on the type of information provided. For a full listing `# man man`. The section is specified by using the number as an option to `man`:

- `# man 1 time` – a command that times another command
- `# man 2 time` – a system call used by programmers to get the current time
- `# man 3 time` – a series of functions for use in the awk programming language
- `# man 7 time` – a general discussion of how Linux views time

Some commands also will have a more advanced style of manual page which incorporates hyperlinks and colors. These can be accessed using the `info` command. If an `info` style page is not available, `info` will display the standard man page. Of particular use is
`# info coreutils`.

For more info, `# info info`.

Module 2: Files and Directories

ls

To list the files in a directory, use the `ls` command. Called without options or arguments, `ls` lists the contents of the user's present working directory. It will only display the names of files and subdirectories, and will not list hidden files (files whose name begins with a dot **.**) when called this way. This is the listing of the directory **/test**.

```
# ls /test
binary   directory   file   link   source
```

There is no information available in this view beyond file names. Let's add some options:

```
# ls -la
total 56
drwxr-xr-x.  3 root root       90 Jun  2 08:32
dr-xr-xr-x. 24 root root     4096 May 19 14:11 .
-rwxr-xr-x.  1 root root    41504 Jun  2 08:25 binary
drwxr-xr-x.  2 root users       6 Jun  2 08:23 directory
-rw-r--r--.  1 root root       58 May 17 09:31 file
-rw-r--r--.  1 root root        0 Jun  2 08:32 .hidden
lrwxrwxrwx.  1 root root       10 Jun  2 08:31 link -> /test/file
-rw-r--r--.  1 root root     2724 Jun  2 08:27 source
```

Here we supplied two options to the `ls` command: `-l` and `-a`. The `-l` option instructs the command to display a **long** listing of directory contents. The `-a` option causes **all** files to be displayed (including hidden files such as **.hidden** in the output). Together, these options provide the results we see above.

As we will be using the `ls` command very frequently, let's take a moment to familiarize ourselves with the output.

<u>**drwxr-xr-x.**</u>   2 root root   6 Jun 2 08:23 directory

The underlined part is the permissions string. The first character indicates the type of file we're dealing with. Here it is **d**, for directory. We might also see an **l** (link), a dash - (regular file), or other characters intended to provide hints about the nature of a given listing.

The rest of the string shows permissions triplets for a file's owner (user), the owning group (group), and anyone else (others). In this string, **r** indicates Read, **w** is Write, and **x** is eXecute. We could read the permissions string above as:

- User: Read, Write, Execute
- Group: Read and Execute (but not Write)
- Others: Read and Execute (but not Write)

The dot **.** on the end of the permission string indicates that there is currently no Access Control List (ACL) associated with this file. If an ACL had been associated with this file, we would see a plus sign **+** rather than a dot. We'll discuss permissions (including ACLs) in detail later.

```
drwxr-xr-x.  2 root users     6 Jun  2 08:23 directory
```

The next field (**2**) is the number of **links** to a file. Links are entries in a directory that point to a file. These come in two flavors: **hard** and **symbolic**. Hard links point directly to a file's underlying inode (a filesystem data structure which contains information about the file and its pointers to the data blocks containing the content of the file), while symbolic links are like hyperlinks, and simply contain a path to another file. The number increments as the number of hard links to a file increases and decrements as links are removed.

After that, two fields indicate the owning user and group. In this case, the owner is the `root` user, and the owning group is the `users` group.

The last three fields represent the size of the file (**6** bytes), the date and time the file was last modified, and the name of the entry: `directory`.

file, stat

Going back to the output above:
```
# ls -la
total 56
drwxr-xr-x.  3 root root      90 Jun  2 08:32
dr-xr-xr-x. 24 root root    4096 May 19 14:11 .
-rwxr-xr-x.  1 root root   41504 Jun  2 08:25 binary
drwxr-xr-x.  2 root users      6 Jun  2 08:23 directory
-rw-r--r--.  1 root root      58 May 17 09:31 file
-rw-r--r--.  1 root root       0 Jun  2 08:32 .hidden
lrwxrwxrwx.  1 root root      10 Jun  2 08:31 link -> /test/file
-rw-r--r--.  1 root root    2724 Jun  2 08:27 source
```

Above each object is named to reflect its nature (`file` is a file, `directory` is a directory). In reality filenames do not control content type. Below we have another directory listing:
```
# ls /usr/lib/udev
accelerometer      mtd_probe         tascam_fw
ata_id             mtp-probe         udev-add-printer
cdrom_id           rename_device     udev-configure-printer
```

Those names are not especially revealing. To find out more about them, we use `file`. The `file` command attempts to determine the nature of a file. It runs three sets of tests against the file: filesystem tests, magic tests, and language tests.

Filesystem tests examine the results of `stat`. The `stat` command reports detailed information about files or filesystems. When called without options against a file, it returns useful information such as a file's type, size, reference inode, timestamps, access rights, and more.

Executing `ls` in the /test directory shows a file called `link`.
```
# ls
binary    directory    file    link    source
```

Running **file** against **link** gives us some interesting results:
```
# file link
link: symbolic link to '/test/file'
```
```
# stat link
  File: `link' -> `/test/file'
  Size: 10            Blocks: 0          IO Block: 4096    symbolic link
Device: fd00h/64768d  Inode: 34218811    Links: 1
Access: (0777/lrwxrwxrwx)  Uid: (    0/    root)   Gid: (    0/    root)
<truncated>
```

When we called **stat** against **link** it returned the metadata associated with that file, including the denotation of **symbolic link**. The filesystem itself could understand what type of file **link** was, and the **file** command found an answer in the first set of tests. If this set of tests fails to get a satisfactory result, the **file** command will attempt identification through magic database files. Trying the same thing with **binary**:

```
# file binary
binary: ELF 64-bit LSB executable, x86-64, version 1 (SYSV),
dynamically linked (uses shared libs), for GNU/Linux 2.6.32,
BuildID[sha1]=bb794ad0b7a9b70f6bb8d757d4423c2a374dabcf, stripped
```

```
# stat binary
  File: `binary'
  Size: 41504         Blocks: 88         IO Block: 4096    regular file
Device: fd00h/64768d  Inode: 27204150    Links: 1
<truncated>
```

Above, **file** successfully identified **binary** as an **ELF 64-bit LSB executable binary**. That is to say a program that can be run. However, **stat** indicates a **regular file** – the filesystem tests did not identify this file. In this case, the magic files were consulted, specific byte patterns were matched in the file's data blocks, and an identification was made.

If both tests had failed, **file** would have attempted to determine if the target file was a text file containing character sequences from a known language.

which

There are many ways to locate files in Linux. The **which** command will attempt to locate the first instance of a named command in a user's **PATH**. The **PATH** environment variable contains a series of directories, separated by colons :, through which the shell will search to find a command. To display the contents of **PATH**:
```
# echo $PATH
/usr/local/sbin:/usr/local/bin:/usr/sbin:/usr/bin:/root/bin
# which cat
/usr/bin/cat
```

Here, which searched sequentially for cat in /usr/local/sbin, /usr/local/bin, and /usr/sbin before locating cat in /usr/bin. If another copy of cat existed in /root/bin, the final directory, or anywhere else on the system; which would not have found it.

The **which** command tells us which instance of a command will be executed when called without specifying a path. If that doesn't seem important, consider this:
```
# echo $PATH
.:/usr/local/sbin:/usr/local/bin:/usr/sbin:/usr/bin:/root/bin
```

The dot at the front of the **PATH** represents the present working directory. If it is present in a user's **PATH**, it can result in unintended execution. For example, if a malicious program called ls existed in a user's present working directory, and the user then attempted to list the contents of that directory, they would inadvertently trigger the script instead.

whereis

The **whereis** command is designed to locate binary, source, and man pages for a command. **whereis** is limited when compared to other search utilities, but it does provide quick answers. It does this by searching:

- a predefined, hard-coded list of directories
- directories in a user's **PATH**
- directories defined by the **MANPATH** variable
- To see the directories to be searched and the file types expected in them:
  `# whereis -l`

Below, whereis found the cp binary in /usr/bin and two man pages in /usr/share/man:
```
# whereis cp
cp: /usr/bin/cp
/usr/share/man/man1/cp.1.gz
/usr/share/man/man1p/cp.1p.gz
```

locate

The `locate` command is a simple tool for finding files by name on your system. It uses an index database `/var/lib/mlocate.db`. This is updated by `updatedb`, which usually run daily by `anacron`. In EL8, this is not the default. We will rectify that in the module on scheduling events. If you wish to run the indexing manually as root run # `updatedb`

Using `locate` is straightforward:
```
# locate locate.me
/lab/02-files/directory/locate.me
```

Here locate returned the absolute path of the located file. There are some drawbacks to locate. The biggest is locate will always treat the supplied argument as a string pattern. It will match this string in whole or in part, regardless of where in the path the pattern occurs. For example:

```
# locate cp | head
/boot/extlinux/cpuid.c32
/boot/extlinux/cpuidtest.c32
/boot/extlinux/ifcpu.c32
/boot/extlinux/ifcpu64.c32
/boot/grub2/i386-pc/acpi.mod
/boot/grub2/i386-pc/cpio.mod
/boot/grub2/i386-pc/cpio_be.mod
/boot/grub2/i386-pc/cpuid.mod
/boot/grub2/i386-pc/lsacpi.mod
/etc/dhcp
<truncated>
```

Note that locate matched the string **cp** regardless of its location in the path. This behavior cannot be modified. To find the **cp** command using `locate`, you would need to resort to silliness like this:
```
#   locate cp | grep /cp\$
/usr/bin/cp
```

The `locate` command has its place, but for serious work `find` is a better option.

Enterprise Linux versions 7 & 8

find

find is one of the most powerful search utilities available in Linux. It can find files based on attributes such as filename, timestamp, ownership, permissions, and more. When working with find, we will typically:

- Define a search space (a place to start looking)
- Specify search criteria (filename, type, timestamps, permissions, etc)
- Optionally specify a command to run against the results

Defining a search space

If we call `find` without any options or arguments, will behave similarly to `ls -Ra`. It will list the contents of the present working directory (including hidden files), and recursively list the contents of subdirectories as well.

```
# find
.
./file
./directory
./directory/subfile
./binary
./source
./link
./.hidden
./pathfile
```

Had we been at **/**, it would have listed every file and directory on the entire system.

A directory, or series of directories, may be provided to **find** as a search space. The depth of search in those areas can be refined with the **maxdepth** and **mindepth** options. Consider the following output:

```
# find /1 -type f
./1/fileInDir1
./1/2/fileInDir2
./1/2/3/fileInDir3
./1/2/3/4/fileInDir4
./1/2/3/4/5/fileInDir5
```

Here we have a stack of directories (**1** through **5**), with a single file in each. We told **find** to look for regular files (`-type f`) in the directory **/1** and all subdirectories beneath it.

To use `mindepth` and `maxdepth` to narrow the scope from **2** to **4**:

```
# find /1 -mindepth 2 -maxdepth 4 -type f
./1/2/fileInDir2
./1/2/3/fileInDir3
./1/2/3/4/fileInDir4
```

Searching by name

Suppose we need to find a configuration file, but we're not sure of the name. We know it ends with **conf** and it starts with a **c**, but we're not sure of the capitalization.
```
# find /etc -iname "c*" -name "*.conf"
/etc/pki/ca-trust/ca-legacy.conf
/etc/abrt/plugins/CCpp.conf
/etc/security/chroot.conf
/etc/openldap/check_password.conf
```
Let's break it down.

- `find` – start finding
- `/etc` – start here and recurse subdirectories
- `-iname` – search by name, ignore case
- `c*` – filename starts with **c**. asterisk translates to "anything or nothing"
- `-name` – search by name, respect case
- `*.conf` – filename can be anything or nothing as long as it ends with ".conf"

The default behavior of `find` when multiple `name` or `iname` options are supplied is to insert a logical **AND** between them. If you would prefer `find` to operate using a logical **OR**, simply pass it the `-o` option.

Note that `find` uses **bash globbing**, the built-in wildcard expansion, not RegEx when searching by name. Full details can be found in **# man 7 glob**, the most relevant differences are these:

Glob	Glob Meaning	RegEx Meaning
*	Zero or more characters	Zero or more of character it follows
?	Any single character	Zero or one of character it follows
.	A literal dot .	Any single character

Enterprise Linux versions 7 & 8

Searching by attribute

Frequently, we may need to find files with unsafe or undesirable ownership, permissions, or attributes. We may wish to find all executable files which are world writeable, a common security concern. Or, we might want to list any files with Special Purpose Access Modes (SUID, SGID, or Sticky bits) set. Maybe we'd like to find files that are owned by a particular individual (or owned by no one at all), or files accessed or modified within a certain time window. `find` can resolve all of these issues. Consider:

```
# find . -type f -perm /o=w -perm /o=x -exec ls -l {} \;
-rwxrwxrwx. 1 root root 2724 Jun  2 08:27 /source
```

Breaking the command down:
- `find` – start finding
- `.` – start looking in PWD and proceed recursively through all subdirectories
- `-type f` – search only for regular files
- `-perm` – match files with the following permissions
- `/o=w` – match any of the bits listed – listed are "o=w", or "write" for "others"
- `-perm` – match files with following permissions (logical AND with previous -perm)
- `/o=x` – match any of the bits listed – listed are "o=x", or "execute" for "others"
- `-exec ls -l {} \;` – run `ls -l` against the `STDOUT`

In English, that is "Find any regular files, in my current directory or beneath, which are writeable **and** executable by the world. Then, run `ls -l` on them."

Let's explore a few examples of finding files that present security concerns:

```
# find / -nouser
```

This will return a list of all unowned files on the system. When files are unowned, this is usually the result of user account deletion. Calling `ls -l` on an unowned file might results in this:

```
-rwxrwxrwx. 1 root root  2724 Jun  2 08:27 source
-rw-r--r--. 1 1002 1002   231 Aug  2  2016 unowned
```

For the file **source**, we can see an owner of **root**, and an owning group of **root**. However, the file **unowned** shows only numbers. These numbers represent a User ID and a Group ID. We are seeing them now because there is no user or group matching these IDs in the `/etc/passwd` and `/etc/group` files. Thus, the file is unowned.

We might also be interested in finding files with undesirable attributes such as SetUID or SetGID. These attributes allow files to be executed with the permissions of the owning user or group rather than the invoking user. This is especially problematic when such files are owned by root or other privileged accounts. To locate these types of files:

```
# find / -type f -perm /u=s -exec ls -l {} \;
-rwsr-xr-x. 1 root root 32008 Nov  5 2016 /usr/bin/fusermount
-rwsr-xr-x. 1 root root 61328 Nov  5 2016 /usr/bin/ksu
-rws--x--x. 1 root root 23960 Nov  5 2016 /usr/bin/chfn
-rws--x--x. 1 root root 23872 Nov  5 2016 /usr/bin/chsh
-rwsr-xr-x. 1 root root 27832 Jun 10 2014 /usr/bin/passwd
```

The switch **-perm /u=s** instructs **find** to locate files with the SUID bit set. The **-exec** option returns a long listing of the located files, allowing us to learn more about the files in question.

While **-exec** allows the execution of any command on the results of a `find`, the full invocation can be awkward. There are several other ways to achieve much the same result:

```
# find /path criteria -exec ls -la {}\;
# find /path criteria | xargs ls -la
# ls -la $( find /path criteria )
# find /path criteria > scratch-file; ls -la < scratch-file
```

All of the above are equivalent. You can also directly list or delete files from within `find`:

```
# find /path criteria -ls
# find /path criteria -delete
```

Enterprise Linux versions 7 & 8

Finally, we may wish to find files that have been accessed or modified within a certain time range. The **find** command offers options for locating files based on these characteristics:

- **atime** – Access Time (the last time a file was opened for reading – may not be recorded)
- **ctime** – Change Time (when the status – permissions, ownership – of a file was changed)
- **mtime** – Modify Time (when the content of a file was altered)

These options are easily misunderstood, and as such, are often misapplied. All three options use 24 hour blocks to define time ranges, and the timeline points backwards in time. Specifying the number 1, for example, causes find to return files with a timestamp **between** 24 and 48 hours old. To locate files created within the last 24 hours, we would instead have used:
```
# find / -atime -1
```

For files more than TWO days (48 hours) old:
```
# find / -atime +1
```

There is another option to find files by time using the –newer option. This can be used to search for files newer than a reference file
```
# touch   -t   202003170000    reference-file
# find /etc -type f -newer reference-file
```

Above we created a file with a modify time of 17 March 2020, then searched **/etc** for newer files. This can be modified using the **-newer**Xt format, where X can be **a**, **c**, or **m** for access, change, modify and the optional **t** tells `find` that a time rather than a reference file argument follows. The search can be inverted using **-not**. These can also be combined to create a range:
```
# find /etc -newermt 2020-03-17
# find /etc -newermt 2020-03-01 -not -newermt 2020-03-17
```

cat, head, tail

The simplest command for viewing text, `cat`, is most often invoked like this:
```
# cat file
these are the contents of file
file contains multiple lines

^ that was a blank line
this is the end of file
```

Above, `cat` was invoked without options, and given a filename as an argument. `cat` dumped the contents of the file to **STDOUT**.

`cat` can place line numbers into the output (`-n`, or `-b` to number non-blank lines only). This is handy for debugging scripts.

If you need to create a quick text file, but don't want to fuss with an editor, use `cat`:
```
# cat >> outfile
we are just typing in the empty space
this is a new line.
when we press CTL-d cat will close and append this to outfile
```

When dealing with log files, it is often helpful to view only the first or last few lines of a file. Logs are sequential, so the latest entries will be at bottom, and the earliest will be at the top. The `head` and `tail` commands will return the first or last ten lines of a file, respectively. The number of lines returned can be altered if desired.

To view the last three lines of the log for cron:
```
# tail -3 /var/log/cron
Dec  2 09:01:01 8 CROND[10091]: (root) CMD (run-parts /etc/cron.hourly)
Dec  2 09:01:01 8 run-parts[10091]: (/etc/cron.hourly) starting 0anacron
Dec  2 09:01:01 8 run-parts[10091]: (/etc/cron.hourly) finished 0anacron
```

If we supply `-f` (follow), `tail` will display the last few lines of a file and continually refresh that output as the file changes.

Conversely, `head` returns the first few lines of a file:
```
# dmesg | head -5
[    0.000000] Initializing cgroup subsys cpuset
[    0.000000] Initializing cgroup subsys cpu
[    0.000000] Initializing cgroup subsys cpuacct
[    0.000000] Linux version 3.10.0-514.el7.x86_64
(builder@kbuilder.dev.centos.org) (gcc version 4.8.5 20150623 (Red Hat
[    0.000000] Command line: BOOT IMAGE=/vmlinuz-3.10.0-514.el7.x86_64
root=/dev/mapper/cl-root ro crashkernel=auto rd.lvm.lv=cl/root
rd.lvm.lv=cl/swap rhgb quiet LANG=en_US.UTF-8
```

Here we used `dmesg`, which displays boot logs as the input for `head`. The underlined portion is a wrapped line. It shows the options supplied to the kernel at boot time.

touch, echo

Much administration of Linux involves manipulating text files. Occasionally, we will need to create a new file from the command line. For most work, we will turn to a fully featured editor such as **vi**, which is addressed later. In other situations, we may only require that a file exist. The file **/.autorelabel**, for example, will cause all files and directories on a system to be relabeled to their default security context if it exists at boot time. The file itself is empty, and does not exist by default.

The simplest way to create such a file would be to use the **touch** command. The intended use of **touch** is updating the access and modify timestamps on a given file. However, if a non-existent filename is supplied as an argument to **touch** as an argument, it will be created.
```
# touch /.autorelabel
```

To create small configuration files, or add lines to simple configuration files, we can use **echo** with redirection. The primary function of **echo** is to read input (typically from **STDIN**) and send that output to **STDOUT**. Combining this with redirection allows the insertion of text into a file. This is useful for appending lines to configuration files, or creating small text files.
```
# echo "this is line 1" > file

# cat file
this is line 1

# echo "this is line 2" >> file

# cat file
this is line 1
this is line 2
```

mkdir, rm, rmdir

Directories are created with the **mkdir** command. The use of this command is straightforward; invoke **mkdir** and provide the path and name of the directory you wish to create:
```
# mkdir -m 0700 -p this/is/insecure

# find this -exec ls -ld {} \;
drwxr-xr-x. 3 root root 16 Jun 16 15:26 this
drwxr-xr-x. 3 root root 22 Jun 16 15:26 this/is
drwx------. 2 root root  6 Jun 16 15:26 this/is/insecure
```

Above, we added two options to the **mkdir** command: **-m** and **-p**. The **-m** option sets the mode (permissions) for the directory and **-p** allows us to create a directory and its subdirectories in a single command. Note that, when the options are combined in this way, the mode option only sets the permissions of the ultimate subdirectory, rather than each directory in the set.

The **rm** command removes (deletes) files and directories. This is an inherently dangerous act as `bash` has no undo function. Thankfully, **rm** has options to limit its scope and effect:
- **-r** – recursive, remove a directory (and everything inside it)
- **-i** – interactive, prompt user for confirmation before deleting
- **-f** – force, do not prompt

In EL, the **.bashrc** file for the root user has a default alias of **rm** to **rm -i**. This causes **rm** to prompt the user for confirmation before deleting any file. From a safety and security standpoint this is a desirable behavior, but it presents a problem when **root** needs to remove a large number of files. In these cases, we may use **rm -f** or invoke the system version of **rm** directly, bypassing the alias:

```
# rm outfile
rm: remove regular file 'cap'? #confirmation prompt
# /usr/bin/rm outfile
#  #no confirmation
```

To remove directories use **rm -f**, or **rmdir** which will only delete empty directories.

cp, mv

To copy and move files, use **cp** and **mv**. There are some factors to consider regarding their usage:

- **Copying** a file requires read permissions on the original file, and read/execute on the directory containing it.
    - When the new file is created, it will be owned by the copying user and access permissions will not necessarily be preserved from the original.
    - The SELinux security context for the new file will be inherited from the directory it is created in.
- **Moving** a file does not require any permissions on the file itself; but does require read, write, and execute privileges on the directory containing the file. This is because moving a file, or deleting one, is a directory operation. Rather than saying a file was deleted or moved, we should say that the directory listings for this file's inode were altered.
    - Moved files retain the original security context, ownership, and permissions.
    - `bash` does not have a separate rename command, to rename a file or directory, use **mv**.

Enterprise Linux versions 7 & 8

sort, wc, tr, uniq, diff

The **sort** command arranges data alphabetically, numerically, or by other characteristics (such as days of the month).
```
# cat list
red
blue
green

# cat list | sort
blue
green
red
```

We can use the **wc** command to get counts of <u>w</u>ords, <u>c</u>haracters, or <u>l</u>ines in a file or input stream:
```
# cat counts
This file contains five lines.
The number of words is 29.
I don't know the number of characters.
But I can use wc to find out.
Let's try it.

# wc counts
  5  29 141 counts

# wc -c counts
141 counts

# wc -l counts
5 counts

# wc -w counts
29 counts
```

The **tr** command allows us to translate specified characters into other characters (or remove them altogether). Here are some simple examples using command line redirection.

Translating lower to uppercase:
```
# ps
  PID TTY          TIME CMD
 3271 pts/0    00:00:00 bash
 3418 pts/0    00:00:00 ps

# ps | tr [:lower:] [:upper:]
  PID TTY          TIME CMD
 3271 PTS/0    00:00:00 BASH
 3419 PTS/0    00:00:00 PS
 3420 PTS/0    00:00:00 TR
```

Squeezing out the repeating spaces to make things more compact:
```
# ps | tr -s [:space:]
 PID TTY TIME CMD
 3271 pts/0 00:00:00 bash
 3428 pts/0 00:00:00 ps
 3429 pts/0 00:00:00 tr
```

Deleting numbers from the output:
```
# ps | tr -d [:digit:]
  PID TTY          TIME CMD
  pts/     :: bash
  pts/     :: ps
  pts/     :: tr
```

Deleting everything that is not a number:
```
# ps | tr -cd [:digit:]
32710000003437000000034380000000
```

Remember that `tr` is translating characters rather than words:
```
# ps | tr 'bash' 'shell'
  PID TTY         TIME CMD
 3271 pte/0    00:00:00 shel
 3463 pte/0    00:00:00 pe
 3464 pte/0    00:00:00 tr
```

Note that **tr** didn't replace "bash" with "shell". Instead, it replaced **b** with **s**, **a** with **h** and so on. This is why **pts** became **pte**.

The **uniq** command can be used to find lines that repeat (or lines that don't), but it can only find lines that repeat immediately. If a duplicate line exists in multiple locations in a file, and the duplicate lines are is separated by some other unique text, **uniq** will not register this as a duplicate. Consider the following example:
```
# cat song
This is the song that never ends
it never ends
it never ends
It just keeps going
it never ends
it never ends
```

```
# uniq song
This is the song that never ends
it never ends
It just keeps going
it never ends
```

The `diff` command is used to compare two files. This is typically used as a form of version control for configuration files or for forensic purposes. Consider the following example:
```
# diff file1 file1.bk
1,4c1,4
< This is the original file
< and nothing has been changed
< but we'll make some changes
< and compare it with diff
---
> This is the copied file
> and something has been changed
> we made some changes
> and compared it with diff
5a6
>  we added this line
```
We can read the output this way:

- `1,4c1,4` – lines 1-4 of the first file need to be changed to match lines 1-4 of the second file
- `5a6` – and we need to add line 6 of the second file after line 5 in the first file.

We can see that only four lines were returned from the first file. Why did `diff` insist that a changed needed to be made after line 5? Let's compare the files side by side with line numbers:
```
# diff -y file1 file1.bk | tr -s [:space:] | cat -n
1  This is the original file        |  This is the copied file
2  and nothing has been changed     |  and something has been changed
3  but we'll make some changes      |  we made some changes
4  and compare it with diff         |  and compared it with diff
5  but this line won't change          but this line won't change
6                                       we added this line
```
Note lines 5 and 6 above. Both files contain an unaltered line 5, which `diff` did not display. Line 6 existed only in the second file.

Module 3: vi

There are several text editors available in Enterprise Linux. There is **gedit** – a graphical, notepad-like editor, **nano** – a text based editor developed originally as part of an email client, and then there's **vi**. Unlike gedit or nano, vi is not intuitive. It has a steep learning curve; even the people who love it admit that it takes weeks or months to get comfortable with **vi**.

To begin with, it uses modes: **Insert** mode allows you to type; **Visual** mode allows you to select; and so-called **Normal** mode allows you to run commands, open and close files, etc. Every beginner finds themselves flopping around in the wrong mode, trying to type in Normal mode and watching weird things happen instead.

If it's not intuitive, takes a long time to learn, and has easier alternatives, why bother?

- If you spend some time getting good with vi, you will find it is the right tool for many jobs.
    - With the extensions provided in **vim** (**vi im**proved), it is a pretty fully featured programming environment, with lots of handy shortcuts and support for most major languages. It is the preferred development environment for many programmers, some people even pay for versions of **vi** to run in Windows.
- Some tasks, such as editing the password file, should **only** be done using vi.
- vi has a small memory footprint and can open very large files.
    - The default maximum is 2 GB
    - This can be customized with: `set mm`, `:set mmt`, and `:set swap`
- In a Unix-like environment, it is the only editor you are sure to have.
    - Graphical editors, like gedit, don't run without graphics, and real servers don't run graphical interfaces.
    - Other editors, like nano, may not be installed.
    - vi is available and installed by default on pretty much every device where you can run ls on to get a directory listing. As long as the computer in front of you isn't running Windows, it probably has vi.

In EL7/8 there are two versions of vi installed: **vim-minimal** and **vim-enhanced**, which has all the pretty colors and extra features. Users with a UID less than 200 will get vim-minimal by typing **vi**, those above (all regular users) will get vim-enhanced. This is set by aliases in **/etc/profile.d/vim.*** The files in this directory are read and processed during the logon sequence. All users will get the enhanced version by invoking **vim**.

This module is broken into three parts: the first is the absolute least you need to know to be an effective administrator; the second is a list of some of the cool things that may make your life easier if you learn to use them, the third addresses safe editing of configuration files.

Basics

At a minimum you need to be able to open a file, edit it, and get out without breaking things. To open a file

`# vi` *newfile*.

You will start in **Normal** mode. You can use the arrow keys to move in any mode. To begin typing you will need to be in **Insert** mode; to get there you can use

- `i` – insert here
- `o` – add a line below and insert there
- `A` – insert at end of current line
- To get back to Normal mode press `ESC`.

To get around in **Normal** mode

- `u` – undo
- `CTL-r` – redo
- `yy` – 'yank' (copy) the current line
- `dd` – cut current line
- `p` – paste
- `^` / `$` – beginning/end of line
- `H` / `M` / `L` – high/mid/low on page
- `gg` / `G` – top/bottom of file
- `*` / `#` – match next/previous word under cursor
- Repeating commands:
    - `.` – (dot) repeat the last thing you did
    - or a number before the command: `10dd` cuts 10 lines, `2p` pastes twice.

To select, you need to be in **Visual** mode. From **Normal** press

- `v` – select characters
- `V` – select lines
- `CTL-v` – select blocks
- `y` – copy
- `d` – delete
- `p` – paste

To exit vi, go to Normal mode then issue a vi command. Commands begin with a colon:

- `:q` – quit without saving, if you made changes it will want `:q!`
- `:e!` – start editing the file over without saving
- `:w!` – write changes to file
    - `:w!` */path/otherfile* – writes to *otherfile*
    - `:w >>` *otherfile* – appends buffer to *otherfile*
- `:wq!` – write and quit, the most common way to leave

Cool Tricks, Pretty Colors

Most of these things apply both to `vi` (vim-minimal) and `vim` (vi-enhanced). Some, such as the syntax-aware highlighting (the pretty colors) only apply to `vim`.

Multiple files

To open a file explorer from `Normal` mode `:Ex`

You can open several files sequentially:
`# vi` *fileone filetwo filethree*

Each file will open in a separate buffer.

- To move between buffers
    - `:n` – next
    - `:N` – previous
- If you haven't written your edits
    - `:wn` – write, next
    - `:n!` – next, discard changes
- To list buffers `:ls`
- To leave all files at once `:wqa!`

You can also open a second file in the current buffer
`# vi` *filethree*, then `:e` *filefour*

To switch between them, use **CTL-^**.

We recommend using either of these methods, but not both, as it can get confusing. If you do get confused while doing these kinds of things **CTL-g** will give you a hint as to where you are.

If you want to open multiple files on a single screen, open one normally then
`:split` *otherfile*

To move between windows **CTL-w** followed by an arrow key.

With no arguments, `:split` will open the current file in two windows – very useful if you want to view the original while making changes.

To view files side by side instead of over and under `:vsplit` (`vim` only).

To highlight differences between two files `:diffsplit`

You can also open multiple files in tabs using `:tabedit`.
To move between tabs **CTL-PgUp** / **CTL-PgDown** or `:tabn` / `:tabp`

vi will open remote files using scp, http, or ftp:
vim scp://user@other.server.com//var/log/messages

Notice the two slashes before `var`. The first ends the url, the second is the beginning of the path.

Inserting stuff

There are lots of ways to get external content into a file. The most basic is to open multiple files, select what you want, switch files and paste. To put the entire contents of **file2** into **file1**:
vi *file1 file2*
  :n – switch to next file
    gg – goto the top
      v – enter Visual mode
        G – goto the bottom
          y – yank
            :N – switch to previous file
              p – paste

That's a lot of keystrokes for a pretty small result. Instead we can:
vi *file1*
:r *file2*

This reads the contents of `file2` into `file1` at the cursor.

To insert the result of a command into a file
:r !date   or
:r !ls -la | grep *pattern*.

There are times you may wish to carry lots of different cut text at the same time. To cut and paste to multiple registers (clipboards) you need to specify a register name. This is done in `Normal` mode. Registers are specified by double quotes and a letter. For instance to copy a line into register **x** and paste it three times **"xdd**, **"x3p**. You can see the contents of all registers with **:reg**.

Avoiding repetition

If you find yourself typing the same thing over and over again you can create an abbreviation for it. For instance, here is a typical address record from a DNS zone file:
`server1    IN    A    10.0.1.5`

These files can go on for hundreds of lines and mistakes can cause service outages. To avoid some of the drudgery and chance of error:
`:abbr ad    IN    A    10.0.1.`
Now you can simply type `server1 ad` followed by a space and `ad` will expand to `    IN    A    10.0.1`

You can add permanent abbreviations to a `vimrc/virc` file.
To find the path to the appropriate file `:version`

There are some global commands which you can use. They take the general form of
`:g/`*pattern*`/`*command*`/`*action*

These go well beyond the scope of this course but some handy ones include:

- `:g/apple` – show lines containing `apple`
- `:g/apple\|orange/d` – delete lines with `apple` or `orange`
- `:v/apple\|orange/d` – delete lines **without** `apple` or `orange`
- `:%s/apple/orange/g` – search for `apple`, replace with `orange`, globally
- `:g/^\s*$/d` – delete lines that are whitespace `\s*` from beginning `^` to end `$`. That is to say, blank lines.

If you want to repeat a `vi` command, use the up arrow after a colon.

If you find yourself doing the exact same set of keystrokes repeatedly you can record a macro to a register from Normal:

- `q`*M* – begin recording to register *M*
    - perform your action
- `esc`, `q` – end recording
- `@`*M* – perform action saved in register *M*
- `@@` – repeat action

Running commands

You can run commands external to `vi` from `Normal` mode:
`:!ip a` or `:!bash`

If you want to run an external command on the entire contents of your file
`:% !sort` – the percent sign represents the contents of the file

To run commands by on part of a file by line number it is best to first see the line numbers
`:set number` – turn line numbers on
`:set number!` – turns them off
Now you can say something like
`:4,12 !sort -u` – sort lines **4** through **12** keeping only the unique lines.

You can also run commands on a selection using `Visual` mode.
Select what you want – (**v** is best for line based operations) then type a colon.
Do not `ESC` to `Normal`, **vi** will do it for you.
It will put this in `:'<,'>` where the tick and bracket collection means the beginning and ending of the selection. Do not remove this!
Now type your command using **!** *cmd*

Moving around quickly

If you find yourself moving back and forth in a large file, you can create marks with letters assigned to them. From Normal, press **m** followed by a letter. To return to that mark, use the single quote (tick) **'** followed by the letter. To list current marks **:marks**. Marks made with a capital letter will carry from file to file (within a session). To perform an action between two marks **:'x,'y !sort -r**. To move to the last position before a jump **''**.

Other quick movement methods include:
- **w** / **b** – move a word forward/backward
- **f** *char* – find *char*, **F** searches backwards
- **%** – find the matching delimiter **)** **]** **}** – useful when programming
- **/***pattern* – search for *pattern*, **n** for next, **N** previous, **?** search backwards

Other things

To find help **:help**. (vim only, help will be completely munged in vi)

To see matching topics **:help** *pattern*, followed by **CTL-D** or **tab**.

In Normal, place the cursor over a word, **K** will take you to the man page for that word.

To enable/disable the pretty colors **:syntax on/off**

If you have a crash or lose connection during a session **:recover** *file* or **vi -r** *file*

If you get discouraged **:help!**

Config files

Most Linux configuration is done by editing plain text files. In most cases even menu-based Text User Interfaces (TUIs), Graphical Tools, and command line utilities are ultimately just making changes to configuration files that you can also edit manually. Most of these files are located in **/etc** and its sub-directories. There are different types of config files with differing conventions but there are generalizations that can be made:

- Anything starting with a hash **#** is a comment and will be ignored by the system.
- The size of white space and blank lines does not matter. Formatting is for humans, not computers.
- If the file has a stanza format or relies on ordered processing, the order will matter.
- Order of options in a simple list will not matter.
- To turn an option on, set it to **1**; **0** will turn it off.
- Changes made to a config file will not be effective until the service calling it is restarted.
    - In EL7/8 this is done with **# systemctl restart** *name.service*
    - In EL6 this is done with **# service** *service-name* **restart**
        - The **auditd** service is still controlled this way in EL7/8

There are exceptions to all of these rules, so read the documentation **before** making changes.

There are several ways to protect yourself when editing a config file. The simplest is to make a habit of making a backup copy using **cp**.

Another way is to not change the base file at all. Many services will have a standard configuration file (such as **/etc/crontab** for the cron service) and a separate directory for user generated changes (**/etc/cron.d/**). The base file will be read first, then anything in the **.d** directory will be read in lexical order (the same order displayed by ls). The last setting applied takes precedence.

Some services will place user-specific files either in a user's home directory or another user-specific directory. For instance user configuration of cron will be in **/var/spool/cron/***username*/. Thus the basic, unchanged configuration can be restored by simply deleting or moving the changed files.

Sometimes a change being made has the potential to break access to a computer, or may make the machine otherwise unusable. Changing the IP address of a machine is one such change. The way around this problem is to backup the file to be changed, then schedule a task in the future that will the restore original unless the task is canceled. If you are locked out, the task will run and everything will be as it was before the change. If your change was successful, you merely need to log in and delete the task before it runs.

Module 4: Users and Groups

When a user is created with the command **useradd**, several things happen:

1. The files **/etc/default/useradd** and **/etc/login.defs** are consulted
2. A primary group is created for that user by adding a line to **/etc/group**
3. A line is created in **/etc/passwd** assigning them a User ID (UID), a primary group, a home directory, and a shell
4. A line is created in **/etc/shadow** (where password hashes are stored) – with no hash
5. A home directory is created in **/home**
6. The contents of **/etc/skel** is copied the home directory. This typically includes any user specific startup or configuration scripts such as **bash_profile** and **bashrc**
7. A mail spool file is created for the user in **/var/spool/mail**

/etc/group, passwd, shadow

When you add a user, a line like this will be created in **/etc/group**:
bob:x:1004: – This says:

- that there is a group called **bob**
- with a Group ID (GID) of **1004**.
    - the GID is simply the next one available
    - This group is assigned to bob as his primary group in **/etc/password**
- If there were additional members of the group, they would be listed after the final colon.

A line is created in **/etc/password**:
bob:x:1002:1004::/home/bob:/bin/bash – This says:

- there's a user **bob**
- he uses a hashed password **x**
- his User ID is **1002**, his primary Group ID is **1004**
- an empty field, which can be used for comments
- bob's home directory is **/home/bob**
- his shell is **/bin/bash**

Beginning in EL8 there is no support for all numeric user or group names

A user's identity is established by User ID. By default **useradd** starts at the first available number, beginning with 1000. The numbers below 1000 are reserved for system use. The UID, along with the Group ID is used for permissions and ownership. UID and GID will increment up by one from the highest currently assigned. If the last created user is deleted and another created the system will reuse the old UID for the new user. The new user could inherit rights from the previous user. Best practice is to manually assign UID and GID on user creation using the **-u** and **-g** options.

Enterprise Linux versions 7 & 8

A line will be created in **/etc/shadow**:
`bob:!!:17312:0:99999:7:::`
This is where the actual security information lives. This file is owned by root and should have no permissions whatsoever on it. This says that bob exists and his password hash is **!!** This is not a valid password hash. This will change when bob's password is set.

The third field is the last time bob's password was changed in days since the epoch (1 January 1970). If this field is set to **0** the user must change their password on next login. The remainder of the fields are related to password expiration and such.

useradd

Almost all the default actions of **useradd** can be overridden by use of command line switches. Commonly used switches include:

- **-G** – add user to additional groups (no space between them, comma separated).
- **-p** – password. This is an encrypted value, not a simple plaintext password.
- **-s** – use a different shell. Often **/sbin/nologin** to prevent interactive login.
- **-e** – expire date in YYYY-MM-DD format, for temporary accounts
- **-u** / **-g** – manually set the user or Group ID
- **-Z** – manually specify an selinux user role for this user.
  - default is **unconfined_u**
  - STIG specifies
    - administrators should be **sysadm_u** or **staff_u**
    - all others should be **user_u**
  - to view available roles
    `# semanage user -l`
  - to view current user-role mappings
    `# semanage login -l`

/etc/default/useradd, /etc/login.defs

For security some settings should be changed in **/etc/default/useradd**. These values will be applied to all users created after making the changes. They will not be applied retroactively, so it is best to make these changes before creating users.

- **INACTIVE** – controls inactivation of accounts with expired passwords, in days
  - **-1** will never disable accounts
  - **0** will disable the account immediately upon password expiration
    - This is the standard for government systems
- **EXPIRE** – date that the user's password expires
  - set either in days since the epoch (1 Jan 1970), or YYYY-MM-DD format
  - do **not** set this to **0** while **INACTIVE** is also **0** as users created this way will never be able to log in
  - in most cases this is left blank, with user expiration set manually during creation
- **SKEL** – default skeleton directory, copied to new user's home directories

- contains files such as `.bashrc` and `.bash_profile` which configure a users environment upon login

There are several fields that must be set in `/etc/login.defs` on government systems:

- `PASS_MAX_DAYS` – the maximum password age. This should be set to **60**.
- `PASS_MIN_DAYS` – minimum time between password changes. Set this to **1**.
- `PASS_MIN_LEN` – the minimum password length. This should be **15**.
- `PASS_WARN_AGE` – the number of days before password expiration occurs. The default is **7**; this may be short for some users.
- `FAIL_DELAY` – the time in seconds between login attempts. This is **not** a default field. It must be added and set to **4**.
- There are several others that must remain at default values:
  - `UMASK 077`
  - `ENCRYPT_METHOD SHA512`
  - `CREATE_HOME yes`

passwd, usermod, userdel

After you have created a user you will need to set their password using `passwd`. Common switches for `passwd` include:

- `-l` / `-u` – lock and unlock a user's account
- `-e` – expire. Forces a password change at next login
- `-x` – set maximum days for expiration
- `-S` – show status of the user's password

Global password parameters are specified in `/etc/login.defs` as discussed above.

Password quality rules are enforced by PAM – Pluggable Authentication Modules. There are many files used to configure PAM and any changes to them should be approached with care, as you can permanently disable a system with a typo.

Account lockout, password encryption, and password reuse policies are configured in `/etc/pam.d/system-auth` and `/etc/pam.d/password-auth`
The guidelines in the STIG should be followed as written.

User account information can be modified by the `usermod` command. Options are similar to, but not the same as `useradd` and `passwd`:

- `-L` / `-U` – lock and unlock
- `-g` / `-u` – change GID / UID
- `-l` – change login name
- `-aG` – append secondary groups (will wipe current group membership with out `-a`)

Users can be deleted with `userdel` (`-r` removes their home directory and mail spool as well). If you wish to create multiple users from a file, this can be done with `newusers`.
Passwords can be set en masse by using the `chpasswd` command.

vipw, vigr

You can also create and modify users and groups by editing the relevant files directly, though this is not recommended as it is possible to break a system completely by making a mistake. If it is at all possible, use the tools mentioned above.

If the normal tools simply will not do the job, there are special editors provided which provide file locking and some level of sanity checking These are **vipw** and **vigr** for the password and group files respectively. With the `-s` switch, they can be used to edit the relevant shadow files. There is also a **visudo** to edit the **sudoers** mentioned below.

groupadd, groupmod, groupdel, groupmems, id

Groups can be manipulated with commands that mirror those for users: **groupadd**, **groupmod**, and **groupdel**.

Users can be added to secondary groups

- on user creation with `# useradd -G` *groupname*
- or after creation with `# usermod -aG` *groupname username*
- or with `# groupmems -g` *groupname* `-a` *username*

Group membership can be determinined using `id` *username*.

su, wheel

As we said before, best practice is to never login as root. A secure system will have strong controls on local root login and will not allow remote root login at all. This is configured by setting `PermitRootLogin no` in `/etc/ssh/sshd_config`. To perform administrative work on such a machine, you must first login as a normal user.

Once logged in there are a few options to elevate your privileges. On a default installation, if you have the root password you can change to root by using the **su** (substitute user) command and entering the root password. If you wish to execute commands in the environment (home directory, startup scripts, $PATH, etc.) that root would have if logged in directly use **su -**

Root can su to any other user with no additional authentication required. By default any user can su to any other user if they know that user's password. At the very least you will want to restrict the ability to su to root to a small group of administrators. The special group **wheel** (GID 10) is customarily the administrative group. To restrict use of **su** to members of `wheel`:

- Add users to **wheel** with **usermod -aG**
- Verify group membership with `id` *username*
- In **/etc/pam.d/su** uncomment this line:
`auth required   pam_wheel.so use_uid`.

sudo, sudoers

Restricting **su** somewhat strengthens the security posture of a computer, but leaves a problem: everyone who has a need for administrative control must have the root password. It is also important to note that a user who has become root via su **is** root and will be audited as such. To avoid these problems we use **sudo**.

When a user runs **sudo** the following command is executed **as if** it were run by root, but the user does not **become** root. The user may be prompted for their password, not for the root password.

A normal user will be required to type `sudo` before every privileged command issued. In `bash` the last command can be reissued by simply typing **!!** If you type a command that requires `sudo` and get the dreaded **Permission denied** response, reissue it with
`# sudo !!`

To grant users the ability to **sudo**:

- Add the users to **wheel**
- Verify group membership with **id**
- Run **visudo** – do not directly **vi**
- Uncomment the line
  `%wheel     ALL=(ALL)         ALL`
- If you wish to change the five minute password timeout for `sudo`, add a line:
  `Defaults  timestamp_timeout=`X
  - Where X is time in minutes
  - `-1` is never timeout
- Test the user's ability to login and use `sudo` **before** further securing the machine

Individual users or groups can be allowed a limited command set with or without a password. For instance, to allow users in the **backup** group to mount and unmount cd/dvd media when logged in locally add this line to **sudoers**
`%backup   localhost=/sbin/mount /mnt/cdrom, /sbin/umount /mnt/cdrom`

After `sudo` is configured and tested, you can lock down the root account:

- change the password to something random
- lock the password with **usermod -L**
- expire the password with **usermod -e**
- change the shell to **/sbin/nologin** with **usermod -s**

who, w, lastlog, last, lastb

As an admin, you need to know who is logged in, when they logged in, and what they are doing.
- **who** – who is logged in, when they logged in and from where
- **w** – all that plus usage stats and the current command
- **lastlog** – last login of each user, sorted by UID
    - For better viewing: **lastlog | grep -v Never**
- **last** – successful logins by time
    - The pseudo-user **reboot** logs in on every startup.
      To see all reboots: **last reboot**
- **lastb** – unsuccessful logins, from newest to oldest.
    - To reverse the order: **lastb | tac**

loginctl

A newer command which is integrated with systemd and logind is **loginctl**. It displays and controls active users and sessions. Useful sub-commands include:
- **list-users** – show active users
- **terminate-user** *username* – end all processes for user
- **kill-user --signal** *XX username* – send a signal to all processes of a user
    - signals are discussed later, for now: **9**=*kill*, **19**=*pause*, **18**=*resume*
- **list-sessions** – show active sessions
- **session-status** *session-id* – show details, including log snippets, of a session
- **terminate-session** *session-id* – end all processes in a session
- **kill-session** *session-id* – send a signal to all processes of a session
- **enable-linger** *username* – allow a user to run processes without logging in

Module 5: Permissions and Ownership

Ownership

There are two entities granted specific permissions to any file or directory: the owning user and the owning group. Users may always change permissions (and ownership) on the files they own, even if they have no access to the files in any other sense. Proper file ownership is an important security concept. To change ownership on a file use the **chown** command:
```
# chown bob:sales file
```

To change only a file's owner, we would supply a username without specifying a group:
```
# chown bob file
```

To change only the owning group, place the group name after a colon:
```
# chown :sales file
```

Permissions

Earlier, we observed output similar to this:
```
# ls -l
total 56
-rwxrwxrwx.  1 root root     58 May 17 09:31 file
```

Where **-rwxrwxrwx** is the permissions string, and **root root** lists the owner of the file and the owning group. The first character of the permission string is not part of the permissions set, and is instead used to identify the type of file we are dealing with. Starting with the second character, we see this: **rwxrwxrwx**.

This string can be broken into 3 sets, denoting permissions this way:
```
Owning User:   rwx (read, write, and execute)
Owning Group:  rwx
Others:        rwx
```

Or stated another way: **U:rwx G:rwx O:rwx**

Enterprise Linux versions 7 & 8

The output of `ls -l` displays the permission string using alphabetic characters; the system sees them as 12 binary bits where Read = 4, Write=2, and Execute=1. Each `rwx` triplet will evaluate to a decimal value between 0 and 7, for a total of 8 possible values. Because of this, these permission strings are called "octal permissions". There is one hidden triplet which precedes the standard permissions. It controls the Special Purpose Access Modes discussed below. The triplets can be treated as 4 concatenated 3 bit strings:

String	Decimal	Binary	Meaning
`---`	0	000	no permission
`--x`	1	001	execute only
`-w-`	2	010	write only
`r--`	4	100	read only
`-wx`	3	011	write, execute – no read
`r-x`	5	101	read, execute – no write
`rw-`	6	110	read, write – no execute
`rwx`	7	111	read, write, and execute

chmod

The owner of a file and `root` can change the permissions on a file by invoking `chmod`. The `chmod` command accepts either octal or symbolic notation:
`# chmod 755 list`   or
`# chmod u=rwx,g=rx,o=rx list`

These are the symbols accepted by `chmod`:
- `u` – set permissions for the owning user
- `g` – set permissions for the owning group
- `o` – set permissions for others (not the owning user or in the owning group)
- `a` – set permissions for all: user, group, and other
- `+` – add a permission to an existing set
- `-` – subtract a permission from an existing set
- `=` – set an exact permission

Special Purpose Access Modes

Earlier, we mentioned that there are twelve bits for permissions, but have only discussed nine bits (three each for User, Group, and Others). The other three control a set of file behaviors referred to as *Special Purpose Access Modes* or SPAMs. This set is comprised of: **SUID**, **SGID**, and the **sticky bit**.

SUID allows a file to be executed with the permissions of the file's owner rather than the user who invoked it. Normally, a process executed by a user could not perform any tasks that the user himself did not have permissions to perform. With SUID, a process will be able to do anything its owner could do, regardless of who runs it. This is obviously dangerous, and must be carefully implemented and monitored.

SGID is similar in concept to SUID, but it applies to the named group as opposed to individual user accounts. SGID is best used on directories, where it causes all new files created in that directory to be owned by the directory's owning group (rather than the primary group of the creating user).

The **sticky bit** prevents anyone other than a file's owner or root from deleting or renaming it, regardless of permissions. Normally, any user with write and execute permissions for the directory a file inhabits can delete or rename the file. The sticky bit prevents this. Often, this is set on the **/tmp** directory (which, by nature, must be writeable and executable by many users). Doing so prevents users from destroying temporary files they do not own.

The binary values for the three SPAMs are: **SUID=4**, **SGID=2**, **sticky bit=1**.

The **chmod** command is used to set or unset Special Purpose Access Mode values:

```
# chmod 7777 file
# ls -l file
-rwsrwsrwt. 1 root root 15 Jun 19 09:49 file
```

The first **7** in the command **chmod 7777 file** causes SUID, SGID, and sticky to be set. These are represented by the underlined characters in the permission string (rw[suid] rw[sgid] rw[sticky]). We can do this in symbolic notation as well:

```
# chmod u+s,g+s,o+t file
# ls -l file
-rwsr-sr-T. 1 root root 15 Jun 19 09:49 file
```

Note the uppercase **T** at the end of the string. This indicates that the sticky bit has been enabled, but that **others** do not currently have execute permission on the file. We would see similar behavior with SUID and SGID.

umask

To control permissions on new files and directories, we may use **umask**. A **umask** consists of a set of permissions to be **subtracted** from the system default of **0777** when new files and directories are created. A final check will remove execute permissions from files, but not directories, when they are created.

For example, if the umask was **0027** the following would occur:

- A new file/directory is created with default permissions of **0777**
- **umask** is subtracted from **0777**, leaving **0750**
- If the target is a file, remove any execute permissions, leaving **0650**

The current **umask** has no effect on existing files. It only affects permissions on new files created after it has been set.

To see the current mask: **# umask**
To temporarily set the mask to a different value: **# umask 0027**.

In EL the default umask for root and system users is **0022** and regular users is **0002**. STIG stipulates that the default for all interactive users should be set to **0077**. This is defined in **/etc/bashrc**, and **/etc/profile** and can be changed there. To set an individual user's default mask, place the desired **umask** command string into **.bashrc** in their home directory.

Access Control Lists

The built-in Linux permissions define access for three sets of users: the owning user, the owning group, and all others. For more granular permissions, we must turn to Access Control Lists.

```
# ls -l
-rw-rwxr--+ 1 root root      30 Jun 19 08:12 file
```

Note the plus **+** at the end of the permission string above. This indicates the presence of an ACL. We can retrieve an ACL with the **getfacl** command.

```
# ls -ld /test
drwx------. 4 root root 100 Jun 22 10:20 /test

# getfacl /test
getfacl: Removing leading '/' from absolute path names
# file: test
# owner: root
# group: root
user::rwx
group::---
other::---
```

Above, we can see that the **/test** directory currently has no extended ACLs applied to it. The permissions in the output of **getfacl** matchs the permissions reported by **ls -l**, and there is no **+** character at the end of the permissions string.

ACLs are set using `setfacl` which has the following options:
- `-m` – modify an ACL
- `-x` – remove an ACL entry
- `-b` – remove all ACLs for file
- `-R` – apply ACL recursively through subdirectories
- `[d]:u|g|o|m:`*UID|GID:perms* – followed by the target, where:
    - `d` – [optional] sets this as default
    - `u, g, o` – user, group, or other
    - `m` – mask, sets effective rights mask (like `umask`)
    - `UID` or `GID` – who we are affecting
    - `perms` – in rwx format

Let's explore some sample usage:
- `# setfacl -m u:bob:rwx /test` – Add user **bob** with full permissions
- `# setfacl -m g:sales:rw /test` – Add the group **sales** with read and write
- `# setfacl -m d:g:sales:rw /test` – Add permissions for **sales** to the default ACL
- `# setfacl -m o::r /test` – Set permissions for **others** to read only
- `# setfacl -m m::rw /test` – Set the effective rights mask to **rw-**, masking execute away from **bob**
- `# setfacl -m d:m::rw /test` – Make that mask part of the default ACL

The result should look something like this:
```
# getfacl /test
getfacl: Removing leading '/' from absolute path names
# file: test
# owner: root
# group: root
user::rwx
user:bob:rwx
#effective:rw-
group::---
group:sales:rw-
mask::rw-
other::r--
default:user::rwx
default:group::---
default:group:sales:rw-
default:mask::rw-
default:other::r-
```

In EL7/8, ACL support is on by default for both `xfs` and `ext4` filesystems. Some filesystems will not support ACLs by default. To enable ACL support, pass the `acl` option during mount:
`# mount -o +acl /dev/sdb1 /testdir`

Or alter the default mounting options stored in the filesystem superblock using `tune2fs`:
`# tune2fs -o +acl /dev/sdb1`

Module 6: Regular Expressions

Linux provides several powerful tools for working with text in files and input streams. These include `grep`, `sed`, and `awk` which perform decidedly different functions, but the central mechanism for each involves **regular expressions** (RegEx).

grep

Regular expressions provide the ability to match patterns in text. This simple description belies the incredible utility of regular expressions. The first tool to be addressed is `grep`, which can be used to search through text, match a defined pattern (regular expression), and print the resulting matches. It uses 3 broad categories of commands to define this pattern:

- **Pattern:** these define the string pattern we are searching for.
- **Anchors:** these define the acceptable position for a matched pattern.
- **Modifiers:** These modify how grep treats the character(s) immediately preceding them.

`grep` also relies on two types of character interpretations:

- **Literal characters:** characters with no special meaning, i.e. the character **a** is the literal lowercase alphabetic character **a**.
- **Metacharacters:** characters with additional meanings beyond the literal, i.e. the dollar sign **$** is interpreted as an anchoring metacharacter, translating to "at the end of a line".

Since `grep` treats characters as literals or metacharacters *situationally*, certain characters must be *escaped*. That is, they must be flipped, depending on the situation, from a literal to a metacharacter or vice versa. This can lead to regular expressions that look something like this:
`'@[a-zA-Z_.]\+\?\.[a-zA-Z]\{2,3\}'`

We will come back to this expression at the end of the module. For now, notice the backslashes in the string above. Each of these escapes the character that follows it. In **basic grep**, the following characters are treated as *literals*: + ? | {} ()

If we wish them to be treated as *metacharacters*, that is to have a special meaning, we must escape them with the backslash: \+ \? \| \{ \} \(\)

Extended grep inverts this logic: these characters are metacharacters by default, and must be escaped if we want them treated as literals. Consider the examples below where `-E` causes `grep` to treat the RegEx as an *extended regular expression*. We could also use the `egrep`, which is equivalent, but deprecated. When dealing with `grep`, always be mindful of whether you are using a basic regular expression or an extended regular expression, and apply appropriate escapes as required.

With escapes:
```
# grep '@[a-zA-Z_.]\+\?\.[a-zA-Z]\{2,3\}' /test/file
tim@honey.net

# grep -E '@[a-zA-Z_.]\+\?\.[a-zA-Z]\{2,3\}' /test/file
###<<< - no results
```

Without escapes:
```
# grep -E '@[a-zA-Z_.]+?\.[a-zA-Z]{2,3}' /test/file
tim@honey.net

# grep '@[a-zA-Z_.]+?\.[a-zA-Z]{2,3}' /test/file
###<<< - no results
```

Character Sets

Moving beyond the backslashes in the example regular expression, we can see groups of characters like this `[a-zA-Z_.]` These are called **character sets**. These evaluate to:

- `[a-z]` – Match any single lowercase alpha character
- `[A-Z]` – Match any single uppercase alpha character
- `[abc]` – Match any one of **a**, **b**, or **c**.
- `[0-9]` – Match any single digit, **0** through **9**.
- `[^a2]` – Match any character which is NOT **a** or **2**
- `[.]` – When enclosed in braces, a literal period.
- `.` – A period not enclosed in braces, match any single character other than line break

Returning to the example `[a-zA-Z_.]` This can be interpreted as "*any upper or lowercase alphabetic character, or an underscore, or a period.*" Note that a dot inside of a character set is never interpreted as a metacharacter, but by default a dot outside of a character set will be a metacharacter representing *any single character*.

Here are some examples of character sets, working with a file called `list` containing the following text :
```
red
road
read
radical
The road is radical.
all lowercase
0123456789
123
789
ALL CAPS
```

Enterprise Linux versions 7 & 8

To find lines in this file that contain either **red** OR **rad**, we would use:
```
# grep 'r[ea]d' list
red
radical
The road is radical.
```

Above, `grep` matched the pattern **red** OR **rad** in three lines. It did not matter if this pattern occurred inside of a larger string. More interesting, however, is what `grep` did not match. Notice that **read** was not matched, despite containing both the **e** and the **a** from the defined character set. Let's look at the expression again: `'r[ea]d'` This evaluates as "Match anything that starts with an **r**, followed by either an **e** OR an **a**, followed by a **d**."

To find lines which contain capital letters, we could do this:
```
# grep [A-Z] list
The road is radical.
ALL CAPS
```

Simple enough. But what if we wanted to find only lines that did NOT contain uppercase letters? We might try this:
```
# grep [a-z] list
red
road
read
radical
The road is radical.
all lowercase
```

This got rid of the **ALL CAPS** line, but still matched **The**. The expression: `[a-z]` evaluates as: "Match any lowercase character." In **The road is radical**, only the **T** is not matched. Every other character was matched, and so the line was returned.

We might also try "negation". This involves the caret **^** metacharacter. When placed inside of a character set, it will *negate* the pattern that follows it. An example:
```
# grep '[^0-9]' list
red
road
read
radical
The road is radical.
all lowercase
ALL CAPS
```

Without the caret, we would have expected this to return any lines containing a digit. Instead, we have returned all lines which contain "characters that aren't digits". If we tried this with our earlier example (lines which do NOT contain uppercase characters), it would still return lines with mixed case (lines containing characters which weren't uppercase letters).

To get lines which did not contain any uppercase characters, use **-v** to invert the match and return only lines which do not contain the given pattern.
```
# grep -v [A-Z] list
red
road
read
radical
all lowercase
0123456789
123
789
```

Anchors

Suppose we wanted to match capital letters only if they occur at the beginning of a line. We can't do this with character sets alone. The dollar sign **$** and caret **^** will find matches at the end or beginning of a line respectively. These are known as **anchors**.

To do find all lines that begin with a capital letter, we will place a caret **^** before the pattern we wish to match:
```
# grep '^[A-Z]' list
The road is radical.
ALL CAPS
```

To find a pattern at the end of a line, we use the dollar sign **$** placed immediately after the pattern we are trying to locate. To match all lines ending with the lowercase letter "d":
```
# grep 'd$' list
red
road
read
```

Note that anchor characters lose their special meaning if they are not placed at the beginning or end of a pattern. To explain this, let's add two lines to our list file and conduct an experiment:
```
# echo '$1.51' >> list
# echo '$1.52' >> list
# grep '1$' list
$1.51

# grep '$1' list
$1.51
$1.52
```

In the second example, the anchor was ignored, or, more specifically, was interpreted as a literal. Any lines containing the character string **$1** were returned.

Enterprise Linux versions 7 & 8

Modifiers and Alternation

We may also modify how often a pattern must be matched in order for **grep** to return it. These characters are modifiers:

- ? – Match the preceding 0 or 1 times
- * – Match the preceding 0 or more times
- + – Match the preceding 1 or more times
- {N} – Match the preceding exactly N times
- {N,} – Match the preceding N or more times
- {N,M} – Match the preceding between N and M times

Let's try pulling some numeric strings out of our target file. This evaluates as "Return any line in which a digit, 0 through 9, occurs at least once."
```
# grep -E '[0-9]+' list
0123456789
123
789
```

This evaluates as "Return any line containing a sequence of 3 digits, 0 through 9."
```
# grep -E '[0-9]{3}' list
0123456789
123
789
```

This evaluates as "Return any line containing a sequence of 4 digits, 0 through 9."
```
# grep -E '[0-9]{4}' list
0123456789
```

If we had wanted to return lines containing *only* a 3-digit number, and *nothing else*, there are two solutions. One way is to use anchors and modifiers, like this:
```
# grep -E '^[0-9]{3}$' list
123
789
```

This instructs grep to return lines in which:

- ^ – the line begins, then
- [0-9]{3} – 3 digits (0 through 9) appear in sequence, and then
- $ – the line ends

We could also use the **-x** option, which instructs **grep** to match the given pattern *against entire lines*, rather than finding the pattern *within a line*:
```
# grep -x '[0-9]\{3\}' list
123
789
```

Finally, we may also use **alternation.** Alternation allows us to specify multiple possible patterns, only one of which must be matched to return a result. The metacharacter for alternation is the pipe | which may be read as OR. To match lines beginning with **r** OR ending with **3**:
```
# grep -E '^r|3$' list
red
road
read
radical
123
```
Here we used **-E** to avoid having to escape the pipe metacharacter.

Backreferences

There are also some situations in which we may have an idea of what sort of pattern we want to match, but not precisely which variant of that pattern will be returned. If we wanted to find all instances in which a word was repeated, we might start by creating a pattern that would match any word. We know it would be composed only of uppercase and lowercase alphabetic characters. A set to match any single character like that might look like this: `[a-zA-Z]`

The problem now is that we have no idea how long a word might be. It would be at least one character long, but could be composed of many. We have a way to address this: `[a-zA-Z]+`

The plus sign (+) functions as a **modifier**; it evaluates as "match the preceding pattern one or more times". In other words, a match for the pattern we're working with would be "one or more alphabetic characters in sequence".

To tell grep that we want to find this pattern ONLY when it repeats we need to introduce a new concept: **backreferences**. A backreference allows regular expressions to store a match and refer to it later. To create a stored pattern, we simply surround the match criteria with parenthesis: `([a-zA-Z]+)`

We can store up to nine backreferences in a single expression, and call them with a backslash, followed by a number (1 through 9, based on order of occurrence). To practice this, let's create a small file and run our test pattern against it:
```
# grep -E '([a-zA-Z]+)' testfile

the the
the these
there thesis
the thesis
there there
one one one
```

This returns the entire contents of the file (though it wouldn't have matched any lines containing only numbers, if they had been present). To match repetition, we'll tell grep to match the pattern, store it at /1, and then try to match that pattern again immediately following a space:

```
# grep -E '([a-zA-Z]+) \1' testfile
the the
the these
the thesis
there there
one one one
```

This is close, but we have some odd behaviors. In the second and third lines the stored pattern was matched inside of a longer string. This isn't exactly the desired behavior. To fix this, we need to tell grep to respect word barriers. We can do this by using less than < and greater than >, but we'll need to escape them.

```
# grep -E '(\<[a-zA-Z]+\>) \<\1\>' testfile
the the
there there
one one one
```

Now we have it. If you're concerned about the last line, remember that grep returns entire lines by default. You may troubleshoot grep to a degree by instructing it to return only the matches it finds, rather than the line in which the match occurs. We can do so using the -o option, like this:

```
# grep -oE '(\<[a-zA-Z]+\>) \<\1\>' testfile
the the
there there
one one
```

By default in both EL 7 and 8 grep is aliased so that the matched portion of the lines will be highlighted with color. If this is not the case use the --color option.

```
# grep --color 'pattern' file
```

Another Look

Let's take another look at the expression we introduced at the beginning of this module.

`'@[a-zA-Z_.]\+\?\.[a-zA-Z]\{2,3\}'`

We should be able to break it down now:

- `@` – a literal @ symbol
- `[a-zA-Z_.]` – any lowercase or uppercase alpha character, an underscore, OR a period
- `\+` – match the preceding expression at least once
- `\?` – match the preceding expression no more than once
- `\.` – a literal period
- `[a-zA-Z]` – any alpha character, upper or lowercase
- `\{2,3\}` – match the preceding either 2 or 3 times; no more, no less

If we apply that search to a file containing this:
```
tim@honey.pot.not
tim@honot.not
tim@sonot.au
tim@bonnot
tim.turner
tim.turner@bon_ney.con
@kim.com
a@b.c
```

- Which of these lines will be matched? Which won't, and why?
- What sort of patterns could we place before the @ symbol?
- Can you think of other ways to achieve the same goals?
- Can you improve readability by eliminating the need to escape some of the characters?

sed

The man pages for sed and awk describe them as follows:

- **sed** – stream editor for filtering and transforming text
- **awk** – pattern scanning and processing language. On EL7/8 this links to **/bin/gawk**

Both make use of regular expressions, and both are complex enough that entire books have been written regarding their usage. We cannot, and will not attempt to, cover these utilities comprehensively. Instead, we will focus on some of the more pedestrian uses of each – commands of value to system administrators.

The basic invocation of **sed** is as follows: **sed** *options commands file*. The **options** alter the standard behavior of **sed**; the **commands** define what **sed** will do.

To understand why **sed** does things the way it does, we must first consider **sed**'s standard behavior. Without options, **sed** will do the following:

- Read the first line of input into the pattern space (sed's workspace buffer)
- Perform the commands from the commands section
- Print the contents of the buffer to output
- Clear the buffer
- Read the next line of input into the buffer

We can demonstrate this process by calling **sed** without commands against a file (we'll use a modified copy of our **hosts** file as a target):

```
# sed '' hosts
192.168.1.166       example-svr         example-svr.example.not
192.168.1.165       example-clnt        example-client.example.not
```

Above, **sed** performed its standard behavior by reading in the first line, doing nothing, printing the line to STDOUT, clearing the buffer, and repeating the behavior.

If this description of **sed**'s behavior seems unnecessary, consider the following: there is a command, **p**, which explicitly instructs **sed** to print whatever is currently in the working buffer to output. We know that, as part of its standard behavior, **sed** will already print the contents of the buffer after running any specified commands. The result? See below:

```
# sed 'p' hosts
192.168.1.166       example-svr         example-svr.example.not
192.168.1.166       example-svr         example-svr.example.not
192.168.1.165       example-clnt        example-client.example.not
192.168.1.165       example-clnt        example-client.example.not
```

Each line was printed twice. We could suppress the automatic printing step from the standard behavior with an option, **-n**. Let's try it:

```
# sed -n 'p' hosts
192.168.1.166       example-svr         example-svr.example.not
192.168.1.165       example-clnt        example-client.example.not
```

Keep in mind that **sed** will perform any commands listed in the commands section in order, from left to right. Let's put multiple commands into a single statement using the semicolon as a separator.

```
# sed 'p;s/example/CHANGED/' hosts
192.168.1.166      example-svr       example-svr.example.not
192.168.1.166      CHANGED-svr       example-svr.example.not
192.168.1.165      example-clnt      example-client.example.not
192.168.1.165      CHANGED-clnt      example-client.example.not
```

Walking through the steps, **sed**:

- Reads a line into the buffer.
- Performs the command **p**: print the unmodified line.
- Performs the command **s**, substituting the first instance of **example** with **CHANGED**.
- Finishes its work on the line and prints the results
- Clears the buffer
- Repeats, reading the next line into the buffer.

Armed with this understanding, we can move on to a discussion of **sed**'s more obvious uses.

Perhaps the most common use for **sed** is performing simple pattern substitution; that is, finding a string and replacing it with something else. This is what was done with the earlier command `'s/example/CHANGED/'`.

Let's take a closer look.

```
# cat hosts
192.168.1.166      example-svr       example-svr.example.not
192.168.1.165      example-clnt      example-client.example.not

# sed 's/example/production/' hosts
192.168.1.166      production-svr    example-svr.example.not
192.168.1.165      production-clnt   example-client.example.not
```

Above, **sed** substituted the word **production** for **example**. It will do this once per line unless directed otherwise. A **g** at the end of a command directs **sed** to perform the action 'globally':

```
# sed 's/example/production/g' hosts
192.168.1.166      production-svr    production-svr.production.not
192.168.1.165      production-clnt   production-client.production.not
```

Let's break this command down:

- **s** – substitute
- **/** – delimiter (or separator)
- **example** – what we want to replace
- **/** – delimiter
- **production** – what we want to replace it with
- **/** – delimiter
- **g** – globally – where to make the substitution in the line

Enterprise Linux versions 7 & 8

To save the results, use command line redirection (**>** or **>>**) to a different file. If you try to overwrite the existing file, it will be emptied before `sed` begins executing. To get **sed** to save its changes in the source file, use the **-i** option (in-place edit).

We might also like **sed** to replace patterns based on regular expressions rather than literal character strings. To test this, let's first make some alterations to our text file:
```
# sed -i 's/example/production/' hosts
```

```
# cat hosts
192.168.1.166        production-svr        example-svr.example.not
192.168.1.165        production-clnt       example-client.example.not
```

Let's suppose we wish to accomplish two things: replace all remaining instances of **example** *in the hostname portion only* with **production**, and replace all dashes with underscores. Here's one way to do this:
```
# sed 's/\(production\|example\)-/production_/g' hosts
192.168.1.166        production_svr        production_svr.example.not
192.168.1.165        production_clnt       production_client.example.not
```

Breaking it down:

- **s** – substitute
- **/** – delimiter
- **\(production\|example\)** – match **production** or **example**, escape to metacharacters
- **-** – where **production** or **example** are followed by a literal dash
- **/** – delimiter
- **production_** – replace the matched items with this string
- **/** – delimiter
- **g** – global replacement

A couple of notes regarding sed

The ampersand **&** has a special meaning in `sed`: it corresponds to a previously matched pattern. `grep` allowed matched patterns to be stored using numeric backreferences **1-9**. `sed` accepts these, and adds **&** for use in the replacement section of a substitution command.

Consider the following file, named `subtest`:
```
1-2-3
1.2.3
1:2:3
```

If we wished to double the dashes, dots, and colons, we could do it by using **&**, like this:
```
# sed 's/[.\:-]/&&/g' < subtest
1--2--3
1..2..3
1::2::3
```

Note that parentheses were not required to use the ampersand. Also note, when using a hyphen in a character set, that the hyphen should be placed last in the list so that it is not interpreted as part of a range.

As a final thought, we would like to point out that the use of forward slashes as delimiters (or separators) in `sed` is by convention only. Really, any character that follows the "s" in the substitution command can be used as a separator. This is also a valid sed expression, using pipe **|** as a delimiter:
```
sed 's|[.\:-]|&&|g' < subtest
1--2--3
1..2..3
1::2::3
```

`sed` is a powerful tool, and the uses of it go far beyond what is covered in this material. We encourage students to further explore `sed` if the opportunity presents itself; it can yield tremendous amounts of utility.

awk

Although **awk** usage can be tremendously complex, there are times when simple invocations of **awk** are the best tool for accomplishing a particular task. In this section, we will briefly discuss how **awk** treats files, then proceed to a series of small examples with accompanying explanation.

awk sees files as a series of records and fields, which it reviews one line at a time. The default field separator is whitespace, and the default record separator is a linefeed. Consider this:
```
Apple $1.95
Pear $0.57
Strawberry $1.26
```

By default, **awk** would see this as a set of 3 records, with 2 fields each.

Let's suppose we only wanted the information from the first field in our file (the fruit names). We could ask **awk** to **print** them in this way:
```
# awk '{ print $1 }' pfile
Apple
Pear
Strawberry
```

$1, in this case, is a built-in variable that **awk** understands as "the first field". We could print the second field with **$2**. **$0** is the entire line, and **$NF** (Number of Fields) functions here as a shortcut to the last field:
```
# awk '{ print $0 }' pfile
Apple $1.95
Pear $0.57
Strawberry $1.26

# awk '{ print $NF }' pfile
$1.95
$0.57
$1.26
```

We can also redefine the field separator from whitespace to something else. Let's try this with **/etc/passwd**:
```
# awk -F: '/1[0-9][0-9][0-9]/ { print $1,$3 }' /etc/passwd
Lisa 1003
caroline 1004
lori 1005
bob 1006
ldapuser1 1007
ldapuser2 1008
```

Let's break that down:

-       **-F:**   – set field separator to colon
- **/1[0-9][0-9][0-9]/** – match this pattern (it's a RegEx!)
- **{ print $1,$3 }** – print fields 1 and 3

awk substitutions

To this point, we've used `awk` in a fashion silmilar to `grep`. It can also be used much like `sed`, to perform substitutions. As with `sed`, we can specify whether we wish those substitutions to be made once per line (record) or globally within a line. To do this, we will use two functions built into awk: **sub** and **gsub**.

Returning to a previous example file, we can demonstrate these functions by replacing the sting "the" with the string "THE":

```
# awk '{ sub(/the/,"THE"); print }' regtest
THE the
THE these
THEre thesis
THE thesis
THEre there
one one one
```

Breaking it down, we see:

- `awk '{ }'` – the invocation of awk and the braces containing the program
- `sub( )` – the substitution function (one replacement per record)
- `/the/,` – the pattern we are searching for, comma is a delimiter
- `"THE"` – what to replace matched patterns with
- `; print` – semicolon separates commands, print prints to STDOUT
- `regtest` – the input file

To replace all matches, rather than a single match per record, we could instead use the **gsub** function, as follows:

```
# awk '{ gsub(/the/,"THE"); print }' regtest
THE THE
THE THEse
THEre THEsis
THE THEsis
THEre THEre
one one one
```

The invocation for the two functions is identical, but we can now see that all matches have been replaced, as desired.

awk programs

We can write **awk** programs as if they were shell scripts. Here is one called `/awkish`:

```
#!/bin/gawk -f

BEGIN { print "Record and Fields of:" }
{ if(NR == 1) { print FILENAME }; }
END { print "\n""Num Recs:\t",NR,"\n""Num Fields:\t",NF }
```

Running that gets us this:
```
# /awkish pfile
Record and Fields of:
pfile

Num Recs:       3
Num Fields:     2
```

awk programs consist of three main sections:

- **BEGIN** – We run these lines first. Often used to make header or set variables.
- **BODY** – Typically where we put the bulk of our work.
- **END** – Runs these lines last. Often used to create a footer.

In the script, we specified a program which should be used to interpret our commands: `#! /bin/gawk -f`. The `-f` option tells it to expect a file as an argument. We passed it `pfile` at runtime, which uses whitespace as a record separator. What would happen if we had passed it something like `/etc/group` instead?
```
# /awkish /etc/group
Record and Fields of:
/etc/group

Num Recs:       88
Num Fields:     1
```

One field? Let's use **awk** and **sed** to get the first line out of that file so we can take a closer look.
```
# awk 'NR==1 { print }' /etc/group
root:x:0:

# sed -n '1p' /etc/group
root:x:0:
```

Human eyes would register at least 3 fields here (technically four – the last field is just empty). We've used `-F` to set the separator to a colon earlier; this time, let's declare it in the **BEGIN** section of our **awk** script.
```
BEGIN { FS=":";print "Record and Fields of:" }
```

We added `FS=":";` to the `BEGIN` section of our script. This sets the **F**ield **S**eparator to a colon. Running it again:

```
# /awkish /etc/group
Record and Fields of:
/etc/group

Num Recs:       88
Num Fields:     4
```

As used above, `FS` and `NR` are built-in variables that **awk** populates based on what it knows about a file. Here's a short list of the more commonly used ones:

- **FILENAME** – the name of the input file; undefined in BEGIN block
- **FS/RS** – input field separator/record separator
- **OFS/ORS** – output field separator/record separator
- **NF** – number of fields in current record
- **NR** – number of current record
- **FNR** – if multiple input files, record number of current file
- **$0** – entire current record
- **$n** – where **n** is a number; field by sequence e.g. **$1,$2**

Let's reexamine a line from the body section of our **awk** script.
`{ if(NR == 1) { print FILENAME }; }`

In the above example, the outer curly braces simply represent the BODY of the script and the semicolon ends the line. We may disregard them for the moment and break down the remainder:
if(*condition* **) {** *action* **};**

This is a conditional statement. As a condition we used **NR==1**. **NR** is a variable which holds the current record number. The double equal signs == are interpreted as "is equal to". In other words, the statement reads: *"if we are currently evaluating the first record of the file"*. If the condition evaluates as true, the action portion of the statement is executed – otherwise, the program simply continues.

Our action was **print FILENAME**. When the script executed, the condition evaluated as TRUE, and the filename was printed exactly once – when we evaluated the first record.

Returning to our example:

```
#!/bin/gawk -f

BEGIN { print "Record and Fields of:" }
{ if(NR == 1) { print FILENAME }; }
END { print "\n""Num Recs:\t",NR,"\n""Num Fields:\t",NF }
```

Finally, The **\n** represents a newline, and the **\t** represents a horizontal tab. Simply put, it made the output prettier.

Consider this example, using echo instead of awk:
```
# echo -e "hi \t there \n"
hi       there
```

Enterprise Linux versions 7 & 8

Module 7: Booting

Boot Sequence

The boot sequence of an EL7/8 system is:
- **UEFI** or **BIOS** – firmware which checks the hardware, initializes it, and specifies (or in the case of UEFI without compatibility support *detects*) the boot device. It will then load the bootstrap program from the either the Master Boot Record (BIOS or CSM) or a separate `/boot` partition (UEFI).
    - Most current implementations of UEFI run with the compatibility support module (CSM) enabled. This will end soon, as support for CSM/legacy BIOS ends in 2020.

- **Bootstrap**
    - UEFI – will read from a special boot partition (either `/boot/efi` or `/efi/BOOT`). The file be named something like `grubx64.efi`.
        - The integrity of `grubx64.efi` and of the kernel are validated using keys stored in a file called `shim.efi`.
    - MBR – the first 512 bytes on the boot device; containing `boot.img` in the first 446 bytes, followed by four 16-byte Primary partition tables, and a two-byte magic number (`xAA55`).
        - `boot.img` in turn loads `core.img`
        - `core.img` is written in the empty space between the MBR and the first partition
            - It loads configuration files, and other modules needed to boot such as filesystem drivers.
            - `core.img` is generated during installation.
    - The `grub2` process then starts.
    - Additional or alternative images may also be loaded, for instance for network boot.

- **grub2** – the bootloader for EL7/8. It will read the appropriate `grub.cfg` and provide a text menu based on it to select an operating system. Typically `grub2` will then:
    - Mount the filesystem in read-only mode
    - Load the kernel from a compressed file (`vmlinuz`)
    - Mount an initial read-write filesystem (the `initramfs`) in RAM and load load an image (the `initrd`) into it which will have the remainder of the necessary modules and instructions to load the actual run-time kernel for use.
        - The image contents can be viewed using `# lsinitrd`
    - Mount the root filesystem in read-write mode, then start the kernel.
        - At this point logging to the kernel ring buffer begins.
        - These logs are viewable with `# dmesg`

- o Much of this is done through a program called **dracut**, which generates the `initramfs`. Any opotions you see beginning with **rd.** are options passed to `dracut`.
- o The kernel will then launch **systemd**

- **systemd** – the first userspace process which initiates all other processes. It will examine all the unit files required or wanted by the destination target using a series of small executables called generators. Using the information from them it will build a dependency tree, and initialize all needed mounts, devices, services, and sockets in an appropriate order.

grub.cfg, grub2-mkconfig, grub2-setpassword

Grub will read either **/boot/grub2/grub.cfg** or **/boot/efi/EFI/redhat/grub.cfg** to determine what menu it should present and how it should boot. This file should not be edited directly. Any changes made to this file will be overwritten by other processes.

Instead changes should be made to **/etc/default/grub** or to files in **/etc/grub.d/**
These changes then are exported to `grub.cfg` using
```
# grub2-mkconfig -o /path/grub.cfg
```

Things you might change in **/etc/default/grub** are:
- **GRUB_TIMEOUT** – number of seconds before executing the default
    - o If set to **0** there will be no grub menu.
    - o This can be overridden by pressing **shift**.
- **GRUB_DISABLE_RECOVERY** – If set to **"false"** (notice the quotes), will show all available kernels and a rescue mode option for each.
- **GRUB_DISABLE_SUBMENU** – If set to **false** (notice no quotes), will collapse all non-default kernels into a sub-menu labeled **Advanced Options**.
- **GRUB_CMDLINE_LINUX** – specifies arguments passed to the kernel at boot.
- **GRUB_DEFAULT** – the default kernel entry.
    - o It can be index number of a menu entry, a menu entry name, or the special string **saved** – which points to the variable **saved_entry**.
        - ▪ You can see all available menu entries with
          ```
          # grep ^menu grub.cfg
          ```
        - ▪ You can view `saved_entry` with
          ```
          # grub2-editenv list
          ```
        - ▪ You can change `saved_entry` with
          ```
          # grub2-set-default
          ```
            - • This can be the number of the menu entry (counting from 0)
            - • Or the name with double quotes around it.
            - • This alters the system generated file **grubenv**.
    - o When you upgrade the kernel, the **grubby** tool will create a new menu entry and update the value of `saved_entry`.
        - ▪ It will also automatically backup the old `grub.cfg`

Enterprise Linux versions 7 & 8

Custom entries can also be placed in files in **/etc/grub.d/**. The files are processed in lexical alphabetic order. In case of a conflict, the option processed last wins. When you are done making changes, it is best to backup the old `grub.cfg` before running **grub2-mkconfig**

Another way to alter `grub.cfg` is with the use of **grubby**. If `grubby` is used, be aware any changes made will be overwritten the next time `grub2-mkconfig` is invoked.

In addition to `grub` menu configuration changes the boot process can be changed during boot. This is done by pressing **e**. This will allow you to edit the currently selected boot entry. Most edits will be done to the line which begins **linux16** or **linuxefi**. To boot **CTL-x**. To return to the menu **ESC**. For a very limited command line **CTL-c**. These kernel command line changes can be made permanent using GRUB_CMDLINE_LINUX as above.

Common edits to the kernel command line are:
- Remove:
    - **rhgb** – prevent Red Hat Graphical Boot, which hides boot messages
    - **quiet** – do not supress detailed boot messages
- Add:
    - **rescue** – mounts all filesystems, root login only, no networking.
    - **emergency** – mounts the root filesystem read only, minimal services
    - **systemd.unit=**some.target – define the target to boot to
    - **rd.break** – when `dracut` exits, drop to a shell.
        - This is similar to emergency mode but there is no need for a password as the 'real' kernel has not yet loaded.
    - **selinux=0** – do not load the SELinux kernel module, prevents SELinux from running at all. Should not be a default, for testing and maintainence only.
    - **enforcing=0** – set SELinux into permissive mode, it will log violations, but not prevent them. Should not be a default, for testing and maintainence only.
    - **audit=1** – turns on auditing for processes which begin before `auditd` initiates.
    - **nosmt=force** – disables simultaneous multithreading as a security measure against exploits such as L1TF and MDS
    - **mitigations=auto** or **auto,nosmt** – further mitigations for L1TF and MDS
    - **spectre_v2=retpoline** – mitigation for the Spectre vulnerability family
    - **fips=1** – require FIPS compliant encryption, should be set during installation

To prevent unauthorized alteration of the boot sequence you have two alternatives. You can set **GRUB_TIMEOUT=0**. Downside: no one, not even legitimate users, can alter the boot sequence. It is better (and required by STIG) to password protect the menu. Use
grub2-setpassword

The technique shown some documentation in which a password hash is manually inserted into a file is outdated and will not work. The grub password should not be the same as root's login password.

To restrict booting of a particular menu entry: Manually remove `--unrestricted` from the menu entry in `/boot/grub2/grub.cfg`. This is the only time you should directly edit this file. The restriction will remain when new kernel versions are installed, but will be lost the next time you use `grub2-mkconfig`. This will require use of the grub password to boot that entry.

To prevent unauthorized access, ensure that ownership of `grub.cfg` is `root:root` and permissions are set to `600`.

Recovering the root Password

If you have lost the root password you can recover it either using an installation disk, or by altering the boot sequence. To use the install disk:
- Choose Troubleshooting, Rescue a System, you will get a prompt (`sh-4.2#`).
- The root partition will be the temporary RAM filesystem, not the **real** system root. Fix this with `# chroot /mnt/sysimage`.
- You can now run `# passwd root`, or any perform any other needed repairs.
- Because you changed files while SELinux wasn't looking, they need to have their security contexts restored.
    - If you only reset a password, `# restorecon /etc/shadow`
    - If you altered other files, you can run `restorecon` against them as well.
    - If you aren't sure, `# touch /.autorelabel`
      This will fix security context on all files in the filesystem on next reboot. It takes longer, but it's safer.
- `# reboot`

To recover a lost password by altering the boot:
- Press **e** to edit at the grub menu.
    - If needed, enter the password
- Add to the `linux` line: `rd.break enforcing=0`
- Start the boot process with **CTL-x**
- Mount the root filesystem and use it as /
    - `# mount -o remount,rw /sysroot`
    - `# chroot /sysroot`
- Change the password and resume boot
    - `# passwd root`
        - In FIPS mode you may receive an error:
          `no entropy gathering module`, to correct this
            - `# /bin/mknod -m 0666 /dev/random c 1 8`
            - `# /bin/mknod -m 0666 /dev/urandom c 1 9`
            - `# /bin/chown root:root /dev/random /dev/urandom`
    - `# exit ; # exit`
- Fix the security context using `restorecon` or `/.autorelabel` as above
- `# reboot`

systemd

When grub launches the kernel (via `dracut`), it hands over control to **systemd**. The first thing `systemd` does is run **systemd.generator**, a series of small programs which can dynamically create symlinks or unit files as appropriate. An example is the **systemd-fstab-generator**, which reads `/etc/fstab` and creates appropriate `.mount` units in a temporary filesystem.

It then reads `/etc/systemd/system/default.target`, which is a symlink to a `.target` unit file. The target specifies which services to start at boot.
- The default target can be set with **# systemctl set-default** *some.target*
- It can be over-ridden with **systemd.unit=** passed as a kernel command line option
- The targets are roughly equivalent to the classic SystemV init-based runlevels and are aliased to them for backwards compatibility.
  - Switch running targets by issuing **# systemctl isolate** *dest.target*
  - **runlevel** and **telinit** will work, but are not recommended.

Valid targets for isolation or default are:
- **emergency** – Bypasses all other services.
Equivalent to passing **emergency** on the kernel command line
- **rescue** – The same as passing **rescue**. Aliased as runlevel 1.
- **multiuser** – Text based, all services. Aliased as runlevels 2, 3 & 4.
- **graphical** – Multi-user plus the pretty stuff. Aliased as runlevel 5.
- **halt** – Stop the system, but don't power off.
- **poweroff** – Full shutdown. Aliased as runlevel 0.
- **reboot** – Restart the system. Aliased as runlevel 6.
  - Can also be invoked by **CTL-ALT-DEL**, this should be disabled
    - **# systemctl mask --now ctrl-alt-del.service**
    - **# systemctl mask --now ctrl-alt-del.target**
  - On GUI systems additional steps are needed to prevent user-induced reboot
- **system-update** – Used for offline installation of software that may otherwise conflict with a running system. See the man page for **systemd.offline-updates**
- **kexec** – used to boot to another kernel, usually not run by a user.

There are also lots of special targets, which are not destinations, but instead are waypoints between destinations. A listing can be found in the man page for **systemd.special**.

After reading the target's unit file and running the generators `systemd` then builds a dependency tree like this:

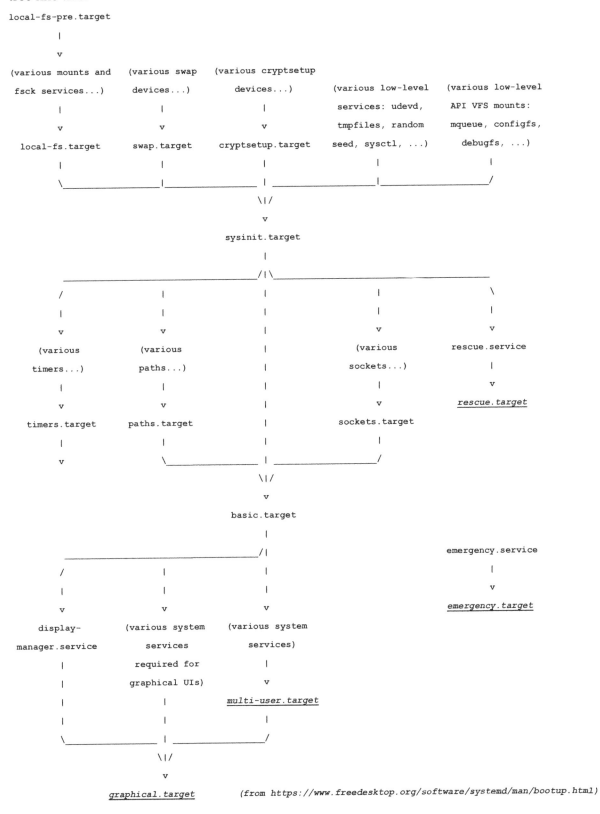

(from https://www.freedesktop.org/software/systemd/man/bootup.html)

Enterprise Linux versions 7 & 8

It builds this tree by analyzing the dependencies as configured in the unit files. There are several ways to visualize the dependency tree:
- `# systemd-analyze critical-chain` – also shows start time information
- `# systemd-cgls` – shows all scopes and slices, but not targets
- `# systemctl list-dependencies` – shows dependencies for a service
    - `--reverse` – shows what depends on a service
    - `--before` / `--after` – shows order of units
- `# systemctl show` – allows reading of the dependencies manually

systemctl

The `systemctl` command has already been mentioned, and will be brought up again in multiple places. It is used to examine and control `systemd` and the service manager. Here are a few of the more common verbs for controlling services:
- `status` – shows general status and state
- `show` – lists all properties
- `list-units` – show units in memory
- `start/stop/restart` – control the running state
- `reload` – force the service to re-read configuration files (.conf, not unit files)
- `daemon-reload` – re-read unit files and re-run the systemd generator for dependencies
- `enable/disable` – turn on/off service auto-start
    - `enable --now` – equivalent to `enable` and `start`
- `mask/unmask` – completely prevent a service from starting
- `is-enabled` – query enable status
- `verify` – check syntax on unit files
- `cat` – print assembled unit files for a service
- `isolate` – change running state to a designated target (`multi-user`, `graphical`)
- `get-default` / `set-default` – control default target
- `halt` / `reboot` / `poweroff` – control power state

To limit the results of `systemctl` you can use:
- `--type=service, socket ,target, device, mount, automount, swap, timer, path, slice, scope`
- `--state=active, inactive, failed, dead, running`
    - more can be found with `--state=help`

Unit Files

Unit files are the way we configure almost everything that `systemd` touches. Many command line tools that involve anything controlled by `systemd` will generate or alter unit files on the fly. Enabling and disabling services does nothing more than create a symlink to a unit file in a directory that `systemd` will read when loading (on boot or when triggered with **daemon-reload**). Masking a service creates a link from that unit file's name to `/dev/null`, preventing it from ever running.

Unit files have a standard syntax common to all unit types, as well as specialized syntax for different unit types. The man pages are the best reference. For the generic unit configuration consult the man pages for **systemd.unit** and **systemd.resource-control**. To see a list of man pages for the specialized unit types
```
# man -k systemd | grep "unit configuration"
```

The **[Unit]** portion is required for all unit files. Among other things, it can contain:
- **Description=** The program description, mandatory.
- **Documentation=** URL/URI for documentation.
- **Requires=** Other units that must be started with this unit. This unit will be deactivated if required units fail or gets deactivated.
- **Wants=** Other units that will be started with this unit. Softer than **Requires=**, this unit will not fail if the wanted units fail.
    - If a *servicename*.**wants/** or *servicename*.**requires/** directory exists, symlinks to other unit files can be placed here. They will be treated as though those units were listed in the **Wants=** or **Requires=** line.
- **Before=** and **After=** Used to modify the start order of **Wanted** or **Required** units. Refers to this unit's relation to the ones listed:
    - **Before=** means that this unit will start before those listed.
    - **After=** wait for the named unit to fully start before attempting to run this unit.
- **Conflicts=** Units that cannot run with this unit. Starting one of these will stop this unit, and vice-versa.
- **AllowIsolate=true** Allows the use of `# systemctl isolate` *target*; a method to switch between destination targets. This will conflict all units which are not required by the named target and then start it.

Unit files may optionally have an **[Install]** section which can contain:
- **Alias=** An alternate name; `syslog.service` is an alias for `rsyslog.service`
- **WantedBy=** / **RequiredBy=** Allows a unit file to be enabled and tells `systemctl enable` which directory to create symlinks to.
    - Some units do not have a `WantedBy` or `RequiredBy` and cannot be enabled. Instead they are triggered by other unit file types which wait for an event such as `.socket` or `.timer`.
- **Also=** Units which will be installed when this unit is enabled.

Enterprise Linux versions 7 & 8

Some units can be used to trigger other unit files (typically a `.service`) or perform an action when a condition is met. Unit types which can be used as triggers include:
- `.automount` – mounts a file system when a directory is accessed
- `.path` – executes a service when the contents of a directory is changed
- `.timer` – executes another unit at a given time
- `.socket` – starts a service when a network connection to it is made

Settings from unit files stored in **/etc/systemd/system** will override settings in any other location, such as **/usr/lib/systemd/system**. Therefore, that is where you usually should make your changes.

The validity of a unit file can be checked with
`systemd-analyze verify` *name.service*

If there are no errors it will not produce an output. If it is valid, run
`systemctl daemon-reload`

This makes `systemd` re-read all unit files and regenerate the dependency tree. Relevant services may also need to be restarted.

Shutdown is nothing more than isolation to another target. The commands **shutdown**, **reboot**, and **halt** are wrappers for this. The dependency tree for shutdown is this:

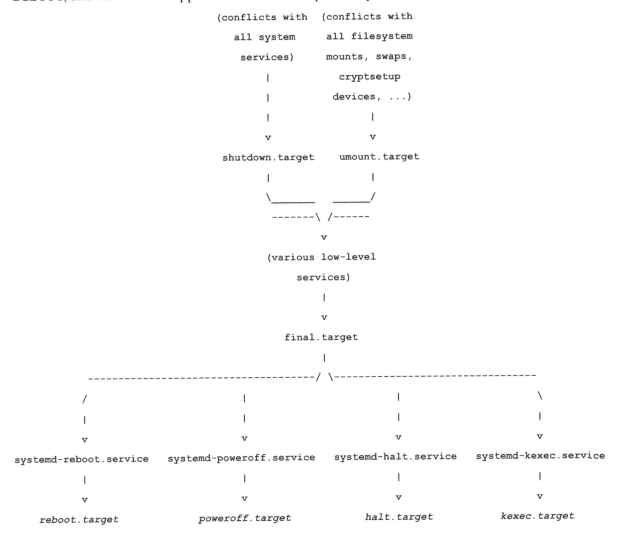

(from https://www.freedesktop.org/software/systemd/man/bootup.html)

Module 8: Processes and Services

When you boot an EL system the BIOS or EFI locates the boot device and begins reading it, the bootloader (`grub2`) loads the Linux kernel and mounts the root filesystem read-only, finally the kernel takes the command line arguments passed to it by `grub` and starts **systemd.**

This is the first process and is ultimately responsible for the initiation of all further processes, from remounting the root filesystem as a read-write device, and configuring networking, to providing a `bash` prompt for you to log in to. The kernel does not really count as a process. Rather it sits below all other running processes and controls the hardware, taking requests from the user-space programs in the form of system calls and returning the results.

Every process is assigned a Process ID (**PID**), a unique number that the kernel uses to track processes. As the first process, **systemd** will receive **PID 1**. In most earlier versions of Unix-like systems this role was taken by the process `init`. Beginning with the release of EL7 in 2014 `systemd` has been the only available initialization process. Some members of the EL family (such as Fedora) adopted it as early as 2011. Most other major distributions including Debian and Ubuntu have also adopted it. We will address `systemd` later, first we need to look at the processes that come after `systemd`, and how to control them.

ps, pgrep, kill, pkill, killall

Before you can control processes, you must first identify them. The most direct way to find processes running on a system is with **ps**. Common invocations include:
- **# ps -ef** – everything, full listing
- **# ps -u** *username* – display only processes from a user
- **# ps -eo pid,user,pmem,args --sort pmem** – everything, with column selection and sorting
    - Column keywords can be found under **STANDARD FORMAT SPECIFIERS** in the man page for **ps**

Long ago there was a divergence from the UNIX/POSIX standard by the BSD group. While you can use the BSD style switches (most commonly **aux** or **-aux** as an equivalent to **-ef**), use of the POSIX standard switches is encouraged.

Another handy way to find processes is by the use of **pgrep**. For instance, if you want to find the PIDs of `ssh` processes being run by a user: **# pgrep -u** *username* **ssh**. If you also want to see the command line that invoked it add **-a**. To see the newest process (other than `pgrep`) currently running **# pgrep -na**.

Processes are controlled by sending them signals. There are 64 signals defined in EL, each defined by a number and a short ALL CAPS word. The important ones from a system administrator's viewpoint are:
- 1 `HUP` – Reread your configuration file and restart
- 2 `INT` – End, gracefully if possible
    - Sent by `CTL-c`
    - Cannot be ignored
- 3 `QUIT` – End now, provide a core dump if possible
    - Sent by `CTL-\`
- 15 `TERM` – End, gracefully
    - Can be ignored
- 9 `KILL` – End now
    - Cannot be ignored
- 19 `STOP` – Pause
- 20 `STP` – Pause
    - Can be ignored
    - Sent by `CTL-z`
- 18 `CONT` – Resume
    - Sent by `fg` and `bg` discussed in the next section

Signals can be sent with the `kill` command. The common invocation is `# kill -9` *PID*
You can also use `pkill` or `killall` to signal multiple processes.
- `# pkill -9` *processname*
- `# pkill -9 -u` *username*
- `# killall -9` *processname*
- `# killall -9 -i -u` *username*

Before you use any of these tools be aware that you can (and likely will) destroy stuff along the way. Terminating the wrong process can forcefully log you out or completely lock a computer. Some things to be aware of:
- `kill`
    - If *PID* is `0`, all processes in the current group are signaled, including your login
    - If *PID* is `-1` is all processes other than systemd are signaled
- `pkill`
    - uses `-v` for invert, like pgrep
        - `# pkill -9 -v sleep` will kill every process not named `sleep`
- `killall`
    - uses `-v` for verbose mode, **unlike** pkill/pgrep
    - has `-i` for interactive, it will ask you before killing things

jobs, bg, fg, disown

Thus far all the processes you have started have been issued from the command line and have run in the foreground while you watched. This is not always what you want to do though. You may not want to give up your bash prompt for half an hour while logs are compressed and moved. To start a command in the background put an ampersand at the end of the line:
```
# tar -cvf /lotsostuff/* tarball.tgz &
```

You also have some options to control a job after you have started it in the foreground. You can suspend a job with **CTL-z**. You can get a list of all stopped and backgrounded jobs with
```
# jobs
[2]     Running                 sleep 99999 &
[3]+    Stopped                 vi
[4]-    Stopped                 man man
```

To bring a job to the foreground, type **fg** and the job number. To resume the job in the background, **bg** and the job number. If you issue **fg** or **bg** with no number the command will be applied to the job with the plus sign; the minus indicates the job which will be assigned the plus sign next.

All job manipulation is shell specific. You cannot **bg** a job in one terminal and **fg** it in another. If you log out, any stopped or backgrounded jobs are lost. To prevent this, you must
```
# disown -h job-number    or   # disown -ha
```
(all jobs)

top, uptime, free, vmstat

You can also view and control running processes using **top**. This displays a header bar summarizing the state of the system:

```
top - 08:36:00 up 17:53,  2 users,  load average: 3.21, 0.76, 0.31
Tasks: 163 total,  12 running, 150 sleeping,  1 stopped,   0 zombie
%Cpu(s):100.0 us, 0.0 sy, 0.0 ni, 0.0 id,0.0 wa,0.0 hi,0.0 si, 0.0 st
KiB Mem:2916168 total, 2053344 free,   384916 used,  477908 buff/cache
KiB Swap:  3776504 total,  3776504 free,      0 used.  2290980 avail Mem
```

The first line displays the current time, **up**time since last boot, number of logged in **users**, and **load average** – the number of processes waiting in the cpu queue over the last 1, 5, and 15 minutes. This line is also displayed by **w** and **uptime**.

The **Tasks** line shows the number of processes: **total**, **running**, **sleeping** (waiting for something to happen), **stopped** (via **CTL-z** or a **STOP** signal), and **zombies** (those that have terminated, but not fully exited).

The **Cpu** display can be switched between cumulative and per cpu statistics by pressing **1**. The numbers on the Cpu line are:
- **us**er – all programs that don't belong to the kernel
- **sy**stem – kernel programs, such as networking or I/O operations
- **ni**ce – time spent running programs that have been niced
- **id**le – time spent doing nothing
- **wa**it – time spent waiting for the outside world such as I/O
- **hi** & **si** – time spent servicing hard and soft interrupts
- **st**olen – only seen on virtual machines hosted on Linux. This is the time spent waiting for cpu because another VM was using it.

The **Mem**ory and **Swap** lines should be self-explanatory, with the exception of **buff/cache** – which is the amount of memory used by the kernel in pre-read buffers and write caches.

This information can also be obtained in a more readable format with **# free -h**; and in a less readable format, with more detail using **# vmstat**.

Below the header is a list of processes:
```
PID USER    PR  NI   VIRT    RES   SHR  S  %CPU %MEM   TIME+   COMMAND
649 root    20   0  228920   6228  4632 S   0.3  0.2   0:41.06 vmtoolsd
```
- `PID, USER, COMMAND` – the PID, user who issued the command and the command name.
- `PR & NI` – The scheduling priority and niceness value
- `VIRT` – Virtual image: the total memory size of the process, including all shared libraries, pages swapped out to disk, and pages allocated, but not used.
- `RES` – Resident memory: the actual physical memory in use.
- `SHR` – Shared memory: or at least potentially shared memory (such as libraries).
- `S` – Status: Running, Sleeping, sTopped, Zombie, Dead (uninterruptible sleep).
- `%CPU, %MEM, TIME+` – Percentages of cpu and memory, as well as total cpu time taken. Note that `%CPU` is based on one core and may exceed 100% in a multicore system.

There are a number of commands that can be issued within `top`. Useful ones include:
- `h` – Display a help screen
- `d` – set update interval in seconds
- `i` – toggle idle processes
- `n` – Change the number of processes displayed.
- `f` – Select fields to display
- `M` – Sort by memory usage.
- `P` – Sort by CPU usage.
- `T` – Sort by cpu time.
- `R` – Reverse sort order
- `<>` – navigate
- `V` – Show parent process relationships
- `c` – show full command line
- `u` – Filter by user.
- `o` – Add filters, for example:
  - `%CPU>0.1`
  - `!USER=root`
  - `COMMAND=httpd`
- `CTL-o` – Display filters
- `=` – Clear filters
- `L` – locate string
- `r` – Renice a process
- `k` – Send a signal / kill a process
- `W`—Save current configuration to `~/.toprc`

If you wish to use a more modern version of `top`, `htop` is available in the EPEL.

nice, renice, ionice, taskset

There are several different ways to limit and prioritize resource usage, the simplest is based on cpu priority. Priority is controlled by the niceness value. This can be found with
`# ps -eo nice,pid,user,comm`

Niceness is an integer from **-20** to **19**, with lower numbers being higher in priority (less nice). A process started from the command line has a default niceness of **0**. To start a command with a different value, use **nice**. If you simply issue `# nice` *command*, that command will be started with a niceness of **10**. Use **-n** to set a different value.

Once a command is running its niceness can be adjusted using
`# renice` *PID*

This can be done for all processes owned by a user `# renice -n -10 -u` *username*.

You can renice groups of processes using either command expansion or **xargs**:
`# renice -n +15 $(pgrep chrome)`
   or
`# pgrep bc | xargs renice -n -15`

Processes also have a scheduling priority for disk access. This can be viewed and controlled using **ionice**, which allows scheduling in classes of **realtime**, **best-effort**, or **idle** time only.

A given process can be assigned to run on a specified processor or processor set. This is known as processor affinity and while not often done, it can have large performance benefits. In EL processor affinity is set using **taskset**.

cgroups: slices, scopes, services

You can also control resource utilization using control groups, known as **cgroups**. EL7/8 uses `systemd` to create a series of `slices`, which can contain `sub-slices`, `scopes`, and `services`. A `scope` is a group of externally created processes such as a user session or a virtual machine. A `service` is a group of processes started by `systemd` based on a unit file. Each of these is a cgroup that can be individually regulated regarding memory, i/o, and cpu usage.

Slices are arranged hierarchically beginning at `-.slice`, where `systemd` lives. Below `-.slice` are a `system.slice`, the default for services; a `user.slice`, where user sessions exist, and a `machine.slice` where VMs and containers are run.

Additional slices, scopes, and services can be created either transiently or permanently. To see all active `cgroups` and the processes contained within them:

```
# systemd-cgls
├─1 /usr/lib/systemd/systemd --switched-root --system --deserialize 21
├─user.slice
│ └─user-0.slice
│   ├─session-158.scope
│   │ ├─9329 sshd: root@pts/2
│   │ ├─9334 -bash
│   │ ├─9502 systemd-cgls
│   │ └─9503 less
│   └─session-157.scope
│     ├─9255 sshd: root@pts/1
│     ├─9260 -bash
│     ├─9470 man systemd-system.conf
│     └─9475 less -s
============================= >SNIPPED HERE< =========================
└─system.slice
  ├─udisks2.service
  │ └─2642 /usr/lib/udisks2/udisksd --no-debug
  ├─wpa_supplicant.service
  │ └─2588 /usr/sbin/wpa_supplicant -u -f /var/log/wpa_supplicant.log
  ├─packagekit.service
  │ └─2587 /usr/libexec/packagekitd
```

Here you can see the `-.slice`, the `user.slice`, and a sub-slice for **user-0** (root). Below `user-0.slice` are two scopes, each representing a separate login session. Below the snip line you can see the beginning of the `system.slice` with several services contained within it.

You can list existing cgroups by type using
`# systemctl -t` *type* where *type* is **slice**, **scope**, or **service**.

Each of these steps in the hierarchy: slices, scopes, and services is a control group and is represented by a unit file (or files). Unit files can be stored in several different directories, these are evaluated in this order with the final setting being the one applied:
- Permanent files created or controlled by the system **/usr/lib/systemd/system/**
- Temporary files created on the fly by the systemd generator **/run/systemd/transient**
    - Additional files may be created in **/sys/fs/cgroup** and **/run/systemd/system**
- Permanent files created by users **/etc/systemd/system/**

Additional files may be placed in separate **.d** directories which override the base unit file. Thus anything placed in **/usr/lib/systemd/system/httpd.service.d/** will override the **httpd.service** unit. In EL8 a full list of paths used by systemd can be found with
 # systemd-analyze unit-paths

Overridden configuration files can be found with
 # systemd-delta

Any unit can be individually configured for resource control by editing the proper unit file. Resource controls are inherited from parent to child. This means that a child process will not exceed the limits placed on a parent, unless explicitly overridden in the child's unit file.

Controls are measured in different ways:
- **Absolute values** – **MemoryHigh=1G** sets a hard 1G limit.
- **Relative to available resources** – Setting **CPUQuota=150%** and **MemoryHigh=33%** will restrict a group to 1½ cpu core's worth of compute and ⅓ of installed memory.
- **Relative to each other** – If there are three cgroups with the first having **CPUWeight=200**, the second **[Not Set]** (default is **100**), and the third with **CPUWeight=50**; they will get cpu in the ration of 4:2:1 respectively.

The controls available and their names have been rapidly evolving and are different from EL7 to EL8, and even vary between minor versions. For instance CPUWeight mentioned above is EL8 specific, replacing CPUShares from EL7. Before configuring, consult the man page for **systemd.resource-control** for your specific version. It should also be noted that **IPAddressAllow** and **IPAddressDeny** do not work in EL8 at this time.

To demonstrate this we will create a default control set for all users, a less restrictive one for root (UID 0), and a more restrictive one for the user bob, who has a UID of 1005.

For these controls to be effective, the user must execute a true login. If # su - is used the secondary bash session will be a part of the original parent cgroup and will inherit the settings appropriately.

Create **/etc/systemd/system/user-.slice.d/defaults.conf**

```
[Unit]
Description=User Slice of UID %j
After=systemd-user-sessions.service
[Slice]
TasksMax=2000
MemoryMax=1G
CPUQuota=100%
```

For root create **/etc/systemd/system/user-0.slice.d/defaults.conf**

```
[Slice]
TasksMax=infinity
MemoryHigh=1G
CPUQuota=200%
```

For bob create **/etc/systemd/system/user-1005.slice.d/defaults.conf**

```
[Slice]
TasksMax=200
MemoryHigh=250M
CPUQuota=50%
```

There are several tools for viewing information about running cgroups:
- `# ps -o args,cgroup | less` – current `cgroup` information
- `# systemctl show user-`*UID*`.slice` – effective options on the current slice
- `# systemd-cgtop` – resource usage by slice, `h` for help

New control groups can also be generated by `systemd-run`, and copied. To do this:
`# systemd-run --unit=`*tempname* `[--scope][--slice=`*slice-name*`] \`
`/`*path*`/`*command* `-options &`

`scope` and `slice` are mutually exclusive. If given a unique `slice` name, a new slice will be created and the service run there. If given `scope` it will run in the current slice, typically `user.slice`. If neither are specified, it will run under `system.slice`.

The command to be run can be anything executable. However it will need to be labeled as a binary (`bin_t`) by SELinux. The easiest way to achieve this is by placing it in a binary directory such as `/usr/sbin/`.

This creates a transient service, scope, or slice with unit files stored in `/run/systemd/` and associated `.d` directories.

You can tune the running properties of the service using like this:
`# systemctl set-property` *tempname*`.service MemoryLimit=10K`

To make the service persistent, you will need to create a unit file. An easy way to accomplish this is to copy the transient file set to a permanent location:
`# systemctl cat` *tempname.service* `> /etc/systemd/system/`*name.service*
Use a destination service name which is different from the running name, otherwise you will have a conflict later. Ensure that the file has permission and ownership of `644 root:root`

It is good practice to then clean up the file, add dependencies (`Wants`, `WantedBy`), enable the service if appropriate, associate it with targets, etc. For the moment it is enough to add:
    `[Install]`
    `WantedBy=multiuser.target`
at the bottom of the just created file. This allows us to then `systemctl enable` the service, ensuring it will start on reboot.

After a permanent unit is created, limits can be placed on it by manually editing the unit file.
    `[Unit]`
    `Description=/root/splat`
    `[Service]`
    `ExecStart=`
    `ExecStart=@/root/splat "/root/splat"`
    `CPUQuota=25% ##### Line added here#####`
    `Slice=spatter.slice`

After making changes, the unit must be reloaded with:
`# systemctl daemon-reload` *name* `&&` `# systemctl restart` *name*

limits.conf, ulimit

An older, but still valid way to limit the resource usage of a given user or group is to use the file `/etc/security/limits.conf`. It takes these columns:
- `<domain>` user, group (preceded by @), or * for default
- `<type>` hard – never to be exceeded or soft – adjustable by the user up to a hard limit
- `<item>` what we are limiting, options include:
    - `fsize` – maximum filesize (KB)
    - `maxlogins` – maximum number of concurrent logins
    - `memlock` – max locked-in-memory address space (KB)
    - `nofile` – max number of open files
    - `cpu` – max CPU time (Minutes)
    - `nproc` – max number of processes
    - `as` – address space limit (KB)
    - `priority` – the priority to run user process with
    - `nice` – max nice priority [-20, 19]
- `<value>`

There is one important security setting to be configured here. To reduce the potential impact of Denial of Service attacks, concurrent logins per user should be restricted to 10 or fewer:
```
*       hard    maxlogins       10
```

Limits can be adjusted on the fly using the `bash` built-in `ulimit`. If you impose default limits using `limits.conf`, it is recommended that `ulimit -u unlimited` be added to root's `.bashrc`.

Module 9: Filesystems

Filesystems organize, structure, and account for files on a device. A device in this case could be a disk, a partition, a logical volume, or any number of other data-holding things. Though there is tremendous variation in the way that filesystems treat data, most modern filesystems share some common concepts. **Blocks** are the smallest chunk of space that a filesystem can track. Each block will have a unique number assigned to it by the filesystem. All data written to a filesystem is stored in one or more of these blocks. The main types of blocks are:

- **Superblocks** – a special type of block that contains information about the filesystem itself (filesystem type, size, available inodes, free space). When utilities like `mkfs.ext4` write the filesystem structure to a device, the superblock will be created in one of the first blocks in that space. Backup copies of the superblock may be created later, and spread throughout the addressable space as data is written into the filesystem.
- **Inodes** – also stored in a special space (where depends on the filesystem; ext4 stores them at the beginning of each block group, xfs dynamically allocates them offset from the beginning of an allocation group). Inodes do most of the heavy lifting in filesystems, and contain metadata about file characteristics and pointers to the blocks holding the data of files.
- **Directory blocks** – provide a way to associate file names with inodes. An entry could be as simple as: `27199300 file`. In this case, the inode number `27199300` is associated with the filename `file`.
- **Data blocks** – where data is stored. For example, if a user created a small text file, the data blocks would hold the text entered into the file by the user. Everything else, including the name of the file, would be metadata. Data blocks can be either direct or indirect, meaning that data is either stored directly in the block, or indirectly at other blocks via pointers.

Inodes

Inodes are integral to filesystem function. Each inode will contain information about a file or directory (including permissions, timestamps, and size. This information is metadata: data *about* data. Interestingly, inodes do *not* contain a file's name. To understand why, we must briefly explore how files are retrieved when a user requests them:

```
# ls -i /test
18073930   file
18073930   link
```

Here, we executed `ls` with the `-i` option, which lists the inode number associated with a directory entry. Let's examine the entry for a file called `file`. The number `18073930` is the index number of the inode associated with that filename. Earlier, we discussed pathing. The absolute path to `file` is `/test/file`. The first directory listed in this path is slash `/`. This is followed by the `test` directory, and finally by `file`. If we display the contents of `file` using `cat` the system has to begin at slash `/` and proceed from there.

```
# cat /test/file
These are the contents of file.
```

Ordinarily, to find the inode of a given file, a directory listing would be consulted (as we saw at the beginning of this section). The root directory, however, is at the top of the hierarchy. No directory exists that contains an entry for it. There is no procedural way to deduce the location of root directory's inode. Because of this, the inode for the root directory will always exist at a known location.

On older filesystems, this was traditionally inode **2**. On a typical EL7/8 deployment the root filesystem is built on a logical volume and formatted with XFS. The root inode here is **128**, which can be determined by examining the superblock of the filesystem using **xfs_db,** is a utility most often used to examine the superblock of an XFS filesystem. It can also make changes, though this is usually done though the **xfs_admin** command (which will call **xfs_db** as needed). Here, we use **xfs_db -r** to open a mounted filesystem read-only, **sb** to set the superblock at AG 0 as our target, and **print** to print out the contents for examiniation:

```
# xfs_db -r /dev/mapper/cl-root
xfs_db> sb
xfs_db> print
<truncated>
uuid = c2580007-023f-413e-b8f2-56c867511429
logstart = 2097158
rootino = 128
```

We can use **stat** to retrieve information about a file or directory (directories are technically also files, with special rules for handling):

```
# stat /
  File: /
  Size: 4096          Blocks: 8           IO Block: 4096   directory
Device: fd00h/64768d  Inode: 128          Links: 19
Access: (0555/dr-xr-xr-x)  Uid: (   0/   root)   Gid: (   0/   root)
Context: system_u:object_r:root_t:s0
Access: 2019-10-23 09:04:15.085292434 -0500
Modify: 2019-10-23 09:04:00.745180318 -0500
Change: 2019-10-23 09:04:00.745180318 -0500
 Birth: -
```

Here we can see that this file is named **/** and that it is a directory. We can see the size, inode number, permissions, ownership, and a few other interesting details.

To retrieve **/test/file** using `cat`, the system first retrieved the inode for the root directory. Then it checked the permission string to see if the invoking user has access to the directory. In this case, read and execute permissions were allowed. The next item in the requested path was **test**, another directory.

To find the inode for **test**, the contents of **/** were examined:
```
# ls -di /test
18073928 test
```

From here the process is repeated: check access, consult directories, find inode, retrieve contents. Ultimately, we arrived at the final item in our path: **file**.
```
# ls -i file
27199300 file
```

A final access check was performed. It succeeded. The inode pointed the way to the data blocks for **file**, the data was retrieved, and the requested functions were performed against it. In our case, we simply wanted the contents listed to **STDOUT**. `cat` performed this function, resulting in the following:
```
# cat file
These are the contents of file.
```

Throughout our traversal of the filesystem, only one piece of information could be considered data. It is this sentence:
These are the contents of file.

Everything else along the way was metadata, including the directories and even the file name.

ln

To understand links, it may help to begin with the idea that files don't have names - at least not as we classically understand them.

Instead, they have locations (data blocks, pointed to by inodes), and labels by which their inodes can be referenced. These labels provide the same function as a name, but in reality, they are simply a mechanism for resolving down to an inode number.

Files *exist* at a location, and will continue to do so no matter what they may be called, *or by how many names they are known.*

Consider the following:
```
# ls -li file
total 4
18073930 -rw-r--r--. 1 root root 81 Oct 23 09:11 file
```

The inode number: **18073930** contains the contents of `file`. The number **1** after the permission string is the link count, which is the number of directory entries pointing to that inode. In this case, that entry was `file`.
```
# ln file link

# ls -li
total 8
18073930 -rw-r--r--. 2 root root 124 Oct 23 09:11 file
18073930 -rw-r--r--. 2 root root 124 Oct 23 09:11 link
```

Above, we used the `ln` command to create a hard link from `file` to `link`. The directory listing indicates that two entries now exist in the directory. The inode numbers are the *same for both files*. We appear to have two files, but the information for each is identical. Only the filenames differ. Notice also that the link count for each is now **2**.

`file` and `link` are in fact the same file, referenced by different names. Modifying one has the apparent effect of modifying the other as well.

Deleting one, however, will not cause the other to disappear. Instead, the link count will simply decrement by one and the directory entry for the deleted "file" will disappear. When link count reaches zero, a file is effectively destroyed.
```
# rm file

# ls -li
total 4
18073930 -rw-r--r--. 2 root root 124 Oct 23 09:11 link

# cat link
These are the contents of file.
```

After removing the "original" file, `file`, the listing shows only `link`, with a link count of **1**. The `cat` command was then invoked to display the contents of `link` returning this:
These are the contents of file.

Hard links do not create new files. Instead, they create additional directory listings for existing files. Hard links are useful, but they have limitations. Foremost amongst these is that they may not cross filesystem boundaries. We would not expect inode `103` in filesystem **/tmp** to contain the contents of inode `103` in filesystem **/var**. This is because inode numbers are unique to each filesystem and are used by a filesystem to keep track of its own contents, not the contents of other systems.

To reference the contents of an inode on another filesystem through a link, we use a symbolic link. Symbolic links are files whose contents consist only of a pointer to some other file.

We can create one in this fashion:
ln -s */path/original-file /path/created-link*

Let's use this to "recreate" **file** from the last section:
ln -s /test/link /test/file

ls -li
```
total 4
18073932 lrwxrwxrwx. 1 root root  19 Oct 23 09:20 file -> /test/link
18073930 -rw-r--r--. 1 root root 124 Oct 23 09:11 link
```

This creates a symbolic link called **file** which points to **link**. The string **file -> /test/link** indicates that **file**, when referenced, will attempt to return **/test/link** instead.

Notice that the inode numbers are different. Unlike hard links, symbolic links do not refer to an inode directly. They *must not*; if they did, they could not cross filesystem boundaries. For this reason, a new inode is created, but only contains a pointer (via a simple path) to resources elsewhere on the system.

One interesting consequence of this behavior is that, should we now choose to delete **link**, **file** will still exist (it is tracked by a separate inode). Attempts to read the contents of **file** would fail, returning an error: **No such file or directory**

If we were to then create another file called **link** and store it in the same location as the original, the link would again function - though it would now point to an entirely different file.

parted, mkfs

To create a filesystem, a device must exist onto which the filesystem may be placed. Although certain types of filesystems may exist purely in RAM, we will focus on disk-based implementations.

Preparing a device

To see a list of available hard disks, we could use **lsblk**:

```
# lsblk
NAME                MAJ:MIN RM  SIZE RO TYPE MOUNTPOINT
sda                   8:0    0   16G  0 disk
├─sda1                8:1    0    1G  0 part /boot
└─sda2                8:2    0   15G  0 part
  ├─cl-root         253:0    0   10G  0 lvm  /
<truncated>
  └─cl-home         253:5    0    1G  0 lvm  /home
sdb                  8:16    0   10G  0 disk
```

In the output above, we can see a listing for two hard drives and their partitions. These are: **sda** with two partitions **sda1** and **sda2**, and **sdb** currently with no partitions.

In Enterprise Linux device files are in **/dev/** and follow one of two general naming conventions. For devices that are not partitioned, floppies (**fd**) and optical media (**sr**), two letters and a number, counting from **0**. So the first CD/DVD drive is **sr0**. For IDE (**hd**) and SCSI (**sd**) drives, the convention is two letters for type, a letter for order (**a**=1, **b**=2...), and a number for partition, counting from 1. So the third partition on the second SCSI drive is **sdb3**. USB and flash drives will typically appear as SCSI devices. In cases of more than 26 devices, the ordinal letters double (**z**=26, **aa**=27...).

According to the output of **lsblk**, the second drive, **sdb**, is not partitioned, and has about 10 GB of free space. Several tools exist for partitioning disks, the most popular of these are **fdisk** and **parted**. **fdisk** is menu driven, and can be simpler to work with, while **parted** offers a quick and powerful command line utility, and a straightforward GUI option called **gparted**.

There are two ways to use **parted**: interactively, opening an interpreter and running commands sequentially with prompts; or on a single command line. Any changes made in interactive mode are written immediately without confirmation. To start **parted** interactively, simply call parted and specify a target device without further commands

```
# parted /dev/sdb
```

Common options and commands for `parted` include:
- `-l` – list partition table information for all devices, or a selected device.
- `select /dev/`*xyz* – choose a device to use
- `mklabel` – create an empty partition table, which will hold partition information.
    - Common labels are **msdos** and **gpt**.
- `print` – show information takes an argument of
    - `devices` – block devices
    - `list` – partition tables
    - `free` – unpartitioned space
- `mkpart` – create a partion by specifying name/type, start and end positions.
- `rm` – delete a partion by specifying the partition number.
- `quit` – exit the program if in interactive mode.

We'll be using `parted` to partition `sdb`, but first we'll need to label the device so that parted understands how to work with it. In this case, we will label it as `gpt`, or GUID Partition Table. GPT is an improvement over the older MBR (Master Boot Record), and adds support for more partitions and a vastly expanded size (around 9 Zettabytes vs 2 TB for MBR).

```
# parted /dev/sdb mklabel gpt
Information: You may need to update /etc/fstab.

# parted -l
Model: VMware Virtual disk (scsi)
Disk /dev/sdb: 10.7GB
Sector size (logical/physical): 512B/512B
Partition Table: gpt
Disk Flags:

Number  Start  End  Size  Filesystem  Name  Flags
```

Above, we called **parted** with the **mklabel** command to set the label (partition table type) of **/dev/sdb** to **gpt**. We then used **parted -l** to list the partition tables of our block devices. The lack of output signifies an empty or missing partition table. To add new partitions

```
# parted /dev/sdb mkpart data 1MiB 1025MiB
Information: You may need to update /etc/fstab.
```

```
# parted /dev/sdb mkpart comp 1025MiB 2049MiB
Information: You may need to update /etc/fstab.
```

```
# parted /dev/sdb print
Model: VMware Virtual disk (scsi)
Disk /dev/sdb: 10.7GB
Sector size (logical/physical): 512B/512B
Partition Table: gpt
Disk Flags:
Number  Start    End      Size     Filesystem  Name  Flags
1       1049kB   1075MB   1074MB               data
2       1075MB   2149MB   1074MB               comp
```

We have now created two new 1GB partitions. We listed the partition table to verify our work in the utility. Now let's verify with **lsblk**:

```
# lsblk
NAME                MAJ:MIN  RM  SIZE  RO  TYPE  MOUNTPOINT
sda                 8:0      0   16G   0   disk
├─sda1              8:1      0   1G    0   part  /boot
└─sda2              8:2      0   15G   0   part
  ├─cl-root         253:0    0   10G   0   lvm   /
        <truncated>
sdb                 8:16     0   10G   0   disk
├─sdb1              8:17     0   1G    0   part
└─sdb2              8:18     0   1G    0   part
```

We can also verify by examining **/proc/partitions** directly:

```
# cat /proc/partitions
major  minor  #blocks   name
  8      0    16777216  sda
  8      1    1048576   sda1
       <truncated>
  8     16    10485760  sdb
  8     17    1048576   sdb1
  8     18    1048576   sdb2
```

To update this list, we could use the **partprobe** command with **-s** for show summary:

```
# partprobe -s
/dev/sda: msdos partitions 1 2
/dev/sdb: gpt partitions 1 2
```

Making the filesystem

Having created a partition table and partitions on a device does not make that space useable. Before use, the partition must be formatted with a filesystem. EL7/8 offers support for several filesystems. Tools for creating these are in **/usr/sbin**:

```
# ls /usr/sbin/mkfs*
mkfs        mkfs.cramfs     mkfs.ext2       mkfs.ext3       mkfs.ext4
mkfs.fat    mkfs.minix      mkfs.msdos      mkfs.vfat       mkfs.xfs
```

These commands may be used to create a filesystem of the type specified in their extension. The default filesystem in EL6 type was ext4. For EL7/8, it is xfs. ext2 and ext3 are still supported. The FAT and VFAT filesystems are popular choices for formatting removable drives. The MINIX and cramfs filesystems are lightweight and mainly used in embedded systems.

XFS provides several benefits which make it an attractive choice on modern systems. It uses extents (contiguous chunks of blocks) as ext2/3/4 would, making space allocation more efficient. It will also delay writes, holding changes in a buffer until modifications are likely finished and reducing the overall number of disk operations. Further, XFS uses Allocation Groups to parallelize filesystem operations. Each allocation group (by default, there are four: AG0-AG3) acts similarly to a subfilesystem, managing and tracking its own inodes and free space.

The following example uses **xfs**. From our earlier work, we know that a free partition exists at **/dev/sdb1**. To format that partition with a label of **data**:

```
# mkfs.xfs -L data /dev/sdb1
```

Now we need to make the filesystem available to the operating system.

mount, umount

In the previous section, we created an xfs filesystem on **/dev/sdb1**. When we did so, the data structures necessary for that filesystem to track data blocks for its files and directories were established. However, these files and directories are inaccessible to us.

This is because we inhabit the root filesystem. The root filesystem, like any other, maintains an inode table and directory structure. Natively, these structures cannot account for information stored in other filesystems.

We can solve this problem through a process called **mounting.** Mounting allows us to make a filesystem available via a directory (also called a mount point) in the root filesystem. After the mounting operation occurs, any calls for the contents of the mount point directory will return the top level of the mounted filesystem (instead of the original contents in root).

Let's explore the concept with an example. Here are the contents of the directory **/testmount**

```
# ls -l /testmount
total 4
-rw-r--r--. 1 root root 67 Oct 23 14:14 NOTmounted
```

```
# cat /testmount/NOTmounted
this file lives in the /testmount directory in the root filesystem
```

Note that a single file is present in this directory. Now we will mount the **/dev/sdb1** filesystem to the **/testmount** directory.

```
# mount /dev/sdb1 /testmount
```

```
# ls -l /testmount
total 16
drwx------. 2 root root 16384 Oct 23 11:42 lost+found
```

The file from earlier is gone, and a directory, **lost+found**, has taken its place. This is a special directory which will appear in the root of an ext filesystem. It holds orphaned or corrupted files discovered during a filesystem integrity check (**fsck**). It is not used with xfs filesystems.

We are seeing it now because we are currently viewing the contents of the mounted filesystem instead of the original contents of the **/testmount** directory. Essentially, the mount operation tells the kernel to take a detour at the **/testmount** directory, flipping over to the filesystem at **/dev/sdb1** instead. We can unmount the filesystem to reverse this.

```
# umount /testmount
```

```
# ls -l /testmount
total 4
-rw-r--r--. 1 root root 67 Oct 23 14:14 NOTmounted
```

Our file is now back.

Options exist to control the behavior and mode of mounted filesystems. You can pass these options via the `-o` option of the mount command. Some common ones include:
- `defaults` – Provides an alias for `async`, `auto`, `dev`, `exec`, `nouser`, `rw`, `suid`
- `async` – Allows the asynchronous input/output operations on the filesystem
- `auto` – Allows the filesystem to be mounted automatically using **mount -a**
- `dev` / `nodev` – Allows / prevents direct hardware access to storage devices
- `exec` / `noexec` – Allows / prevents the execution of binary files
    - Remote filesystems and removable media should be mounted **nodev, noexec**
- `suid` / `nosuid` – allows / prevents action of suid and sgid bits
    - Remote filesystems, removable media and **/home** should be mounted **nosuid**
- `nouser` – Prevents mounting and unmounting by ordinary users
- `rw` – Mounts the filesystem for both reading and writing
- `ro` – Mounts the filesystem read only
- `loop` – Mounts an image as a loop device
- `noexec` – Disallows the execution of binary files on the particular filesystem
- `remount` – Remounts the filesystem in case it is already mounted
- `user` – Allows mounting and unmounting by ordinary users
- `noauto` – Default behavior, disallows the automatic mount of the filesystem using the mount `-a` command
- `noatime` – do not update access time; for performance and longer SSD life

systemd.mount

In the previous sections, we discussed the concepts behind mounting, and the manual process for mounting and unmounting filesystems. Manual mounts are non-persistent. They will disappear when the system is rebooted.

Several processes exist for mounting filesystems either at boot time, or on when needed. Traditionally, these involved a file called **/etc/fstab** and/or **autofs**.

EL7/8 still supports these concepts, but **systemd-fstab-generator** will run behind the scenes to convert the entries in `fstab` into the unit files that `systemd` needs. It is possible to build these files by hand, and we will work through some examples of this. However, it is generally considered a simpler and safer practice to use `fstab` and let the generator do the heavy lifting. The man page for `systemd.mount` concludes "In general, configuring mount points through /etc/fstab is the preferred approach."

Here is a line from /etc/fstab:

/dev/sdb1   /testmount   xfs   defaults   1   0
- **/dev/sdb1** – what to mount
- **/testmount** – where to mount it
- **xfs** – filesystem type
- **defaults** – options (defaults = rw,suid,dev,exec,auto,nouser,async)
- **1** – dump? (**1**=yes; **0**=no)
- **0** – fsck? (**1**=yes,chk 1st; **2**=yes,chk 2nd; **0**=do not fsck)

Lines added to this file will be mounted at boot and any other time that **mount -a** is called, unless the **noauto** keyword is used in the options. This also allows mount operations to be performed with a shorter invocation: **mount** /mount-point, with no backing device specified.

To do the same time with **systemd** we would create a unit file in **/etc/systemd/system** with the extention **.mount** and content like this:

```
[Unit]
Description = Mount /dev/sdb1 to /testmount

[Mount]
What = /dev/sdb1
Where = /testmount
Type = xfs
Options = defaults

[Install]
WantedBy = multi-user.target
```

The name of a **.mount** or **.automount** unit must correspond to the absolute path of the mount point. Any slashes in the path must be replaced by dashes. For example **Where = /mnt/foo/bar** requires a filename of **mnt-foo-bar.mount** Conversion of complex paths or those with special characters can be accomplished with
 # systemd-escape -p *"/some/complex/path with spaces"*

The **[Unit]** header and **Description** are required for all systemd unit files.

The **[Mount]** header declares this is a mount unit. Below this header is the information necessary for systemd to successfully perform the mount. Specifically, we tell systemd:
- **What** – the location of the filesystem we wish to mount
    - This can be a device, a filesystem label, or a UUID. UUID is preferred
- **Where** – the mount point we wish to attach to
- **Type** – the type of filesystem we will be mounting
- **Options** – any mount options we would like to apply

This maps directly to the information supplied in /etc/fstab, only differing in structure.

The **[Install]** section says when or if this unit file will be loaded. In this case:
WantedBy = multi-user.target

To mount this filesystem
```
# systemctl start testmount.mount
```

To mount it automatically on boot
```
# systemctl enable testmount.mount
```

After it has been started we can verify our work with:
```
# systemctl status testmount.mount
● testmount.mount - Mount /dev/sdb1 to /testmount
   Loaded: loaded (/proc/self/mountinfo; disabled; vendor preset:
   Active: active (mounted) since Tue 2019-10-20 12:52:28 CDT; 3min
    Where: /testmount
     What: /dev/sdb1
  Process: 21004 ExecUnmount=/bin/umount /testmount (code=exited,
  Process: 21024 ExecMount=/bin/mount /dev/sdb1 /testmount -t xfs -o
defaults (code=exited, status=0/SUCCESS)
```

or

```
# mount | grep /testmount
/dev/sdb1 on /testmount type xfs (rw,relatime,seclabel,data=ordered)
```

systemd.automount

We can also cause this filesystem to be mounted dynamically on demand by creating an automount unit. Automount units cause their associated mount units to be started by `systemd` whenever a user accesses the targeted mount point. This is frequently done for removable media. For this we create a **.mount** unit as before, omitting the **[Install]** section. We also create a **.automount** unit with the same name as the **.mount**. It is the `.automount` rather than the `.mount` which will be enabled. It should have a format like this:

```
[Unit]
Description = Automatically mount /dev/sdb1

[Automount]
Where = /testmount
TimeoutIdleSec=600

[Install]
WantedBy = local-fs.target
```

The **[Automount]** section specifies the mount point from **testmount.mount** and an automatic unmount after ten minutes of idle. This can be enabled and started:

```
# systemctl enable --now testmount.automount
# systemctl status testmount.automount | grep Active
   Active: active (running) since Tue 2019-10-20 10:26:15 CDT; 3h
```

To test it we need to ensure that `testmount.mount` is inactive:

```
# systemctl stop testmount.mount
# systemctl status testmount.mount | grep Active
   Active: inactive (dead) since Tue 2019-10-20 13:41:36 CDT; 11min
```

To reactivate the mount we only need to access **/testmount**:

```
# cd /testmount
# systemctl status testmount.mount | grep Active
   Active: active (mounted) since Tue 2019-10-20 13:56:19 CDT; 10s ago
```

Changing to the **/testmount** directory caused the automount file to trip, which in turn executed the **testmount.mount** unit mounting the directory. If we change out of the directory it will unmount itself when the timeout expires.

/etc/fstab

Earlier, we stated that placing our mount preferences into **/etc/fstab** was generally considered to be a simpler option. Let's explore that process and its results.

Filesystems can be mounted by specifying a device location (/dev/sdb1), a filesystem label (created with mkfs -L), or by UUID. UUID is the safest and most secure. To get the UUID of a filesystem use the **blkid** command:

```
# blkid /dev/sdb1
/dev/sdb1: LABEL="data" UUID="cfcab82e-2f87-46d0-838e-1afef5ec96e6" TYPE="xfs" PARTLABEL="data" PARTUUID="80defbb6-012c-4376-8af6-36f463"
```

This value is inserted into **/etc/fstab** in place of the device name, like this:
UUID=cfcab82e-2f87-46d0-838e-1afef5ec96e6   /testmount xfs defaults 0 2

This will work immediately, but if we want to see what **systemd-fstab-generator** creates for us, we'll need to execute **systemctl daemon-reload**. Once this is done, we can look in **/run/systemd/generator** for a corresponding unit file.

```
# ls /run/systemd/generator
boot.mount   'dev-mapper-cl\x2dswap.swap'   home.mount   local-fs.target.requires   -.mount   swap.target.requires   testmount.mount

# cat /run/systemd/generator/testmount.mount
# Automatically generated by systemd-fstab-generator

[Unit]
SourcePath=/etc/fstab
Documentation=man:fstab(5) man:systemd-fstab-generator(8)
Before=local-fs.target
Requires=systemd-fsck@dev-disk-by\x2duuid-cfcab82e\x2d2f87\x2d46d0\x2d838e\x2d1afef5ec96e6.service
After=systemd-fsck@dev-disk-by\x2duuid-cfcab82e\x2d2f87\x2d46d0\x2d838e\x2d1afef5ec96e6.service

[Mount]
Where=/testmount
What=/dev/disk/by-uuid/cfcab82e-2f87-46d0-838e-1afef5ec96e6
Type=xfs
```

Either of these approaches can produce working results; ultimately it is up to administrators to decide which is the best fit.

swap

Swap is a form of virtual memory, backed by a disk or similar device. When RAM is overcommitted, the system may page inactive memory out to swap, and then back into memory again when needed.

To view free swap space, we can use **# free -m**. This will report free memory and swap space. To create swap space, we use **mkswap**, and to activate or deactivate a swap device or file, we would use the **swapon** and **swapoff** commands. We can also use **# swapon -s** to view swap currently in use.

When creating swap we may designate disk, partition, or file. Below, we explore each of these possibilities in turn.

To create new swap space on a disk or partition, begin by listing available disk space
```
# lsblk
NAME                  MAJ:MIN  RM   SIZE  RO  TYPE  MOUNTPOINT
sda                    8:0      0   16G    0   disk
├─sda1                 8:1      0   1G     0   part  /boot
<truncated>
sdb                    8:16     0   10G    0   disk
├─sdb1                 8:17     0   1G     0   part  /testmount
└─sdb2                 8:18     0   1G     0   part

# free -m
              total        used        free      shared  buff/cache   available
Mem:           3941         339        2888           9         714        3338
Swap:          1023           0        1023

# swapon -s
Filename                          Type         Size       Used    Priority
/dev/dm-1                         partition    1048572    0       -2
```

Here, we've used **lsblk** to identify a free partition in **/dev/sdb2** and **free -m** to see that we currently have **1023** MB of free swap space. The **swapon -s** command shows one currently assigned swap location: **/dev/dm-1**.

To use **/dev/sdb2** as an additional swap partition, we'll need to use **mkswap** to set up the partition for swapping:
```
# mkswap /dev/sdb2
Setting up swapspace version 1, size = 1024 MiB (1073737728 bytes)
no label, UUID=5fea4e5b-4461-45ef-b6a4-c726cdf6221a
```

We need to edit **/etc/fstab** so that our new swap space will be mounted at boot, adding an entry that looks like this:
```
/dev/sdb2               swap                swap        defaults        0 0
```

Finally, we need to inform the kernel that it has new swap space available.
```
# swapon -v /dev/sdb2
swapon: /dev/sdb2: found signature [pagesize=4096, signature=swap]
swapon: /dev/sdb2: pagesize=4096, swapsize=1073741824, devsize=1073741824
swapon /dev/sdb2
```

We can verify our work with `free -m` and `swapon -s`:
```
# free -m
        total    used     free     shared   buff/cache   available
Mem:    3941     345      2881     9        714          3332
Swap:   2047     0        2047
# swapon -s
Filename              Type           Size       Used    Priority
/dev/dm-1             partition      1048572 0          -2
/dev/sdb2             partition      1048572 0          -3
```

If we do not have a free device for swap we can use a file instead. To create and zero the file we can use the `fallocate` command.
```
# fallocate -l 1G /swapfile
```

In EL7 with xfs this will not work, instead use
```
# dd if=/dev/zero of=/swapfile count=1024 bs=1024
```

Since this file will hold the unencrypted contents of memory swapped down to disk, we should also ensure that it has sane permissions applied
```
# chmod 0600 /swapfile
```

```
# ls -l /swapfile
-rw-------. 1 root root 1073741824 Oct 25 11:10 /swapfile
```

We've now created an empty 1 GB file to use as swap. From here, the process of creating swap is the same as when we are using a device. Use `mkswap` to prepare it and `swapon` to activate.

When we're done with a swap device or file, we can remove it with `swapoff`.

systemd.swap

Rather than configuring swap in `/etc/fstab`, you can use a `.swap` unit file. Swap units, like `.mount` units must be named after the controlled device with the slashes converted to dashes. A `.swap` for `/dev/sdb2` must be named `dev-sdb2.swap`.

The `[Install]` section is typically not needed as systemd will automatically create the required dependencies. The format for a `.swap` unit is this:

```
[Unit]
Description=Swap for sdb2

[Swap]
What=/dev/sdb2
Priority=2
```

Logical Volume Manager (LVM)

Logical Volume Manager (LVM) can aggregate physical storage (physical volumes) into pools called volume groups. This pool of space can then be divided into smaller chunks called logical volumes, and handed out with a much greater degree of freedom than traditional systems allow.
- **Physical Volumes** (PVs) can be created from whole disks, partitions, or LUN-based external storage such as iSCSI or Fibre Channel.
- **Volume Groups** (VGs) consist of one or more physical volumes. We must assign at least one physical volume to a volume group at the time of creation, and can add more as needed.
- **Logical Volumes** (LVs) consist of a portion of the space belonging to a volume group. It may span many physical volumes, but can only ever belong to a single volume group.
- **Filesystems** can be written to a logical volume using the same tools that would create them on a disk or partition.

Let's briefly discuss the procedure, and a list of associated commands (and their descriptions).

Physical Volume→Volume Group→Logical Volume→Filesystems

The first step in the process is to create a physical volume. For that, we must identify an available disk, partition, or LUN. We would then run `pvcreate` against the selected device(s). The resulting PV(s) would then be available for use by a volume group.

The commands to create, modify, and destroy or inspect physical volumes are:
- `pvcreate` – create a PV
- `pvdisplay` – display detailed information about a PV
- `pvremove` – remove (destroy) a PV
- `pvresize` – resize PV to reflect size of underlying device
- `pvs` – display information about PVs on a system
- `pvscan` – scan devices for LVM (PV) data; update cache

Physical Volume→**Volume Group**→Logical Volume→Filesystems

A **volume group** is a *group* of physical *volumes*. To create a volume group, we require at least one physical volume. More may be specified at volume group creation, or added later with the `vgextend` command.

The commands to create, modify, and destroy or inspect physical volumes are:
- `vgcreate` – create a VG
- `vgdisplay` – display detailed info about VG(s)
- `vgextend` – add PV(s) to VG
- `vgreduce` – remove PV(s) from VG (CAUTION!)
- `vgremove` – destroy a VG
- `vgs` – display information about VGs
- `vgscan` – scan devices for LVM (VG) data; update cache

Physical Volume→Volume Group→**Logical Volume**→Filesystems

Logical volumes are a portion of the physical storage managed by a volume group. This storage can come from any of the physical volumes backing the volume group. This is normally not specified, rather we allow LVM to manage the physical space for us.

A simple way of stating this:

- Logical volumes can span multiple physical volumes
- Logical volumes may only ever belong to a single volume group

The commands to create, modify, and destroy or inspect physical volumes are:
- `lvcreate` – create an LV
- `lvdisplay` – display detailed information about an LV
- `lvextend` – add physical extents to an LV
- `lvreduce` – remove physical extents from an LV
- `lvremove` – destroy an LV
- `lvresize` – shrink or grow an LV (-r autoresize resident FS)
- `lvs` – display information about LVs
- `lvscan` – scan devices for LVM (LV) data; update cache

Once a logical volume has been created, a filesystem can be written to it using `mkfs` and mounted using any of the methods discussed above.

Putting this process together we can walk through an example using two free partitions: **sdb3** and **sdb4**. We'll use sdb3 to create a new VG, then create a logical volume on that VG.

```
# pvcreate /dev/sdb3
  Physical volume "/dev/sdb3" successfully created.
# vgcreate ExampleVG /dev/sdb3
  Volume group "ExampleVG" successfully created
# lvcreate -n ExampleLV -l 100%FREE ExampleVG
  Logical volume "ExampleLV" created.
# vgs
  VG          #PV #LV #SN Attr   VSize    VFree
  ExampleVG    1   1   0  wz--n- 1020.00m   0
  cl           1   6   0  wz--n-  <15.00g   0
```

Above, we directed **lvcreate** to use 100 percent of free space. We could have also specified a specific size with different invocations of either the **-l** or **-L** options. Let's take a moment to review our work.

```
# vgdisplay -v ExampleVG
  --- Volume group ---
  VG Name                ExampleVG
<truncated>
  VG Size                1020.00 MiB
  PE Size                4.00 MiB
  Total PE               255
  Alloc PE / Size        255 / 1020.00 MiB
  Free  PE / Size        0 / 0
  VG UUID                IUZLT6-mrEt-vwJp-8zpI-Xo66-NY4z-4awMkn

  --- Logical volume ---
  LV Path                /dev/ExampleVG/ExampleLV
  LV Name                ExampleLV
  VG Name                ExampleVG
  LV UUID                e6dDD2-2cBl-cLjH-wGIb-iCWI-Ouyn-SbX8r7
  LV Write Access        read/write
  LV Creation host, time Book-8-C-Client.el8.not, 2019-10-25 14:35:37 -0500
  LV Status              available
  # open                 0
  LV Size                1020.00 MiB
<truncated>
```

We can see in the output above that our logical volume, ExampleLV, has taken all available space on the volume group. The sole PV backing our volume group has been completely consumed. We'll make a note of this, and return to it in a moment.

Ultimately, the purpose of a logical volume is to serve as backing for either swap or a filesystem.

Let's format our logical volume with an ext4 filesystem.

```
# mkfs.ext4 -L Class /dev/ExampleVG/ExampleLV
mke2fs 1.44.3 (10-July-2018)
Creating filesystem with 261120 4k blocks and 65280 inodes
Filesystem UUID: efa40f33-b81d-44d0-98dd-dd71e5a67b1d
Superblock backups stored on blocks:        32768, 98304, 163840,
<truncated>
# mount /dev/ExampleVG/ExampleLV /mnt
# df -h
Filesystem                          Size  Used Avail Use% Mounted on
/dev/sdb1                           1014M   40M  975M   4% /testmount
/dev/mapper/ExampleVG-ExampleLV      988M  2.6M  919M   1% /mnt
```

Enterprise Linux versions 7 & 8

Note that the device listed as backing this filesystem is /dev/**mapper/**ExampleVG-ExampleLV instead of the supplied device **/dev/**ExampleVG/ExampleLV. This is expected in EL7/8; the device mapper handles mapping block devices onto virtual block devices for LVM2. Device mapper also plays a role in disk encryption and software RAID.

Finally, when our LV-backed filesystems become full, we may extend the filesystem and the logical volume it rests on. First, increase the size of the logical volume. Logical volumes will take their space from any of the physical volumes belonging to its volume group. In our case, there is no space currently available. To remedy this, we will need to add a new physical volume to the volume group.

```
# pvcreate /dev/sdb4
  Physical volume "/dev/sdb4" successfully created
# vgextend ExampleVG /dev/sdb4
  Volume group "ExampleVG" successfully extended
# lvextend /dev/ExampleVG/ExampleLV -L +500M
  Size of logical volume ExampleVG/ExampleLV changed from 1020.00 MiB
(255 extents) to 1.48 GiB (380 extents).
  Logical volume ExampleLV successfully resized.
```

At this point, we would use **resize2fs** to resize the filesystem into the newly available space. This command can be used to shrink or grow an ext2, ext3, or ext4 filesystem. We could also have called **# lvextend -r**, which would have handled filesystem resizing for us automatically.

LUKS

There are a variety of methods for securing access to data on EL7/8 systems, but many of these can be circumvented if an attacker has access to a disk directly. To combat this, administrators may choose to encrypt disks (possibly even the boot device of a system). Encrypting a drive scrambles the data such that, should an attacker gain direct access to a hard drive, backup, or disk image, the data on the drive will be completely obscured and unrecoverable without the accompanying passphrase or key file which unlocks and de-scrambles the underlying data.

The most common method of encrypting disks in EL7/8 is the **dm-crypt** module with the **Linux Unified Key System**, or **LUKS**. Though dm-crypt can be invoked without LUKS, this is rarely done. This is because LUKS provides many features, such as salting, key management, and error checking that plain dm-crypt does not.

To encrypt a device with these features we invoke **cryptsetup**, which can apply disk encryption in the following ways:
- Encrypt a device (such as a hard drive, partition, or LUN) directly.
- Encrypt the physical volumes of an LVM volume group (LVM over LUKS).
- Apply encryption to logical volumes (LUKS over LVM).
- Encrypt an entire system from the boot device up (Whole Disk Encryption)

Whole disk encryption is not required by STIG for virtual machines or servers in a secure environment. For laptops, however, it is. The reasoning here is that, if employed, it will render a system completely unbootable without supplying a passphrase or key at boot time. This is desirable for laptops and other such devices where physical theft or loss is a concern. It is less desirable in virtual environments, where console access to a virtual machine would be required each time a VM boots. Implementing whole disk encryption is best done during installation. Converting a non-encrypted system to a whole disk encryption model AFTER installation is a complicated and difficult process.

LUKS on a Device

Let's walk through the direct application of LUKS encryption to a hard disk. The steps we implement here will also, in large part, be applicable to later sections dealing LVM encryption.

To begin, we need to identify a target device. We can list block devices on our system with the **lsblk** command:

```
# lsblk
NAME               MAJ:MIN RM  SIZE RO TYPE MOUNTPOINT
sda                8:0     0   16G  0  disk
├─sda1             8:1     0   1G   0  part /boot
<truncated>
sdb                8:16    0   10G  0  disk
```

Here we've identified a device, **/dev/sdb**, as our target. Now we need to create the encryption layer, supplying the target disk and a passphrase:

```
# cryptsetup luksFormat /dev/sdb
WARNING!
========
This will overwrite data on /dev/sdb irrevocably.

Are you sure? (Type uppercase yes): YES
Enter LUKS passphrase: Passphrase
Verify passphrase: Passphrase
```

Our next step is to open the LUKS device for reading and writing using **cryptsetup luksOpen**, supplying the name of the base device and the passphrase to open it, along with a MAPPING name:

```
# cryptsetup luksOpen /dev/sdb encDisk
Enter passphrase for /dev/sdb: Passphrase
```

```
# lsblk
NAME                MAJ:MIN  RM   SIZE  RO  TYPE   MOUNTPOINT
sda                 8:0      0    16G   0   disk
├─sda1              8:1      0    1G    0   part   /boot
<truncated>
sdb                 8:16     0    10G   0   disk
└─encDisk           253:6    0    10G   0   crypt
```

From this point forward, all commands will use the name of the **mapped device**, **encDisk**, rather than the base disk. We now need to format the disk with a filesystem, in this example ext4; and mount it:

```
# mkfs.ext4 /dev/mapper/encDisk
mke2fs 1.44.3 (10-July-2018)
Creating filesystem with 2619392 4k blocks and 655360 inodes
<truncated>
```

```
# mount /dev/mapper/encDisk /mnt
```

```
# ls /mnt
lost+found
```

LUKS and LVM

When working with whole disks, or partitions, encryption is applied to the base device as has been demonstrated. When working with LVM, the encryption may be applied **either** at the logical volume layer **or** at the physical volume layer. These situations are referred to as "LUKS over LVM" or "LVM over LUKS".

For most purposes, applying encryption to the logical volume is the best answer, or "LUKS over LVM". This is because volume groups may (and frequently do) contain multiple physical volumes. Applying encryption at the PV layer and then incorporating the encrypted volumes into a volume group is problematic; loss of a key on one PV could lead to loss of an entire volume group.

In any case, the encryption process is ultimately the same for logical volumes as for physical devices; we simply need to supply the location of a logical volume in place of a physical disk or partition.

Automating the Mount Process for Encrypted Devices

The standard process for automating mount operations involves entries in the `/etc/fstab` file. This is also the case for encrypted disks, but we have additional considerations.

As we have seen, encrypted devices cannot be accessed until they have been opened and mapped. Nothing in the `/etc/fstab` file accommodates this operation directly. To address this, we turn to another file: `/etc/crypttab`.

The purpose of `/etc/crypttab` is to contain mapping information for encrypted disks. In other words, it will automate the work performed by the `cryptsetup luksOpen` command. Note that this file *is only consulted at boot time for fstab operations*.

The example below shows how an `/etc/crypttab` entry may be created, and what the corresponding entry in `/etc/fstab` might contain:

```
# tail -1 /etc/crypttab
encDisk /dev/sdb none
# tail -1 /etc/fstab
/dev/mapper/encDisk    /secret        ext4      defaults       1 2
# mount /secret
```

Above, the example commands succeed because the targeted LUKS device was already open and mapped. If it had been closed, `/etc/fstab` would not have automatically consulted `/etc/crypttab` to open the device.

Enterprise Linux versions 7 & 8

Keys

When encrypted disks are opened, a passphrase must ordinarily be supplied. In the case that a boot device is encrypted, this prompt will stop the system from booting until manual intervention occurs. To avoid this, we may create a cryptographic key, assign it to the device, and supply the key location in **/etc/crypttab**. This file takes one line per encrypted device, with the format:

```
#    name      device                [optional password]    [options]
     secret    UUID=XXXX-YYYY...     none                    nofail
```

This will map the device **secret** to the specified UUID prompting for password (**none**), but not delaying boot if the unlock fails or is delayed (**nofail**).

It should go without saying that these keys must be protected. Below, we demonstrate the creation and assignment of a key:

```
# dd if=/dev/urandom of=/root/keyfile bs=1024 count=4
4+0 records in
4+0 records out
4096 bytes (4.1 kB) copied, 0.00206224 s, 2.0 MB/s
# chmod 0400 /root/keyfile
# cryptsetup luksAddKey /dev/sdb /root/keyfile
Enter any passphrase: Passphrase
# umount /secret
# cryptsetup luksClose encDisk
# cryptsetup luksOpen /dev/sdb encDisk --key-file=/root/keyfile
# mount /secret
```

With this done, we now need to edit **/etc/crypttab**, informing it of our new key:

```
# tail -1 /etc/crypttab
encDisk /dev/sdb /root/keyfile luks
```

After a reboot, the new encrypted filesystem will automatically be mounted at **/secret**.

Module 10: Scheduling Events

EL7/8 has several ways to schedule events for later execution. The newest, **systemd.timers**, is the most useful and flexible, but can require more work. There are older tools: **cron**, **anacron**, **at**, and **batch**, each of which have their function. As systemd matures and admins become more comfortable with the concepts and interfaces to it, the traditional tools may go away (or at least not be installed by default). A comparison of the tools:

- **systemd.timers** – provided by **systemd**
    - can specify
        - exact time with accuracy of up to one microsecond (**us**)
        - intervals such as **daily** or **hourly**
        - relative time: boot time, last job start/end time, start time of the timer itself
        - any combination of the above
        - can include randomization
    - run either by the owning user, or a pseudo-user named after the service
    - can start a missed job
    - jobs can be independent of or dependent on eachother
    - configured as unit files
        - transient unit files can be created with **systemd-run**
- **cron** – provided by the package **cronie**
    - exact time specified with granularity of one minute
    - available to normal users by default
    - also runs any file in **/etc/cron.hourly**
    - can run jobs simultaneously
    - will not run a job if the time to run is missed
- **anacron** – provided by the package **cronie-anacron**; dependent on cron
    - rough time with a granularity of one day
    - includes start time randomization
    - restricted to root
    - will start a missed job when possible
    - runs jobs sequentially
    - will run all executable files in **/etc/cron.**[**daily**, **weekly**, **monthly**]
- **at**
    - creates a single job from the command line
    - flexible time specification
    - can execute multiple commands in a single job
    - stores jobs on disk – persistent across reboots
- **batch** – a special invocation of at
    - will execute jobs when cpu load average falls below a configured threshold

Enterprise Linux versions 7 & 8

systemd.timer

The most flexible method for scheduling jobs is **systemd.timer**. You get a rich interface using the standard **systemd.unit** file format and time specifications as laid out in the man page for `systemd.time`.

As an example we will use a problem mentioned in earlier. The `locate` database needs to be updated regularly by running `updatedb`. In EL6 this was done using a default job in `anacron`. In EL7/8 this is not done by default. In EL8, there is a timer-based solution provided, **mlocate-updatedb**; but it is not active. There are several other timers which are included for normal maintenance tasks including **dnf-makecache** and **fstrim**.

There are three parts to any **systemd.timer**:
- An executable to run – **mlocate-run-updatedb**
- A `.service` unit which calls the executable – **mlocate-updatedb.service**
- A `.timer` unit which calls the .service – **mlocate-updatedb.timer**

The `.timer` and the `.service` for `mlocate-updatedb` are in **usr/lib/systemd/system**. Timer and service unit files can be located in any of the `systemd` directories, viewable with **# systemd-analyze unit-paths**. These are the paths evaluated by `systemd` during boot and when `systemctl daemon-reload` is called.

If the `.timer` and `.service` have the same name, they are automatically associated. If they do not, you can specify the `.service` name with **Unit=** in the timer.

The `.service` unit file is what runs the actual executable; its format is this:

```
[Unit]
Description=Update a database for mlocate

[Service]
ExecStart=/usr/libexec/mlocate-run-updatedb
Nice=19
IOSchedulingClass=2
IOSchedulingPriority=7

PrivateTmp=true
PrivateDevices=true
PrivateNetwork=true
ProtectSystem=true
```

The `.timer` unit triggers the `.service` unit; its format is this:

```
[Unit]
Description=Updates mlocate database every day

[Timer]
OnCalendar=daily
AccuracySec=24h
Persistent=true

[Install]
WantedBy=timers.target
```

The `[Install]` section specifies when the timer will become active, and allows this unit to be enabled using `systemctl`. It is the `.timer` which is enabled, not the `.service`.

The `[Timer]` section says when the `.service` unit will be called. This particular one says:
- run every day
- at some time during a 24 hour period, we don't really care when
- run immediately if a run was missed because the system was off

systemd.time

Time specification is complex. For details see the `systemd.time` man page. You can specify:
- Time from an event (`OnActive=`, `OnBoot=`)
    - ranges from microseconds (`us`, `usec`) to years (`y`, `year`, `years`)
    - can be expressed in multiple ways (`minutes`, `minute`, `min`, `m`)
        - Don't confuse `m` = `minute` with `M` = `month`
    - can be mixed and matched: `23 h 15 min`
- Specific time (`OnCalendar=`)
    - can be a simple interval: `daily` or `weekly`
    - or formatted as: `Day    YYYY-MM-DD    HH:MM:SS`
        - `Day`(of week) is the English three letter abbreviation
        - all others are numeric
        - portions can be omitted
    - Ranges are expressed with two dots: `Mon..Fri`
    - Asterisks can be used as wildcards: `Mon *-*-1 09:00`
    - To specify every Day or Date, omit that portion of the specification
    - An omitted Time will evaluate as 00:00:00
    - Incrementing is done with a slash and a number: `* *-*-1/7 01:00`
    - Interpretation is liberal and fairly reasonable: `mon..Fri 21-1-*`
    - Days from the end of month is indicated a by tilde: `*-05~1`
    - Takes `RandomizedDelaySec` option to prevent job overlap
    - Takes `AccuracySec` to coordinate timers within a system
    - Uses local timezone time unless otherwise specified

Some examples:
- Run fifteen minutes after activation of the timer:
  `OnActiveSec=15 min`
- Run one hour after boot, and then weekly:
  `OnBootSec=1h`
  `OnUnitActiveSec=1w`
- Run at 11:15 am on even numbered weekdays:
  `OnCalendar=Mon..Fri *-*-02/2 11:15`
- Run at 1 am on the first day of the quarter:
  `OnCalendar=*-1,4,7,10 01:00`
- Run hourly:
  `OnCalendar= *-*-* *:00:00`
- Run after noon on the next to last day of every month:
  `OnCalendar=*-*~1 12:00`
  `RandomizedDelaySec=11h 59m`
- Run in the morning of the last Friday of odd numbered months:
  `Oncalendar=Fri *-1/2~1..7`
  `AccuracySec=12h`

In EL8, time specifications can be checked with
`systemd-analyze calendar` *some-time-spec*

This will evaluate the day, date, and time portions of the specification separately; you will still need to do some combining in your head. It will at least give an idea of how `systemd` is going to read what you typed.

systemd-run .timers

A transient timer stored in memory can be created using **systemd-run**. This can run a single event based on relative time from now, a fixed time event, or a recurring event which will persist until next boot. The temporary timer and service files are placed in **/run/systemd/** or **/run/systemd/transient/**

Arguments mimic the time specification pattern. Days must be all lowercase and any specification with a space must be in double quotes. For example:

```
# systemd-run --on-active="1 h 30 m" command
# systemd-run --on-calendar="wed 12:01" command
# systemd-run --on-active="1 hour" --on-calendar=daily command
```

anacron

If installed, **anacron** (part of **cronie-anacron**) is a convenient way to schedule a recurring task. Unlike **cron** it will run a task that was missed. However, it does not support precise time.

Jobs are scheduled by simply creating a symlink to the executable from the appropriate directory: **/etc/cron.daily**, **cron.weekly**, or **cron.monthly**.

By way of example, if we wanted to use anacron rather than systemd to automate the updatedb task mentioned above, we would do this:

- `# vi /usr/local/sbin/updatedb.task`
- Edit the file to contain the following:

    ```
    #!/bin/sh

    nodevs=$(awk '$1 == "nodev" && $2 != "rootfs" && $2 != \
    "zfs" { print $2 }' < /proc/filesystems)
    ## the above should be one line

    renice +19 -p $$ >/dev/null 2>&1
    ionice -c2 -n7 -p $$ >/dev/null 2>&1
    /usr/bin/updatedb -f "$nodevs"
    ```

- Set permissions and ownership of **500 root:root**
- Create a symlink to it from **/etc/cron.daily**

You can also add a line directly into **/etc/anacrontab** in this format:

```
# IntervalDays   DelayMin   Name       Path/Command
    3              21       bob.job    /home/bob/custom.script
```

This will run a job every three days, **21** minutes after the beginning of the **START_HOURS_RANGE**, plus a random amount up to **RANDOM_DELAY**. These values can be adjusted in **/etc/anacrontab**

cron, crontab

The `crond` service provided by the `cronie` package allows precise scheduling of recurring tasks. On older systems this was done by directly editing `/etc/crontab`. Some documentation will still lead you this way. This is no longer considered best practice. That file should only be altered if you wish to change the global behavior of `cron`.

To schedule a task, use `# crontab -e`.
This creates a separate file per user in `/var/spool/cron`.

All users can use `cron` by default. For security create a file:
`/etc/cron.allow` with a single line: `root`

To further restrict access edit `/etc/security/access.conf` and add:
`-:ALL EXCEPT root:cron`

If you do allow use of cron by other accounts (such as service accounts), when making an entry for that account, do not simply `su - username` instead use
`# crontab -e -u username`

You will now be editing an empty file. Its format is this:
```
# Min  Hour  Date      Month  Day      Path/Command
  15   11    2-31/2    *      mon-fri  /usr/bin/wall "Rus buys lunch!"
```

This means:

Field	Accepted Values	Example	Meaning
minutes	0-59	15	15 minutes after the hour
hour	0-23	11	11 am
date (day of month)	1-31	2-31/2	even numbered days
month	1-12 or jan-dec	*	any month
day	sun-sat or 0-7 (0 & 7 = sun)	mon-fri	weekdays

There are some special statements:
- The asterisk * is used to specify a value of any.
- Incrementing is specified with a forward slash (/3 means increment by 3).
- Values can be separated by commas (no spaces).

To run at 1 am on the first day of the quarter:
```
# Min  Hour  Date  Month     Day  Path/Command
  0    1     1     1,4,7,10  *    /usr/bin/report.job
```

`cron` will check for matches every minute. If all time fields in an entry match the command will run. Be careful with your `*`; if there were one where the `0` is in the above line, the job would run every minute from 1:00 to 1:59.

at, atq, atrm, batch, atd

A fast way to run a job once is with **at**, or its related command **batch**. They allow you to create a multi-line job which runs either at a specific time (**at**), or when cpu load gets low enough (**batch**).

To create a job, type **at** followed by a time specification. Then press **ENTER**.
You will then have an **at>** prompt to enter commands. When done exit with **CTL-d**.

All commands will be run at the time specified in **/bin/sh** with the environment you had when at was invoked (**$PATH** and such). If you wish to run the commands in `bash` instead, make the first command issued **bash**.

Creating a message for everyone 10 minutes from now would look like this:
```
# at now + 10 minutes
warning: commands will be executed using /bin/sh
at> wall "Break Time"
CTL-d

at> <EOT>
job 2 at Mon Oct 28 08:52:00 2019
```

Time specification can take a number of forms:
- `midnight`
- `now + 1 hour`
- `4pm`
- `16:00 Aug 10 2018`
- `noon tomorrow`

View scheduled jobs with **# atq**; remove them using **# atrm** `job-number`.

If you wish to run a computing intensive job when there is less load on the system, you can use **batch**. It is used just like `at` only without the time specification. Jobs queued using batch will wait for the one minute load average to fall below a specified level before running. By default, that load average is 0.8. It can be adjusted temporarily using **atd -l** `0.5` or set permanently in **/etc/sysconfig/atd**.

It is worth noting that `at` runs jobs sequentially, and it will not start the next until the first has completed; while `batch` will overlap jobs, starting them with a default 60 second offset.

As with **cron**, create a file **/etc/at.allow** with the single entry of **root** for security.

Module 11: Networking

On older systems IP configuration was done by editing **ifcfg-** files in **/etc/sysconfig/network-scripts/** or using commands such as **ifconfig** or **ip**. This is no longer the case. The ip command is still used to view status but should not be used for configuration.

Unlike Red Hat and CentOS, by default Amazon Linux uses the older style networking and firewall configuration. It can either be treated as if it were an EL6 machine or you can install **NetworkManager** and **firewalld**.

nmcli, nmtui, ip

In EL7/8 the network stack is controlled by the **NetworkManager** service. You can issue commands to NetworkManager in several ways. The best tool for controlling NetworkManager is **nmcli**. It has the capability to bond multiple physical connections into a trunk. It can even be used to configure a Wi-Fi hotspot. The full use of nmcli is beyond the scope of this book. We will concentrate on basic static IP configuration

To get the name of the current connection:
```
# nmcli connection show --active
NAME  UUID                                    TYPE      DEVICE
ens3  d9ba4dd0-4197-4a82-bb70-28764c1c47cf    ethernet  ens3
```

This shows that both the connection name and the device name is **ens3**. Ethernet devices begin with **en**, wireless lan with **wl**, wireless wan with **ww**. It is important to distinguish between the **device** (the physical interface) and a **connection** (the configuration applied to a device). By default the connection and the device will have the same name.

To get full details on that connection:
```
# nmcli connection show ens3
```

Unset properties will show as a pair of dashes: --. To only display set properties:
```
# nmcli connection show ens3 | grep -v "\-\-" | less
```

To rename this connection
```
# nmcli connection modify ens3 con-name Old-DHCP
```

To create a new connection we write an exceedingly long line specifying all the details:
```
# nmcli connection add type ethernet con-name Static-123 ifname ens3 \
ipv4.addresses 192.168.122.123/24 ipv4.gateway 192.168.122.1 \
ipv4.dns 192.168.122.1,192.168.122.2 ipv4.dns-search mydomain.com \
connection.autoconnect yes  ipv4.method manual
```

To activate the newly created connection:
```
# nmcli connection up Static-123
```

A running connection can be modified and reinitialized:
```
# nmcli connection modify Static-123 \
ipv4.addresses 192.168.122.123/24,192.168.122.111/24
# nmcli connection up Static-123
```

Alternatively you can interactively create or edit a connection:
```
# nmcli connection edit Static-123
nmcli> set ipv4.addresses 192.168.122.123/24
Do you also want to set 'ipv4.method' to 'manual'? [yes]: y
```

One common error when using the **ipv4.addresses** option: if you do not specify a slash notated subnet mask with the address, it will presume **/32**, which is a network of one host and not very useful.

Network configuration can also be accomplished from the GUI if available, or from a text menu interface using **nmtui**. While more limited than nmcli, these can be useful tools.

It should be noted that nmcli produces the traditional configuration scripts in **/etc/sysconfig/network-scripts**. While changes can be made directly there, this is not recommended, as the scripts will be overwritten the next time you use nmcli or nmtui. All changes should be done only with **nmcli**, or another **NetworkManager** based tool.

While still partially supported, the older commands ifconfig and arp should no longer be used for configuration or even trusted even to simply report information, as they will give incomplete results. To view IP information either use **nmcli** with no argument, or use the **ip** command. Common arguments for **ip** include:
- `# ip addr` – view addresses
    - `# ip addr show dev` *devicename*
- `# ip neigh` – view the address resolution tables, arp for IPv4 and ndisc for IPv6
    - `# ip neigh flush all` – remove all cached arp and ndisc entries
- `# ip route` – view routes

hostnamectl

In other Unix-like operating systems you might have set hostname with `hostname`, or by editing a file. The `hostname` command is still available on EL7/8, but only for backwards compatibility (for instance with old scripts). Today we use **hostnamectl**. If you set the hostname in any way other than `hostnamectl`, the change will either be reverted at the next boot, or simply ignored.

With no arguments `hostnamectl` gives a status report:

```
# hostnamectl
Static hostname: localhost.localdomain
      Icon name: computer-vm
        Chassis: vm
     Machine ID: dee4216aa08c497c97bf5aea0ae00478
        Boot ID: d63fdfa01928421fa0fe3a5ba1b0a895
 Virtualization: vmware
Operating System: CentOS Linux 7 (Core)
    CPE OS Name: cpe:/o:centos:centos:7
         Kernel: Linux 3.10.0-514.el7.x86_64
   Architecture: x86-64
```

In addition to the hostname, `localhost.localdomain`, we also got a lot of other information such as the exact kernel version, the distro and its version. It even let us know that we're running in a virtual machine using VMware virtualization. **hostnamectl** distinguishes three types of hostname:

- **transient** – the current hostname, which may or may not be retained at next boot
- **static** – the hostname you will have at next boot
- **pretty** – a display name, can contain characters that would otherwise be illegal

To set the hostname:
```
# hostnamectl set-hostname class-129.vm.not
```

nsswitch.conf, /etc/hosts

To resolve hostnames to addresses, EL first looks to the file **/etc/nsswitch.conf**. This file is a bit of a catch all, with lines for many services. For hostname resolution, the relevant line is:
hosts: files dns myhostname mymachines

Which simply says: "When resolving **hosts:** look in
- **/etc/hosts**, then ask the
- **dns** servers, then run
- **nss-myhostname**, which returns all locally configured IP addresses, then run
- **nss-mymachines**, which resolves locally hosted virtual machines

Address and hostname combinations can be added to **/etc/hosts**. This is often done because the name in question is not served by a DNS server (as in a test network), to provide faster resolution, or for redundancy in case of DNS or network failure. If you do add entries to the hosts file, remember that when an address changes, you must manually change **/etc/hosts**.

One line that should be added on an EL7/8 system is an entry for the local machine's static IP. It should be the first line, and takes the order of IP, FQDN, hostname:
```
192.168.1.129 class-129.vm.not class-129
127.0.0.1     localhost localhost.localdomain localhost4 <truncated>
::1           localhost localhost.localdomain localhost6 <truncated>
```

firewall-cmd

EL7/8 by default comes with a host-based firewall installed and active. It uses **firewall-cmd** to interface with the backing service **firewalld**, which in turn is backed by low-level programs: **iptables**, **ip6tables**, or **nft**, which in turn speak directly to the kernel.

Changes are usually made to the firewall with **firewall-cmd** while it is running. By default all changes are transient and will be lost on a reload or reboot. Permanent changes can be made with the firewall not running using **firewall-offline-cmd**.
- To make persistent changes append **--permanent** to each command
- Or issue # **firewall-cmd --runtime-to-permanent** when you have finished
- After changes the firewall should be reloaded using # **firewall-cmd --reload**

The firewall is broken into zones. There are nine built-in zones ranging from **trusted** (ACCEPT everything) to **drop** (don't respond to anything). If you do not specify a zone name in a command the default zone will be used. Sub-commands for zone manipulation:
- **--list-all-zones** – show all available zones
- **--get-default-zone** / **--set-default-zone** – view/set default
- **--info-zone**=*public* – list rules of a zone
- **--list-all** – display active zone(s) and rules

A zone can be associated with:
- **Services**
    - **--get-services** – list configured services
    - **--info-service**=*ftp* – get details of a service
    - **--zone**=*public* **--add-service**=*ssh* – add service to a zone
    - Services are defined in **/usr/lib/firewalld/services/**
    - Custom services can be created in **/etc/firewalld/**

- **Sources** – an IP range or MAC address
    - **--zone=trusted --add-source**=*192.168.2.0/24* – add a range

- **Ports**
    - **--add-port**=*443/tcp* – add a port

- **Protocols**
    - **--zone=drop --add-protocol**=*icmp* – add a protocol
    - Valid protocols are listed in **/etc/protocols**

- **Rich Rules** – these are more free form, see `man firewalld.richlanguage`
    - Restricting ssh to a local network:
    `--add-rich-rule=' rule family="ipv4" source address="192.168.0.0/24" service name="ssh" accept'`
    - Allow a single address to connect for remote auditing:
    `--add-rich-rule=' rule family="ipv4" source address="192.168.238.6" port protocol="tcp"  port="60" accept'`

- **Interface** – to add an interface to a new zone three steps are required:
    - `# firewall-cmd --zone=`*`public`* `--remove-interface=`*`ens224`*
    - `# firewall-cmd --zone=`*`drop`*`    --add-interface=`*`ens224`*
    - `# nmcli connection modify` *`ens224`* `connection.zone` *`drop`*

- **IP-Sets** – These are lists of addresses which can either be input individually, or loaded from a file and used as either a whitelist or blacklist. For usage consult the Red Hat Security Guide.

Rules are evaluated until a match is made. The order of evaluation is:
- Match **sources** from the zones in alphabetical order:
    - `block, dmz, drop, external, home, internal, public, trusted, work`
        - Source can be: `ip, ip range, mac address`, or an `ip-set`
    - If there is a source match perform the target action for that zone:
        - `block` – REJECT with an error message sent to source
        - `drop` – DROP with no response at all
        - `trusted` – ACCEPT without question
        - all other zones – `default`, which is:
            - If there is a next step go to it
            - Otherwise ACCEPT icmp, REJECT all else
- If the **interface** has a specified zone, check that zone for:
    - `services, ports, protocols, rich rules`
        - If there is a match, ACCEPT, or take the rich rule action
        - Otherwise perform the zone's target action.

The behavior of the `default` target is hard-coded and cannot be changed. The default zone is `public` with `target=default`. This means we will ACCEPT icmp and REJECT with a message everything else. This is not a good practice, disallowed packets should be dropped silently. To correct this:
`# firewall-cmd --permanent --zone=public --set-target=DROP`

In case of emergency, the firewall can be configured to drop all new connections, using
`# firewall-cmd --panic-on`

The configuration for `firewalld` is in **/etc/firewalld/firewalld.conf** (general configuration) and **/etc/firewalld/zones/**`zonename`**.xml** (direct rule configuration). The default zone configuration is in **/usr/lib/firewalld/zones/**. To restore the defaults, simply delete any zone files in **/etc/**.

If you want to see what configuration changes `firewall-cmd` is making at the lowest level, it depends on your particular EL version. Older versions place configuration in **iptables**, newer versions depend on **nft** (net filter tables). If your distro allows a choice between the two, it is configured in `firewalld.conf` as **FirewallBackend**. If this directive is missing, it means that `iptables` is the only option. To see all effective rules:
- On older systems:
    - `# iptables -vL` or
    - `# iptables -S`
- On newer systems:
    - `# nft list ruleset` or
    - `# nft list tables | grep firewalld`
        - `# nft list table` `inet firewalld`
        - `# nft list table` `ip firewalld`, etc.

While you could make configuration changes using `iptables` or `nft`, that is a very bad idea. Likewise you should not install, enable, or start any non-default firewall services as conflicts between them and `firewalld` may occur with unexpected results.

You may interact with firewall configuration while `firewalld` is stopped by using **firewall-offline-cmd**. The options for this command are very similar to **firewall-cmd**. When using **firewall-offline-cmd**, please note that all changes will be permananent, as there is no runtime configuration when the service is not running.

network tools

There are lots of useful tools for network diagnostics. To test connectivity we have **ping**, **arping**, **traceroute**, and **tracepath**.

To ping a computer at 10 second intervals 4 times:
```
# ping -i 10 -c 4 192.168.122.123
PING 192.168.122.123 (192.168.122.123) 56(84) bytes of data.
64 bytes from 192.168.122.123: icmp_seq=1 ttl=64 time=0.246 ms
```

ICMP, the protocol that `ping` relies on is frequently filtered or ignored. Within a subnet `arping` can be used instead. Note that it will not work across a router.
```
# arping 192.168.122.123
ARPING 192.168.122.123 from 192.168.122.139 eth0
Unicast reply from 192.168.122.123 [52:54:00:6F:82:05]  2.323ms
```

`traceroute` and `tracepath` perform similar functions, attempting to map the full route to a remote computer. They use slightly different methods to do this: `traceroute` by default uses ICMP packets, `tracepath` uses UDP. There are other small differences: some features of `traceroute` are only available to root; `traceroute` is not typically installed by default; and `tracepath` will return an MTU value for the entire path.

```
# traceroute www.google.com
traceroute to www.google.com (64.233.185.105), 30 hops max, 60 byte
1  gateway (192.168.122.1)  0.407 ms  0.350 ms  1.261 ms
2  192.168.208.1 (192.168.208.1)  3.919 ms  3.499 ms  3.317 ms
# tracepath www.google.com
 1?: [LOCALHOST]                                      pmtu 1500
 1:  gateway                                               0.251ms
 2:  192.168.208.1                                         2.261ms
```

There are several ways to query and test DNS resolution: `dig`, `host`, `nslookup`, and `resolvectl`. Most of these are part of the `bind-utils` package which must be installed separately. To find the mail exchangers (MX records) for gmail.com, by asking a google.com nameserver:

```
# dig @ns1.google.com gmail.com MX
```

For an interactive tool, use `nslookup` (output has been truncated in these examples):

```
# nslookup
> set type=NS
> google.com
google.com      nameserver = ns1.google.com.
google.com      nameserver = ns3.google.com.
> server ns1.google.com
> set type=MX
> gmail.com
Server:         ns1.google.com
Address:        216.239.32.10#53
gmail.com       mail exchanger = 40 alt4.gmail-smtp-in.l.google.com.
gmail.com       mail exchanger = 20 alt2.gmail-smtp-in.l.google.com.
```

For a simple name to address or address to name resolution, use `host`:

```
# host gmail.com    or
# host 192.168.122.123
```

Another way to do this is with `resolvectl`, which if issued with no arguments will show current DNS configuration

```
# resolvectl query google.com
google.com: 64.233.185.113
            64.233.185.100
```

To explore and see the state of sockets and connections to a computer you can use **netstat** or **ss**. In general ss is preferred; netstat has been deprecated and will no longer be maintained. By itself ss will display all sockets, including the unix-family sockets, shown as **u_str** and **u_dgr**, used for inter-process communication. While sometimes useful, it is normal to restrict the output down a bit. To display all tcp and udp listening ports except ssh:
`#ss -tu state listening sport != :ssh`

To show only the ssh ports, and to add PID, memory, and SELinux information is this:
`# ss -tplm src :ssh`

To continuously display connections to the web server from a specific network:
```
# watch -n 5 "ss  \( sport = :http or sport = :https \) dst 192.168.0.0/16 "
Every 5.0s: ss  \( sport = :http or sport = :https \) dst 192.168.0.0/16      Wed

Netid State     Recv-Q Send-Q Local Address:Port        Peer Address:Port
tcp   ESTAB      0     0     [::ffff:192.168.122.139]:http [::ffff:192.168.122.1]:40286
tcp   FIN-WAIT-2 0     0     [::ffff:192.168.122.139]:http [::ffff:192.168.122.1]:40284
```

There are several ways of interacting with URL/URI based resources (like the web): **curl**, **wget**, **elinks**, and **lynx**. These will be addressed in the section devoted to **httpd**.

There are also some more advanced tools that are beyond the scope of this course, but which you should at least be aware exist. These can be very useful, but need knowledge, consideration, and possibly approval from your security team before use:
- **ncat** – easy provider of network connectivity
- **tcpdump** – wire-level level listener/parser
- **nmap** – network exploration tool

Module 12: Remote Access

ssh

ssh is a replacement for insecure shell protocols such as `telnet`, `rlogin`, and `rsh`, which should no longer be used under any circumstances. It allows the secure passing of credentials and an encrypted channel between machines. It also provides the underlying protocol for secure copy protocol (**scp**) and secure FTP (**sftp**).

Improperly configured **ssh** can be a very large security hole. To configure it correctly:

- In `/etc/ssh/sshd_config`
    - Uncomment and/or change:
      ```
      Protocol 2    ## and only 2
      PermitEmptyPasswords no
      PermitUserEnvironment no
      GSSAPIAuthentication no
      ClientAliveInterval 600
      ClientAliveCountMax 0
      IgnoreRhosts yes
      PrintLastLog yes
      PermitRootLogin no
      IgnoreUserKnownHosts yes
      KerberosAuthentication no
      StrictModes yes
      Compression delayed   ##(or no)
      ```
    - Add:
      ```
      HostbasedAuthentication no
      Ciphers aes128-ctr,aes192-ctr,aes256-ctr
      MACs hmac-sha2-256,hmac-sha2-512
      banner=/etc/issue    ## insert your banner in /etc/issue
      ```
    - Leave at default:
      ```
      UsePrivilegeSeparation sandbox
      X11Fowarding yes
      ```
- In `/etc/bashrc` add a line: `TMOUT=600`
- Find and remove any file with the name `*.shost`, `*.rhost`, or `*hosts.equiv`.
- Check permissions on the host keys:
    - ```
      # chmod 0644 /etc/ssh/*.key.pub
      # chmod 0600 /etc/ssh/ssh_host*key
      ```
- Add the following line in an appropriate `audit.rules` file:
    - `-a always,exit -F path=/usr/libexec/openssh/ssh-keysign -F perm=x -F auid>=1000 -F auid!=4294967295 -k privileged-ssh`
    - This is correct for EL7, for EL8 use **auid!=unset**, rather than **auid!=4294967295**.

Use of ssh is simple: `# ssh user@remotehost`

Enterprise Linux versions 7 & 8
      ```

ssh-keygen, ssh-copy-id

You can also perform fully certificate-based logins. This adds an additional layer of security, and has the advantage of allowing the use of different locally stored passwords on each machine, without having to keep track of them individually.

To do this correctly the source user and destination user must exist on both machines – and should have the same UID. If the UID is used by another user on the destination machine, there is a possibility of conflict. To avoid this, it is best practice to specify UID and GID when creating users. This also avoids the possibility of reuse of UID in the case of a deleted user.

To use certificate-based `ssh`, you must first create a key:
ssh-keygen

Follow the prompts. Then copy the key to the remote server:
ssh-copy-id -i */path/to/key user@remotehost*

You can now log in using the key, rather than the password:
ssh -i */path/to/key user@remotehost*

If you will always use the same username and key for connection to a given destination, add the following lines to `~/.ssh/config`:

```
    Host destination.server
    User username
    IdentityFile /path/to/key
```

This allows connection to the specified host without having to supply a username or key.

The permissions and ownership of keys should be checked. Private keys should be **600**; public **644**. Both should be owned by the user and the users personal group.

If you wish to unlock a passphrase protected key for the duration of a session:
eval $(ssh-agent); ssh-add */path/to/key*

For ease of use, this can be aliased in `.bashrc`.

scp

As mentioned, you can also use the `ssh` framework to transfer files using **scp**. This allows secure and simple transfer between hosts, without requiring the configuration of an ftp server. You can even use certificates. The basic invocation is simple:
scp -i */path/to/key localfile user@remotehost:/path/remotefile*

It will accept wildcards such as **/path/*.conf**, and can recurse entire directory trees with **-r**.

sftp

If you want more interactivity than is provided by `scp`, use **sftp**. The sftp-server is a subsystem of `sshd`. By default it is enabled and configured by the following line of `sshd_config`:
Subsystem   sftp   /usr/libexec/openssh/sftp-server

This allows system-wide inbound sftp rights to any authenticated users controlled by standard permissions, of course.

If you wish to limit access for certain users (in this example the group **sftp-users**), you can make them capable of only using `sftp`, not `ssh`. This is done by replacing the Subsystem line in `sshd_config` with
Subsystem   sftp   internal-sftp
and appending
Match Group sftp-users
ForceCommand internal-sftp

Restart `sshd` after making changes.

To restrict those users further still, such that they can only see a single directory add
ChrootDirectory /sftp/%u

The `%u` will be replaced with the username upon login.

Then create a directory for that user: **/sftp/**_username_**/home**
chown the home directory *only* (not the path above it) to **user:sftp-users**.

cockpit

EL7/8 has a web interface known as **cockpit**. The cockpit interface provides an easy way to accomplish some of the more common administrative tasks, as well providing a terminal for standard command-line access. It is typically installed by default on EL8, in some EL7 versions it must be manually installed. To use `cockpit`:
`# firewall-cmd --permanent --zone=public --add-service=cockpit`
`# firewall-cmd --reload`
`# systemctl enable --now cockpit.socket`

If you have a web server certificate it can be placed in **/etc/cockpit/ws-certs.d/**

You will notice that we enabled and started `cockpit.`**socket**, not `cockpit.`**service**. In an effort to be as lightweight as possible, `cockpit.service` will not run until called by `cockpit.socket`. An **ss -tlpn** will show that the listener for port 9090 is `systemd`. When a user connects, `systemd` will start the service. It will exit after 90 seconds of inactivity.

Browse to **https://**_hostname-or-ip_**:9090** and log in as a user capable of using `sudo`, checking the "Reuse my password" box if you wish to avoid prompting for reauthentication.

Enterprise Linux versions 7 & 8

vsftpd, lftp

Use of FTP is generally discouraged, as it is no longer considered secure. But there are times when it is the right solution; such as when providing an appropriately firewalled software repository for internal use, providing kickstarter files for unattended installation, or when making large files available to the public.

The standard ftp server for EL7/8, **vsftpd**, is not installed by default. When installed it will create the three units in **/usr/lib/systemd/system**. For a simple installation, you will only want to enable **vsftpd.service**; the other units are templates for advanced configuration using multiple .conf files. The configuration file is **/etc/vsftpd/vsftpd.conf**. Relevant options are:

- `anonymous_enable` – set to **NO** unless needed
- `write_enable` – set to **NO** unless needed
- `anon_upload_enable` – default **NO**. Also enforced by SElinux booleans
- `ftpd_banner` – leave commented out instead use banner_file
- `banner_file` – point to **/etc/issue**
- `listen_ipv6` – slightly deceptive, as this enables both IPv4 and 6
- `ssl_enable` – a pain to configure and affected by the several flaws, use sftp instead
- `delay_failed_login` – if allowing authenticated connections, set this to 10 or more.

Before starting the service, check permissions and SELinux context on **/var/ftp/**. This is the default directory for anonymous users. Anonymous users are logged in as user `ftp`. To change the default directory, change the `ftp` user's home directory. You will also need to add the **ftp service** to the appropriate firewall zone, which should be as restrictive as possible.

The usual ftp client for EL7/8 is **lftp**, which supports protocols beyond ftp, including http. The common syntax is **lftp** *[user@]hostname*. Many commands (such as **put** and **get**) are retained from older ftp clients. Others such as **lls**, have been replaced with the syntax **!ls**, where the **!** invokes the local shell. The one exception to this **lcd** which is the only way to change the local directory.

httpd, apachectl

Providing simple web services is a fairly common administrative task. Advanced configuration needs and tasks vary wildly based on site and application specifics, and are beyond the scope of this course. To get a basic web server running on EL7/8:
- Install the Apache webserver: `httpd`
    - If you wish to use authentication, `httpd-tools` is required
    - `httpd-manual` will place documentation for Apache at `http://localhost/manual`
- Create a file `/var/www/html/index.html`
    - otherwise `/etc/httpd/conf.d/welcome.conf` will display
- Add the http service to the firewall:
  `# firewall-cmd --zone=public --add-service=http --permanent`
  `# firewall-cmd --reload`
- Enable but don't start the service:
  `# systemctl enable httpd.service`
- Start the service:
  `# apachectl start`
    - The `apachectl` tool is a wrapper for `systemctl`. It allows graceful shutdown and restart of Apache, preventing unwanted user disconnection. It also tracks down and kills errant child processes.

The primary configuration file for Apache is `/etc/httpd/conf/httpd.conf`. The options contained within it are called directives. The quick reference guide to the directives is over 30 pages long, and configuration can be quite complex, but some relevant directives include:
- `Listen` – This should have both an IP and port.
- `DocumentRoot` – the base directory for service.
- To prevent DoS attacks the following should be set:
    - `LimitRequestFieldSize    8190` – or less
    - `LimitRequestLine    8190` – or less
    - `LimitRequestBody    1` – or more
    - `LimitRequestFields    1` – or more
    - `KeepAliveTimeout    15` – or less
    - `KeepAlive    On`.
    - `Timeout    300` – or less
- All `<Directory/>` entries should have a directive `AllowOverride    None`

After making changes to the configuration files:
- Verify the validity with
  `# apachectl configtest`
- Reload using
  `# apachectl graceful`

Enterprise Linux versions 7 & 8

curl, wget, lynx, elinks

There are times when you will need to get content from a webserver, but only have a command line. There a few tools that you can use to solve this problem. `curl` and `wget` both work from the command line and can be encapsulated in scripts. Both support ftp, http, and https protocols as well as cookies and POST requests, but there are some differences:

- `curl`
  - acts like `cat` for network sources
  - output can be piped
  - will not recurse a website
  - supports many protocols including SFTP, SCP, TFTP, POP3, IMAP, and LDAP
  - provides automatic decompression for HTTP deflate and gzip
- `wget`
  - output goes into a file or files
  - can recurse a website, creating a directory structure matching that of the source
  - will automatically resume if a connection is interrupted

Both `curl` and `wget` have their place and are exceedingly useful at times, but to actually browse the web, you need something that understands html. For that you need `lynx` or `elinks`, which are text interface browsers. While they don't support all the features of a graphical browser, they are useful. They also can be used to verify the accessibility features of a website. Which one is available to you depends on your version of EL: Beginning with EL8 `lynx` is not available, and availability of `elinks` for EL8 has also been variable.

Navigation in either is similar:
- `space` / `shift-space` – page down / up
- `Insert` / `Delete` – scroll up / down
- `up` / `down` – move between hyperlinks
- `right` – select link
- `left` – go back
- `ESC` – show menus
- `q` – quit

NFS

NFS (Network File System) is a file sharing protocol common to Unix-like operating systems. Like many other network protocols, NFS was not designed with security in mind. Older versions (v2 and v3) did not support ACLs, SELinux labeling, or Kerberos integration. They also required multiple services and ports requiring more overhead and a large potential attack surface.

Modern NFS (v4) addresses many of these problems. It uses a single service and port (2049), runs over TCP, and can be integrated with Kerberos authentication. However it still should not be considered secure. It should only be used on enclaved networks. The default version of NFS in EL8 is NFSv4.2. Support for versions 2, 3, and 4 is available in EL7, while EL8 supports only versions 3 and 4.

The software package for both server and client is `nfs-utils`. This package provides everything needed to serve all supported versions of NFS and to access exported filesystems as a client.

To create an NFS server:

Add the service to the default zone (or an appropriate limited zone):
```
# firewall-cmd --add-service nfs --permanent
# firewall-cmd --reload
```

Update the configuration file `/etc/nfs.conf`:
```
    [nfsd]
    vers2=n
    vers3=n
```

This causes `nfsd` to not answer requests for NFS versions 2 and 3, but won't prevent the services that back those versions from starting. To do that, `mask` the unwanted services and start NFS:
```
# systemctl mask --now rpc-statd.service \
rpcbind.service rpcbind.socket
```

```
# systemctl enable --now nfs-server.service
```

Define which filesystems we wish to share (or export), and which hosts and networks they will be shared with. This is done in the `/etc/exports` file. Each line represents an exported file system and will contain:
- **local filesystem to export** – /home, /svr/share, /var/pub
- **hostname to share with** – client, client.local, www.site.not
- **network to share with** – 192.168.0.0/24, 172.16.0.0/28 (note the slash notation)
- **options**:
    - `rw` – allow read and write access
    - `sec=` – define a list of allowable security flavors (sys:krb5:krb5i:krb5p)
    - `sync` – do not reply to NFS request until a write has occurred
    - `fsid=0` – sets the "root" of the virtual file system in NFSv4
    - `anonuid` – set the system UID to be assigned to anonymous users
    - `no_root_squash` – do not map UID 0 requests to `anonymous`

This is a sample **/etc/exports** file from the man page:
```
/              master(rw) trusty(rw,no_root_squash)
/projects      proj*.local.domain(rw)
/usr           *.local.domain(ro) @trusted(rw)
/home/joe      pc001(rw,all_squash,anonuid=150,anongid=100)
/pub           *(ro,insecure,all_squash)
/srv/www       -sync,rw server @trusted @external(ro)
/foo           2001:db8:9:e54::/64(rw) 192.0.2.0/24(rw)
/build         buildhost[0-9].local.domain(rw)
```

Create an export, in this case allowing a one IP read/write access to the local directory **/share**:
```
# cat /etc/exports
/share 192.168.238.73/32(rw,sync)
```

Now export (share) the file system with **exportfs -va**. This command runs when **nfs-server.service** starts or restarts on EL8, on EL7 it is called **nfs.service**). It will export anything listed in the **/etc/exports** file.
```
# exportfs -va
exporting 192.168.238.73/32:/share
```

We can verify the export with **exportfs** which will display the currently exported filesystems.

On the client install the **nfs-utils** package. Configuration is performed in **/etc/nfsmount.conf** which controls how NFS mounting operations are performed. There are dozens of options here. At a minimum set the default and required protocol to TCP, and the default and required NFS version to 4.

```
[ NFSMount_Global_Options ]
Defaultvers=4
Nfsvers=4
Defaultproto=tcp
Proto=tcp
```

We may now attempt a mount:
```
# mkdir /netshare
# mount 192.168.238.73:/share /netshare
# mount -v | grep /netshare
192.168.238.71:/share on /netshare type nfs4
(rw,relatime,vers=4.2,rsize=524288,wsize=524288,namlen=255,hard,proto=
tcp,timeo=600,retrans=2,sec=sys,clientaddr=192.168.238.73,local_lock=n
one,addr=192.168.238.71)
```

This can be automated by adding an entry to /etc/fstab or by making a .mount or .automount unit file. Either way note that what you will mount takes the form of *remote.server:/directory* and type is **nfs**.

NFS and Authentication

NFS uses two layers of permissions: those defined in the export options, and local file permissions on the server. By default, an NFS server relies on the client to provide UID/GID information for users accessing the share. The server will then determine local permissions based on the UID/GID of the accessing user using AUTH_SYS (same process used for local determinations). This leaves NFS servers vulnerable to spoofed UID/GID information, or host impersonation.

This weakness can be mitigated by implementing Kerberos authentication, which would allow authorization of both the server and the client, and, potentially, authorization of user accounts directly through that same system. Configuring NFS to authenticate via Kerberos would be ideal, but at the time of this writing there are issues with Kerberos integration on FIPS enabled systems. FIPS is mandatory on government systems. We expect these issues to be addressed in an upcoming minor release, and will update the material at that time.

Lacking Kerberos, administrators may choose to implement read-only exports, or rely on squashing to limit user interaction on shared filesystems. Squashing involves a series of options:

- `all_squash` – all access attempts are "squashed" to a single, typically unprivileged UID/GID
- `root_squash` – squash the root account, always
- `anonuid` / `anongid` – set the destination account and group for squashing

Again, NFS should not be considered a secure protocol. Certain configurations may, as we have shown, make it *less insecure*; sensitive data should not be shared over NFS unless risk has been assessed and mitigated through other means.

x2go

While most servers do not require and should not have graphics installed, there are some applications which require a GUI. One way to access a graphical desktop is by using X2go. At current it is only supported on EL7, as some dependencies are missing from the EPEL for EL8. It also does not play well with the gnome desktop, so an alternative desktop environment must be installed. It is inherently more secure than vnc as it uses ssh as its primary transport.

To configure the X2go server:

- In **/etc/ssh/sshd_config**:
  ```
  X11Forwarding yes
  AllowTcpForwarding yes
  X11UseLocalhost yes
  X11Displayoffset 10
  ```
- `# yum -y install x2goserver-xsession`
- `# yum -y groupinstall "Xfce" or "KDE Plasma Workspaces"`
- `# systemctl set-default graphical.target`
- `# reboot`
  or isolate to **multiuser.target**, then to **graphical.target**

The client simply needs **x2goclient** installed. The Windows client is at
https://code.x2go.org/releases/binary-win32/x2goclient/release

vnc

Another way to access a GUI is by using the vnc (Virtual Network Computing) protocol. This is not a secure protocol and should not be used on any public facing network.

If you are **not** running in FIPS mode and you want to simply share a single user's desktop, you can run the vnc server built into the `gnome` desktop suite. This is done by simply enabling sharing of a user's desktop in the desktop settings. This will run **vino-server** on port **5900**.

If you are running in FIPS mode (and you should be), you must use **tigervnc-server**. The configuration is involved and diverges substantially between EL7 and EL8.

The EL8 installation is interesting in that it uses a user-owned `systemd.unit`. These can be useful for things like custom mounts and services dedicated to a particular user. User unit files must be `WantedBy=default.target`.

To implement vnc:
- Ensure you have graphics installed, and have `graphical.target` set as your default
- Install **tigervnc-server**
- Open the firewall:
    - `# firewall-cmd --permanent --add-service=vnc-server`
    - `# firewall-cmd --reload`

On EL7:
- Each user will need their own unit file, as each user's instance runs as a separate service:
    - `# vi /usr/lib/systemd/system/vncserver@\:XXX.service`
        - Where *XXX* is a number, such as **1**.
    - The contents should be:
    ```
    [Unit]
    Description=Remote desktop service (VNC)
    After=syslog.target network.target
    [Service]
    Type=forking
    User=<USER>
    Group=<USER>
    # Clean any existing files in /tmp/.X11-unix environment
    ExecStartPre=/bin/sh -c '/usr/bin/vncserver -kill %i > /dev/null 2>&1 || :'
    ExecStart=//usr/bin/vncserver %i
    PIDFile=/home/<USER>/.vnc/%H%i.pid
    ExecStop=/bin/sh -c '/usr/bin/vncserver -kill %i > /dev/null 2>&1 || :'
    [Install]
    WantedBy=graphical.target
    ```
        - Replace *<USER>* with the desired username.
- Reload using `# systemctl daemon-reload`
- Set the user's vnc password:
  `# su - <user>`
  `# vncpasswd`
    - This must be done as the user as it creates a file in the user's home directory
    - Passwords must be at least 6 characters, and unique

- o Skip the view-only password
- o Exit out of that user's session
- Start and enable the session:
systemctl enable --now vncserver@\:1.service

On EL8:

All steps must be run as the target user
- # **ssh** to the server using the desired username
    - o do **not su -** It will not work
- Set the user's vnc password:
vncpasswd
    - o Passwords must be at least 6 characters, and unique
    - o Skip the view-only password
    - o Do **not** exit from the users session
- [optional] If you want to customize the user's startup, create a service just for them.
    - o # **mkdir -p ~/.config/systemd/user**
    - o # **cp /usr/lib/systemd/user/vncserver@.service \
      ~/.config/systemd/user/**
- Enable the vnc server
    - o # **systemctl --user enable vncserver@:***XXX*.**service --now**
        - where *XXX* is a unique number for that users session
- Make the user's login persistent across reboots.
    - o # **loginctl enable-linger**
        - This allows systemd to start the server as the user at boot

Connect to hostname:XXX where XXX is the session number for that user.

If you encounter problems with the lock-screen resetting when trying to enter a password turn off screen lock for that user. This is a security risk, but is currently the only way to make this work. This must be done in the GUI, either in a terminal started from the GUI:
gsettings set org.gnome.desktop.lockdown disable-lock-screen false
or under System Tools > Settings > Privacy.

If you wish to be more secure, create an ssh tunnel from your local machine to the server:
ssh -C -L 590*X***:localhost:590***X*   **server** where *X* is the session number.
Then attach with your vnc client to **localhost:***X*.

Module 13: SELinux

SELinux is a security module for the Linux kernel, which provides a means of implementing Mandatory Access Controls in a secure system. **Access controls** provide a method for preventing the use of a resource by an unauthorized party or in an unauthorized manner.

In **Discretionary Access Control (DAC)** models, users are given control over the resources that they own. Standard Linux permissions and ACLs are discretionary access controls. While this model can prevent unauthorized users and processes from reading, writing, or executing disallowed files, it does not provide way to prevent a user or process from performing undesirable actions against resources they would otherwise be permitted to control.

For example, DAC cannot prevent a user from giving other users access to or even ownership of files they own. Similarly, DAC cannot prevent processes a user spawns from accessing or modifying files accessible to the invoking user. If a process running with root privileges is hijacked by a malicious actor, the entire system is at risk.

Mandatory Access Control (MAC) models provide a way to resolve these issues. The SELinux implementation of MAC accomplishes this by labelling and classifying the resources and participants on a system, and specifying rules for if and how they may interact. These rules cannot be violated by any user or process. Administrators may change policies or place SELinux into permissive mode, but they are still subject to the SELinux enforcement rules that they create.

SELinux does not replace DAC permissions; it is provides controls beyond them. It cannot grant permissions that DAC permissions have denied. DAC is always consulted first. SELinux may, or may not, apply additional controls. The following occurs every time a user-space program asks the kernel to do something:

- System Call – a command is issued.
- Error Check – is it a valid command?
- DAC (Permissions / ACLs) – is the user allowed to read, write, execute as needed?
- MAC (SELinux) – is this allowed under the security context?
- Return – execute command, or exit with error, possibly logging.

The central mechanism of SELinux is Type Enforcement. Type Enforcement controls interactions between different types of system resources. Every resource in SELinux will be assigned a **type**. These resources could be processes (which are often referred to as Subjects) or files, directories, ports, etc. (often called Objects, or "those things that the Subjects interact with and manipulate").

Here is some basic terminology that will help us understand how SELinux protects a system:

- **OBJECT** – a system resource; the target of interaction by SUBJECTS. These can be files, devices, ports – practically any sort of system resource.
- **SUBJECT** – an active component, something that attempts to interact with OBJECTS and other SUBJECTS. In other words, these are processes.
- **TYPE** – a way of categorizing resources on a system. When we assign a type to a process, we would say that we have assigned that process to a DOMAIN. When we assign types to OBJECTS, we simply retain the designation of "type".
- **DOMAIN** – a context in which processes are executed. Policy rules are applied to these.
- **POLICY** – the driver for SELinux enforcement. Policy modules can be created which contain rules and definitions for types and domains (and more). These rules can take a variety of forms, from granting or revoking access and privileges to controlling transitions between domains, to controlling object type transitions inside a domain, to controlling auditing behavior, etc.
- **SECURITY CONTEXT** – made up of an SELinux User, a role, a type, and a sensitivity/classification level in a colon delimited label. Here is a label showing user=`system_u`, role=`object_r`, type=`var_t`, and sensitivity=`s0`: system_u:object_r:var_t:s0.
- **SELINUX USER** – a class of user, such as `sysadm_u`, `staff_u`, or `system_u`. These aren't classic Linux users. Rather, classic Linux users (and every other resource on the system) would be assigned to one of these classes. If Role Based Access Control (**RBAC**) is not being implemented, these aren't typically an object of consideration; instead, processes run under `system_u`, and users default to `unconfined_u`. For STIG compliance, normal users should be confined to `user_u`, and administrators should be confined to either `sysadm_u` or `staff_u`.

Enforcement

SELinux configuration information is stored in the file `/etc/selinux/config`.

It can be configured in three states. They are:

- `Enforcing` – SELinux is active and enforcing policy, default, required by STIG
- `Permissive` – SELinux logs policy exceptions, but does not enforce
- `Disabled` – SELinux is disabled in the kernel and cannot run

The type of enforcement is also configured here

- `Targeted` – default, important processes are protected
- `Minimum` – like targeted, with a smaller selection of targets
- `MLS` – Multi Level Security

The first option sets the state that SELinux will be in at boot. SELinux operates in one of two modes, which it can swap between upon request: `enforcing` and `permissive`. When `enforcing` SELinux monitors all confined entities, logs policy violations, and prohibits any actions that are not specifically allowed by policy. When permissive it will monitor confined entities and log infractions, but will NOT prohibit actions from occurring (helpful for diagnosing SELinux behaviors). Regardless of the settings in `/etc/selinux/config`, SELinux will not run if disabled on the kernel command line.

We can check the current mode with the **getenforce** command, and transiently change it using **setenforce**. The options for `setenforce` can either be numeric (**1, 0**) or a word (**enforcing, permissive**). Changes made with `setenforce` will not persist through a reboot:

```
# setenforce 1
# getenforce
Enforcing

# setenforce permissive
# getenforce
Permissive
```

SELinux cannot be `disabled` using `setenforce`. To disable SELinux entirely, we must alter `/etc/selinux/config` and reboot. This prevents the SELinux kernel module from being loaded at all. SELinux should never be `disabled` on a government system and it should only be run in `permissive` mode for diagnostic and recovery purposes. If SELinux is not `enforcing`, any newly created files or other objects will NOT receive a security context label. When SELinux is functioning, it expects these values to be present. When SELinux is returned to `enforcing` on a system which had been operating in a `permissive` or `disabled` state, serious errors may occur. To prevent this create a file in the root directory: `/.autorelabel`. This forces SELinux to reapply the correct labels at the next boot.

The second option sets the **SELINUXTYPE** (or Enforcement Type). This defines the behavior of SELinux when it is enforcing. The default is **targeted**, which means that most common system services will operate in a confined domain. If set to **minimum** a smaller set of services will be confined; **MLS** is for compartmentalized secure systems.

User Classes and Roles

SELinux operates by confining or restricting actions on a secure system. Any class, type, role, or domain created by policy will operate in this way, with subjects and objects being confined at greater or lesser levels of restriction.

Each user class will have access to one or more roles. A system user assigned to a user class can use any of the roles available to the class, but only inhabit a single role at any given time. The active role can be switched using the **newrole** command. These roles, in turn, have access to domains, and the domains have access to types as defined by policy.

When using the default **targeted** policy, the user class **unconfined_u** will be the default class for all interactive users on the system. This class has access to the **unconfined_r** role which is, as the name suggests, not confined by SELinux. In other words, this user class is only restricted by other security mechanisms available in the operating system, such as permissions or individual service configurations. The processes this user invokes may be confined, or the services this user interacts with - but the user class itself will not be. For example, an unconfined user may be given permission to use **sudo** or to run commands with SUID set; SELinux would not prevent this.

We can get a list of user classes and the logins assigned to them using the **semanage** command:

```
# semanage login -l
Login Name           SELinux User         MLS/MCS Range
__default__          unconfined_u         s0-s0:c0.c1023
root                 unconfined_u         s0-s0:c0.c1023
system_u             system_u             s0-s0:c0.c1023

# semanage user -l
SELinux User    SELinux Roles
guest_u         guest_r
root            staff_r sysadm_r system_r unconfined_r
staff_u         staff_r sysadm_r system_r unconfined_r
sysadm_u        sysadm_r
system_u        system_r unconfined_r
unconfined_u    system_r unconfined_r
user_u          user_r
xguest_u        xguest_r
```

Above, we can see that the `_default_` user class is unconfined_u. If a system user has no specifically defined user class, this entry declares what context the user will receive.

From a STIG perspective, there are three of classes to be dealt with:
- **sysadm_u** - has access to only the **sysadm_r** role. This class can use **sudo** and **su**. It is restricted from login via GUI or **ssh** by default, though this can be altered with booleans:
  `# setsebool -P ssh_sysadm_login 1`
- **staff_u** - is assigned the **staff_r**, **sysadmin_r**, **system_r**, and **unconfined_r** roles. This class can perform any tasks that **sysadm_r** could, with the exception of calling **su**. **staff_u** is not restricted from GUI or **ssh** login by default, as **sysadm_u** is.
- **user_u** - is assigned only the **user_r** role. This class has access to GUI/terminal login and networking and can execute scripts in his/her home directory. Cannot use **su** or **sudo**.
  - In EL7 the range flag **-r** must be passed to semanage in order to place a user in the correct mls context for **user_u**
    `# semanage login -a -s user_u -r s0 username`

Below are a set of commands and tips that can help configure your system to standard:
- We can check user classes and the roles assigned them with
  `# semanage login -l` and `# semanage user -l`
- Users can be added to a user class with
  `# semanage login -a -s userclass username`
- Once assigned, the userclass can be changed with
  `# semanage login -m -s userclass username`
- Groups of users can be added as well by using a percent %
  `# semanage login -a -s staff_u %wheel`
- New users can be confined at time of creation with
  `# useradd -Z userclass`
- The STIG mandates that all administrators be assigned to **sysadm_u** or **staff_u**, and that all nonadministrators be assigned **user_u**. To change the default user mapping to user_u
  `#semanage login -m -S targeted -s "user_u" -r s0 __default__`

Enterprise Linux versions 7 & 8

Types and Policy

Every resource on an SELinux system will be assigned a type. We can determine the type assigned to a resource by examining the label applied to it. Labels are a representation of the security context assigned to a resource.

From our perspective the most important component in these labels is the type (such as **unconfined_t**, or **kernel_t**). Labels are comprised of five colon-delimited sections, the third of which is the type. Labels can be applied to files, processes, even users. In many commands, the standard option, **-Z**, which will cause these labels to be displayed.

```
# ls -Z /var
system_u:object_r:acct_data_t:s0 account
system_u:object_r:public_content_t:s0 ftp

# id -Z
unconfined_u:unconfined_r:unconfined_t:s0-s0:c0.c1023

# ps -eZ
LABEL                                   PID TTY          TIME CMD
system_u:system_r:init_t:s0               1 ?        00:01:38 systemd
system_u:system_r:kernel_t:s0             2 ?        00:00:01 kthreadd

# ps -eo label,args
LABEL                                   COMMAND
system_u:system_r:init_t:s0             /usr/lib/systemd/systemd --switched-
system_u:system_r:kernel_t:s0           [kthreadd]
```

SELinux policies consist primarily of rule sets which define allowed interactions between types. We can inspect these rules with the **sesearch** command. The invocations of **sesearch** below use the following options:

- **--rule** – type of rule sought: **allow**, **type**, **neverallow**, **audit**, **dontaudit**, etc.
- **-s** – source domain: the domain attempting to interact
- **-t** – target: the domain or object being interacted with
- **-c** – class of object: **file**, **dir**, **socket**, **filesystem**, etc.
- **-p** – permission type: **read**, **write**, **ioctl**, **create**, etc.

For this example, we'll use the **httpd_t** type (assigned to the Apache webserver daemon, httpd) and the **httpd_sys_content_t** type (the generic web content type assigned to many of the directories the httpd daemon is expected to interact with or serve content from).

We can ask what permissions the **httpd_t** domain has against **httpd_sys_content_t** using the **sesearch** command:
```
# sesearch --allow -s httpd_t -t httpd_sys_content_t
```

Here, we've asked for rules that allow a source type of httpd_t to interact with a target type of httpd_sys_content_t in some way. This returns more than twenty rules. Let's examine one of the results in detail:
```
allow httpd_t httpd_sys_content_t:dir { getattr ioctl lock open read search };
```

This states that a resource from security context httpd_t is allowed to interact with resources of type httpd_sys_content_t and kernel object class directory in the following ways: retrieving attribute information (file permissions and the like), manipulating ioctl, locking files, opening the directory, reading, and searching directory contents.

Using the seinfo command, we can get more information about our current policy:
```
# seinfo
Statistics for policy file: /sys/fs/selinux/policy
Policy Version:             31 (MLS enabled)
Target Policy:              selinux
Handle unknown classes:     allow
   Classes:             129      Permissions:         452
   Sensitivities:         1      Categories:         1024
   Types:              4934      Attributes:          251
   Users:                 8      Roles:                14
   Booleans:            327      Cond. Expr.:         376
   Allow:            112614      Neverallow:            0
   Auditallow:          162      Dontaudit:         10294
   Type_trans:       244549      Type_change:          74
   Type_member:          35      Range_trans:        6015
   Role allow:           39      Role_trans:          425
   Constraints:          71      Validatetrans:         0
   MLS Constrain:        72      MLS Val. Tran:         0
   Permissives:           0      Polcap:                5
   Defaults:              7      Typebounds:            0
   Allowxperm:            0      Neverallowxperm:       0
   Auditallowxperm:       0      Dontauditxperm:        0
   Initial SIDs:         27      Fs_use:               33
   Genfscon:            105      Portcon:             627
   Netifcon:              0      Nodecon:               0
```

In the output above, we can see that our current policy accounts for 129 classes (`service`, `file`, `socket`, `dir`), with 452 associated permissions (`read`, `ioctl`, `search`, `lock`). Further, we can see that there are 4934 known types (`httpd_t`, `kernel_t`, `var_t`) and 112,614 Allow rules like the one we examined above.

This policy is loaded by default. Administrators typically do not need to create new rules or types. Instead, we can focus on properly applying these predefined types to resources on our systems and letting the policy work for us.

Security Context Labels

When SELinux is configured with the default `targeted` policy, most common daemons and their associated files and directories are confined. This means that security contexts have been created for them, labels have been applied, and rules have been written against them.

In EL7/8 `httpd` has a great deal of default policy. We can examine the context of the default document root for `httpd`:
ls -dZ /var/www/html
system_u:object_r:httpd_sys_content_t:s0 /var/www/html

The type listed here, `httpd_sys_content_t`, is one for which we've already discovered rules in our current policy. The effect here is that, if `httpd` is configured to use its default document root (`/var/www/html`), SELinux will allow the daemon to interact with the files and directories needed to serve web content. But what if we wished to serve content from some other directory? Let's create a new directory, **/web**, and examine the resulting context:
ls -dZ /web
unconfined_u:object_r:default_t:s0 /web

The type defined for /web is `default_t`. This is, as the name suggests, a default type that applies to new files and directories which are created in locations without predefined contexts. When new files are created, SELinux checks a set of context files to determine how they should be labeled.

We can get a list of all the file contexts that SELinux knows about using **semanage**. We'll limit our discussion to one result:
semanage fcontext -l | grep /var/www
/var/www(/.*)?   all files   system_u:object_r:httpd_sys_content_t:s0

The portion **/var/www(/.*)?** is a regular expression. This particular expression is essentially matches **/var/www** and everything under it.

This is called a *default file context*. The default file contexts for every file in the targeted environment are located in the **/etc/selinux/targeted/contexts/files/** directory. Built-in contexts are in **file_contexts**, custom ones are in **file_contexts.local**.

The /web directory doesn't have an entry in these files, so it inherits the default context. Further, SELinux has no rules currently loaded which will allow `httpd_t` to interact with objects of type `default_t`, nor, as a security best practice, should it.

We can configure `httpd` to serve content from /web by editing the `DocumentRoot` directive in `httpd.conf` and create a simple `index.html` there. With permissions and firewall exceptions accounted for, and SELinux in **permissive** mode, these are the results of a `curl` operation:
curl localhost/index.html
this is a success

Enterprise Linux versions 7 & 8

Let's place SELinux into **enforcing** mode and try that again.
```
# setenforce 1
# curl localhost/index.html
```
```
<!DOCTYPE HTML PUBLIC "-//IETF//DTD HTML 2.0//EN">
<html><head>
<title>403 Forbidden</title>
</head><body>
<h1>Forbidden</h1>
<p>You don't have permission to access /index.html
on this server.<br />
</p>
</body></html>
```

When `enforcing` SELinux prevents access. We can check our logs to get a better idea of what's happening. In **/var/log/messages** we find this line:
SELinux is preventing /usr/sbin/httpd from map access on the file /web/index.html. For complete SELinux messages run: sealert -l 3b1ca295-6c8b-482e-bb57-4890f60defc4

We could also check **/var/log/audit/audit.log**, but this file is sometimes difficult to read directly. We can use `ausearch` to pull out what we're interested in:
```
# ausearch -i -m avc -c httpd -ts today | tail -1
type=AVC msg=audit(11/04/2019 15:27:29.204:1987) : avc: denied {
getattr } for  pid=8094 comm=httpd path=/web/index.html dev="dm-0"
ino=1691716 scontext=system_u:system_r:httpd_t:s0
tcontext=unconfined_u:object_r:default_t:s0 tclass=file permissive=0
```

The command above translates to: "Fetch any AVC (Access Vector Cache – basically SELinux) messages related to the common name `httpd` which occurred today, and only show the last entry. Also, please translate as many ID numbers as you can into the names of the things they represent." The results are still somewhat dense, but present a significant improvement over the raw logs. From this, we can determine that:

- SELinux **denied** an attempt by **httpd** to interact with **/web/index.html**
- The source security context was: `system_u:system_r:`**httpd_t**`:s0`
- The target security context: `unconfined_u:object_r:`**default_t**`:s0`

We can confirm that our current policy doesn't allow the `httpd_t` domain to access files of the type `default_t`. Further, we also know that SELinux should not block access to files with context `httpd_sys_content_t`, such as those in **/var/www/html**.

Our simplest solution is to alter the context of the /web directory (and its contents) to match that of the /var/www/html directory. To do that, we will use **semanage**:

```
# semanage fcontext -a -t httpd_sys_content_t /web"(/.*)?"
```

The results of this operation will not immediately be apparent. The /web directory and its contents will still retain their original labels. However, `semanage` will now report our intended contexts, and /etc/selinux/targeted/contexts/files/file_contexts.local will contain an entry reflecting this change:

```
# semanage fcontext -l | grep ^/web
/web(/.*)?         all files      system_u:object_r:httpd_sys_content_t:s0

# cat file_contexts.local
# This file is auto-generated by libsemanage
# Do not edit directly.
/web(/.*)?    system_u:object_r:httpd_sys_content_t:s0
```

To apply our intended contexts to the targeted files and directories, we will need to run **restorecon** with a target of /web using the **-r** (recurse) and **-v** (verbose) options. Then we'll create a new file inside this directory to verify that files are inheriting the proper contexts.

```
# restorecon -rv /web
Relabeled /web from unconfined_u:object_r:default_t:s0 to
unconfined_u:object_r:httpd_sys_content_t:s0
Relabeled /web/index.html from unconfined_u:object_r:default_t:s0 to
unconfined_u:object_r:httpd_sys_content_t:s0

# touch /web/test
# ls -Z /web
total 4
unconfined_u:object_r:httpd_sys_content_t:s0    index.html
unconfined_u:object_r:httpd_sys_content_t:s0    test
```

To remove this custom context, pass the `-d` option to `semanage`:
```
# semanage fcontext -d "/web(/.*)?"
```

This removes the line from `file_contexts.local`, but the changes will not be applied until we run `restorecon` again.

A final note regarding file contexts: some directories defined in the default contexts contain many and various type definitions for the sorts of files that would logically be created inside of them. It may not be sufficient, therefore, to simply match the label of a top level directory like `/web` to the label of `/var/www`.

In cases like these, we may use the concept of *equivalency* to resolve the disparity. We can use semanage to accomplish this:
```
# semanage fcontext -a -e /var/www /web
# restorecon -Rv /web
```

This tells SELinux to treat `/web` as if it were `/var/www` for the purposes of labeling going forward.

Booleans

When files and directories are not set to a context that properly reflects their contents, SELinux will often prohibit actions against them. Defining and applying contexts can resolve these issues, but SELinux also prohibits certain actions as a matter of policy, rather than as the result of a labelling mistake.

In situations where otherwise desirable actions are being prohibited by policy, the only remedy is to alter the policy itself. This can be done in a variety of ways, from writing our own modules and compiling them directly, to using tools like **audit2allow** which converts denials in a log into policy modules which allow the behavior. However, the simplest and most common way to alter loaded policy is with SELinux booleans.

SELinux booleans are like security toggle switches. These are common policy changes that operators might want to enable, and are provided so that we will not be required to create and apply policy modules (which may result in degraded security posture).

We can get a list of SELinux Booleans with **# getsebool** or with **# semanage boolean -l**. The two commands are similar, but the `semanage` version includes a description column.

Let's get a list of booleans that start with "nfs":
```
# semanage boolean -l | grep ^nfs
nfs_export_all_ro          (on   ,   on)  Allow any
files/directories to be exported read/only via NFS.

nfs_export_all_rw          (on   ,   on)  Allow any
files/directories to be exported read/write via NFS.

nfsd_anon_write            (off  ,  off)  Allow nfs servers to
modify public files used for public file transfer services.
Files/Directories must be labeled public_content_rw_t.
```

From this list, we'll choose `nfs_export_all_rw` for further exploration. The description supplied for this boolean is `Allow any files/directories to be exported read/write via nfs`. The (`on, on`) bit indicates that the boolean is currently on and is set to be on by default. We can use `sesearch` to find out more about this boolean and the rules changes it effects.

```
# sesearch -b nfs_export_all_rw -A
allow kernel_t non_security_file_type:dir { add_name getattr ioctl
lock open read remove_name search write }; [ nfs_export_all_rw ]:True
<truncated>
```

Let's walk through the result:

- **allow** – allow
- **kernel_t** – the source domain
- **non_security_file_type** – the target, here an `attribute`.
- **:dir** – (kernel object class of dir, e.g. directories)
- **{add_name getattr ioctl lock open re**<truncated>**};** – the permissions granted
- **[nfs_export_all_rw]** – the name of the boolean these rules are a part of
- **:True** – the state the boolean must be set to for the rules to take effect

The target section of this rule points to **non_security_file_type**, which is actually an SELinux **attribute** rather than a `type`. An `attribute` is a category that `types` can be assigned to. In other words, the rule above takes effect whenever a domain of `kernel_t` targets anything with an attribute of `non_security_file_type`. We can get a list of the types this attribute has been assigned to with **seinfo**. This list is rather large:

```
# seinfo -xa non_security_file_type | wc -l
2998/*9
```

Enterprise Linux versions 7 & 8

There is a converse attribute, `security_file_type`, which we can more easily list:
seinfo -xa security_file_type

```
Type Attributes: 1
   attribute security_file_type;
        audit_spool_t
        auditd_etc_t
        auditd_log_t
        default_context_t
        dnssec_t
        file_context_t
        krb5_keytab_t
        random_seed_t
        selinux_config_t
        selinux_login_config_t
        semanage_store_t
        shadow_t
```

Here we see types that would be, as the name suggests, assigned to security related files such as the kerberos keytab, the shadow password database, SELinux configuration, and more.

When a boolean is toggled, its rulesets are loaded or unloaded from the active policy set. To toggle a boolean use **setsebool**. Before doing this it is best to check the effects, as some booleans can pose substantial security risks. To permanently (-P) set the boolean httpd_read_user_content to on:
setsebool -P httpd_read_user_content 1

audit2allow

When all of the aforementioned techniques have been tried and tested, but SELinux issues still persist, there is a tool that we can use to resolve policy errors. This tool is called **audit2allow**, and it should be used sparingly, if at all.

This is because **audit2allow** will take, as input, AVC error messages from the audit log. It will then transform these error messages into policy modules which will allow the blocked behavior. The tool is so powerful, that it may take the entirety of /var/log/audit/audit.log as input, and generate a policy module which will allow *all* of the blocked behaviors.

```
# cat /var/log/audit/audit.log | grep AVC | grep denied \
| audit2allow -o /test/source.te
```

Above, we used the **-o** option to generate an uncompiled, human readable source file. The extention .te stands for Type Enforcement. As input we took all AVC denials in audit.log.

This has not yet been applied as policy. Before we can apply it, we need to compile the type enforcement file into a policy package (.pp). This can be done using the .pp as a source by running **make** or **checkmodule**. It is easier to generate the policy package file directly by using audit2allow -M.

```
# cat /var/log/audit/audit.log | grep AVC | grep denied \
| audit2allow -M polfix
******************** IMPORTANT **********************
To make this policy package active, execute:
semodule -i polfix.pp
```

We can then load it as suggested in the output, and unload it with **# semodule -d polfix**

One final thing worth noting: some SELinux rules prevent logging of activities to the audit log. This is not malicious behavior; rather it is simply designed to stop certain frequent and innocuous occurrences from spamming the logs. If we would like to turn on auditing temporarily for everything that may be audited, we may do so like this:

```
# semodule -DB
```

If we would like to disable this behavior again, we would do this:

```
# semodule -B
```

Moving and Copying Files

Moving and copying files in SELinux presents additional considerations beyond what we would see on an unsecured system. This is because of the security context, or labels assigned to files. Often, when SELinux problems occur, it is because we failed to account for these behaviors.

Moving a file is a directory operation: data is not copied from one place to another (unless we moved the file to a new filesystem). Rather, we simply change the referring entries in the appropriate directories. Labels are stored in a file's inode, and they will not be updated by a move. This is also why files retain ownership and standard permissions metadata when moved in a classic system.

Copying results in the creation of a new file, and a newly populated inode with new metadata. This new file will be assigned a label based on the defined contexts of the directory it inhabits.

Passing the -Z option to **cp** or **mv** will should cause one to behave like the other regarding labels. However in EL7/8, **cp** -Z has no effect, the destination directory default context will be assigned.

Module 14: Logs

When a Linux machine boots it immediately begins logging kernel messages to the kernel ring buffer. This is simply a 16 KB first-in/first-out over-writable block of memory. These messages will be passed to the system logger services (**rsyslogd** and **journald**) when they become available. Kernel messages will continue being written here even after the logging services start.

The kernel ring buffer is readable using **dmesg**. Here you can see the command line switches passed to the kernel by grub, device driver messages, systemd beginning, etc. Useful switches for **dmesg** include **-H** (human formatted) and **-T** (use clock time instead of boot time).

There are two logging systems which run by default on an EL7/8 system. The traditional syslogd has been replaced by rsyslogd. This provides compatibility with older systems; it will take configuration files of the older syslogd format and store traditional plain text log files. With the introduction of systemd, journald has been added. Both serve distinct purposes:

- **journald** – is tightly integrated into the systemd architecture. It stores data in binary format which is more compact, and easily searched. It can upload signed and encrypted logs to a centralized server using **systemd-journal-remote**. Ideally all logs would be here and accessed via a single tool: **journalctl**. Eventually this may be the case, but it isn't yet.
- **rsyslogd** – conforms to the legacy syslogd standards and is better understood. Some programs have not yet integrated with journald. Most importantly, sending logs to an aggregation server using systemd-journal-remote only works with other journald servers. If you are using a log aggregation and analysis server, chances are it doesn't understand journald natively, so messages are instead routed through rsyslogd.

rsyslogd, logrotate

rsyslogd is nothing but a message router with dynamically configurable inputs and outputs. It can take inputs from journald, /dev/log/, and/or a network socket. It then parses, filters, and formats the inputs. It can output the messages to a file, a database (mariadb, journald), or a remote system. It supports digital signature and encryption of messages sent to a remote system, using Kerberos. The main configuration file is **/etc/rsyslog.conf**.

The first portion of this file, **MODULES** loads and configures input and output modules using the **$ModLoad** directive. Two modules are provided to allow interaction between journald and rsyslogd: **imjournal** inputs to rsyslog, while **omjournal** outputs to journald. There are many other modules allowing everything from the reading of kernel messages to direct interaction with an SQL database.

Below MODULES is **GLOBAL DIRECTIVES**. Some systems will have **$OmitLocalLogging on**, in this section. This usually means that rsyslogd is receiving all messages from journald instead of directly collecting them.

The **RULES** section controls how messages are handled. Each line will have a message classification and destination. The message classification has two parts: the **facility** – where it from, and the **severity** – how important it is. There are several special statements: asterisk * is a wildcard, tilde ~ means discard, and .**none** means do not log. The facilities and severities are:
- Facilities:
    - `kern` – kernel messages
    - `user` – user-level messages
    - `mail` – mail system
    - `daemon` – system daemons
    - `authpriv` – security/authorization messages
    - `cron` – scheduling daemon
    - `local7` – local use 7 (boot messages)
- Severities (aka priority):
    - 0 `emerg` – System is unusable
    - 1 `alert` – Action must be taken immediately
    - 2 `crit` – Critical conditions, such as hard device errors
    - 3 `err` – Error conditions
    - 4 `warning` – Warning conditions
    - 5 `notice` – Normal but significant conditions
    - 6 `info` – Informational messages
    - 7 `debug` – Debug-level messages

Destinations can be:
- A file
    - Standard logs include **/var/log/**...**messages**, **secure**, **cron**, **maillog**, **boot.log**
- A standard out, such as **/dev/console**
- A remote machine
    - @*hostname:port* – sends UDP
    - @@*hostname:port* – sends TCP
- An output module
    - **:omusrmsg:*** – message everyone using `wall`
    - **:omjournal:** – send to journald
    - **:omrelp:** – use the Reliable Event Logging Protocol
- A filter – if you have advanced needs
- Discard – specified with tilde ~
    - Any messages discarded will not be processed by a subsequent rules
    - ***.*** ~ ends all processing.

The STIG requires that logs be sent to a remote server. The recommended way to do this does not take into account the inherent unreliability of the standard transfer method. If the remote server is not available or the local machine crashes, messages will be lost.

Rather than issuing `*.* @@`*`servername`*`:514` – as specified in the STIG, you should use RELP, the Reliable Event Logging Protocol, if available. To configure RELP:
- On the Aggregator:
    - In `rsyslog.conf`:
        - `$ModLoad imrelp`
        - `$InputRELPServerRun 2514`
    - `#firewall-cmd --zone=public --add-port=2514/tcp --permanent`
    - `#firewall-cmd --reload`
- On the Sender:
    - In `rsyslog.conf`:
        - `$Modload omrelp`
        - `*.* :omreplp:`*`10.1.1.250`*`:2514`
- On Both:
    - `#semanage port -a -t syslogd_port_t -p tcp 2514`

If RELP is not available, uncomment and configure the sample forwarding rule at the bottom of `rsyslog.conf`. This creates an on-disk queue which will be retransmitted if need be.

The STIG specifies that unless this machine is an aggregation server and documented as such, it should not receive logs from other machines. This is done by ensuring that the modules `imupd`, `imtcp`, and `imrelp` are not loaded. The STIG only mentions `imtcp`.

Retention and rotation of `rsyslogd` files is accomplished by `logrotate`, which is called from `cron.daily` by `anacron`. It is configured in `/etc/logrotate.conf`. These settings should be adjusted to meet your retention requirements.

You can generate your own messages that will be sent to the logging services using the utility `logger`, with priority `-p`. To put "`test`" in the log as a `warning` from `cron`:
`# logger -p cron.warning test`

Enterprise Linux versions 7 & 8

journald, journalctl

By default `journald` only stores data in `/run/log`, which is in volatile memory and lost at each reboot. To make the journal persistent, create a directory: `/var/log/journal/` and restart `systemd-journald.service`.

File rotation is accomplished automatically, based on disk usage. Retention and other behaviors are configured in `/etc/systemd/journald.conf` and the associated `conf.d/*.conf` files. Some relevant parameters include:
- `Storage` – default `auto`, which will log to `/var/log/journal/`... if it is present
    - `persistent` will create the directory if it is not.
- `Compress` – `on` by default.
- `SystemMaxUse` / `RuntimeMaxUse` – maximum disk and ram used. Default `10%`.
- `SystemKeepFree` / `RuntimeKeepFree` – disk and ram left free. Default `15%`.
- `MaxFileSec`/`MaxRetentionSec` – Time to store entries in seconds.
    - Can be suffixed with `year`, `month`, `week`, `day`.
    - 0 equals forever.
- `MaxLevelStore` – the severity of messages to keep. Default `debug`.
- `MaxLevelWall` – severity of messages to send to all logged in users. Default `emerg`.

The journal produced by `journald` is in binary format and is not directly readable. To view the contents of the journal, use `journalctl`. Common switches include:
- `-f` – show the last few lines and follow new messages
  (roughly equivalent to `# tail -f /var/log/messages`)
- `-u` *unitname* – filter by `systemd` unit.
- `-p` – filter by priority
- `-o` – format output, good options are `verbose`, `short`, and `cat` (very brief)
- `-r` – reverse, show newest messages at the top, incompatible with `-f`
- `-S` / `-U` – since and until.
    - Takes time `YYYY-MM-DD HH:MM:SS` or parts thereof.
    - Has aliases for `yesterday`, `today`, and `tomorrow`.
- `--list-boots` – show index numbers of boot cycles for use with `-b`
    - `-b` *index* – show messages generated during the specified boot cycle

All messages can be sent from `journald` to `rsyslogd` or vice-versa. It is possible to send all messages from `rsyslogd` to `journald`, **and** from `journald` to `rsyslog` simultaneously, creating an infinite loop. Do one or the other, not both.

Given that most current security specifications are built around `rsyslogd`, that's probably where you want to send all messages.

- To send everything to **rsyslogd**:
    - in **rsyslog.conf**:
        - `$ModLoad imuxsock`
        - `$OmitLocalLogging off`
    - in `/etc/rsyslog.d/listend.conf`:
        - `$SystemLogSocketName /run/systemd/journal/syslog`
    - in `journald.conf`:
        - `Storage=volatile`
    - `# rm -rf /var/log/journal/`
- To send everything to **journald**:
    - in **rsyslog.conf**:
        - `$Modload omjournal`
        - `*.* :omjournal:`
    - in `journald.conf`:
        - `Storage=persistent`

auditd

In addition to the standard system and security logs, Enterprise Linux also has the **auditd** service which can be configured to record a wide variety of security related events in **/var/log/audit/audit.log**. By default auditd will record events related to SELinux, authentication, authorization, and sudo. Additional events can be audited with the addition of rules. Audit rules can be manipulated using **auditctl**. To list existing rules: **# auditctl -l**

There are four types of rules:
- Watch a file or directory for activity, often paired with **-p** permission type:
  `# auditctl  -w /etc/passwd -p wa -k identity`
  watches /etc/passwd for write or attribute change, making a record with key "identity"
- Audit a specific kernel system call:
  `# auditctl  -a always,exit -F arch=b64 \`
  `-S sethostname -F key=system-locale`
  audits the 64 bit system call sethostname when it exits and logs as "system-locale"
- Audit (or in this case not audit) everything done by a specific user:
  `# auditctl  -a never,user -F auid=100`
  will never audit events associated with audit User ID 100
- Exclude a given group of events:
  `# auditctl  -a always,exclude -F msgtype=CRYPTO_KEY_USER`
  excludes messages about ssh and ssl keys presented to the server

The rules can get quite complex:
`# auditctl -a always,exit -F arch=b64 -S clock_settime -F a0=0x0`
`  -F subj_type!=ntpd_t -F key=time-change`

This makes a record only when the first argument (**a0**) to the **clock_settime** systemcall is **0** (the realtime system clock) and the user process doing it is not (**!=**) labled **ntpd_t** by SELinux.

Fortunately, we don't have to bother coming up with all the rules and typing them in using **auditctl**. In any case that will only affect the current running system, and all the rules will go away at the next restart of auditd. Instead we need to place our configuration in **/etc/audit/rules.d** and run **augenrules**. This will evaluate the rule sets placed in **rules.d**, validate them, aggregate them in order, and place them in **/etc/audit/audit.rules**, which is the file actually read by auditd.

Even more fortunately the authors of auditd work closely with the groups that make the STIG and other security standards and have provided a set of rules and scripts to meet the baseline. These it should meet the minimum requirements, but it is a good idea to check the results against the STIG. To use these:
- `# cd  /usr/share/doc/audit-version-number/rules/`
- `# vi 31-privileged.rules`
  - remove the leading hashes after the comments
- `# chmod 700 31-privileged.rules`

- `# ./31-privileged.rules`
    - this makes a new file `./priv.rules`
- `# mv priv.rules  35-priv.rules`
- `# vi 99-finalize.rules`
    - remove the leading hash # on `-e 2`
- copy `10-base`, `30-stig`, `35-priv`, and `99-finalize` to `/etc/audit/rules.d`
- `# augenrules --check`
    - this verifies the syntax
- `# augenrules --load`
    - this copies the contents of `rules.d/` to `audit.rules`
- `# reboot` to make the audit system immutable (`-e 2`)

This is sufficient for most use cases. But auditing can take a substantial toll on performance as each rule needs to be evaluated in order until there is a match, and this happens every time a userspace program asks the kernel to do anything. There are a number of performance tuning steps that can be taken within the rule set:
- Combine multiple system calls to reduce the number of total rules.
- Create `never` and `exclude` rules and place them at the top
- Move the most used rules to the top, the least used to the bottom
    - One way to determine which are most used is to add unique identifiers to the key fields, let run for a while, then analyze the results.
- Move the rules for 32 bit architectures (`arch=b32`) toward the bottom. The only reason there are dual rules are because the system call identifiers are different between 32 and 64 bit versions. On a modern system the 32 bit calls should be rare.
- Monitor the memory used by `auditd` during busy times; if needed increase the buffer size (`-b` in `10-base-config`)
- Always leave `-e 2`, the immutable flag, as the final statement.
    - All rule processing ends when this flag is set and the configuration is locked until the next boot. Any rules below it will be ignored.

As noted in the section on `grub`, the kernel argument `audit=1` should always be passed during boot. This ensures that all processes, including those that start before `auditd` are audited.

Because of its unique position in the security hierarchy, the `auditd.service` is protected from direct manipulation by `systemd`. To restart it, use:
`# service auditd stop && service auditd start`

audisp-remote

In EL7 `auditd` needs the plugin **audisp** to be enabled to send logs to a remote server. Set the **active** line in `/etc/audisp/plugins.d/syslog.conf` to **yes**.

In EL8 the functions of `audispd` have been incorporated into `auditd`. **audispd** configuration options are now part of **auditd.conf**. In addition, the `plugins.d` directory has been moved under `/etc/audit`. The current status of `auditd` and its plug-ins can now be checked with
`# service auditd state`

To enable remote auditing:
On the sending machine:
- Install **audispd-plugins**
- In `/etc/audit/audisp-remote.conf` (EL7 `/etc/audisp/`)
    - `remote_server = `*`destination.ip.address`*
    - `port = 60`
    - `local_port = any`
- In `/etc/audit/plugins.d/au-remote.conf` (EL7 `/etc/audisp/plugins.d/`)
    - `active = yes`
    - `direction = out`
- `# service auditd restart`

On the aggregator:
- Install **audispd-plugins**
- In `/etc/audit/audisp-remote.conf` (EL7 `/etc/audisp/`)
    - `local_port=any`
- In `/etc/audit/plugins.d/au-remote.conf` (EL7 `/etc/audisp/plugins.d/`)
    - `active = yes`
    - `direction = in`
- In `/etc/audit/auditd.conf`
    - `tcp_listen_port = 60`
    - `tcp_client_ports = 1024-65535`
- Configure firewall
    - `# firewall-cmd --permanent --zone=public --add-rich-rule=' rule family="ipv4" source address="`*`sender.ip.address`*`" port protocol="tcp"  port="60" accept '`
    - `# systemctl reload firewalld.service`
    - `# firewall-cmd --list-all`
- Confirm:
    - `# tail -f /var/log/audit/audit.log | ausearch -i` on the aggregator
    - perform an auditable event (such as creating a user) on the sender

aureport, ausearch

There are two special tools for parsing audit logs: `aureport` and `ausearch`. A full dive into these tools is beyond the scope of this book, but here are some handy examples:

Find and explore failed authentication events occurring today:
```
# aureport -au -ts today -failed
<truncated>
3. 09/26/2019 13:12:30 root 192.168.210.246 ssh /usr/sbin/sshd no 427
```

The last number is an event ID. This can be used to get an interpreted, detailed output:
```
# ausearch -i -a 427
----
type=USER_AUTH msg=audit(09/26/2019 13:12:30.460:427) : pid=3878 uid=root auid=unset ses=unset subj=system_u:system_r:sshd_t:s0-s0:c0.c1023 msg='op=PAM:authentication grantors=? acct=root exe=/usr/sbin/sshd hostname=192.168.210.246 addr=192.168.210.246 terminal=ssh res=failed'
```

Provide a report on events since the last boot:
```
# aureport -ts boot --summary | head
Summary Report
======================
Range of time in logs: 05/29/2019 13:13:05.153 - 09/26/2019 14:23:06.175
Selected time for report: 09/26/2019 10:42:16 - 09/26/2019 14:23:06.175
Number of changes in configuration: 109
Number of changes to accounts, groups, or roles: 37
Number of logins: 3
Number of failed logins: 1
Number of authentications: 3
```

Find all useradd commands run:
```
# ausearch -c useradd
```

Find all events for a given user
```
# id student
uid=1000(student) gid=1000(student) groups=1000(student),10(wheel)
```
```
# ausearch -ua 1000
```

timedatectl, chronyc, hwclock

Logs are worthless if they don't have valid timestamps. Keeping good time is a part of security, as well as being essential for most certificate based services such as Kerberos. To set the time:
- First check the system time and timezone:
  `# timedatectl status`
- If the timezone is wrong, change it using
  `# timedatectl set-timezone` *America/Chicago*
    - A list of available timezones viewable by using:
      `# timedatectl list-timezones`
- If the time is more than about 10 minutes out you should set the clock before enabling ntp.
  `# timedatectl set-time` *"2012-10-30 18:17:16"*
  or
  `# chronyc manual on && chronyc settime` *18:17* `&& chronyc manual off`
- Determine the appropriate ntp server. Most networks will have a local ntp server; if so use it. If not, some alternatives are:
    - For government networks
        - `time.nist.gov`
        - `tick`, `tock`, and `ntp2.usno.navy.mil` for east and central regions
        - `tick`, and `tock.usnogps.navy.mil` for mountain and pacific
    - In the civilian world you can leave the default pools
- Configure the appropriate ntp servers:
  `# vi /etc/chrony.conf`
    - Comment out any `pool` lines. Add `server` lines in order of preference:
      `server` *192.168.1.1* `iburst`
      The `iburst` directive allows for faster initial synchronization.
- Enable network time protocol (ntp) with
  `# timedatectl set-ntp true`
- Restart or enable the chronyd service with `systemctl`
- Check the status using
  `# chronyc sources`
  `# chronyc sourcestats`
  `# chronyc tracking`
    - or by comparing to another server
      `# clockdiff -o` *other.server*
- The last step of the time setting process is writing the system (software based) time to the hardware (BIOS) clock. This is accomplished with
  `# hwclock -w`
  On a virtual machine this is less important as the hardware clock is reset at each power on. If you find that the clock is consistently incorrect, the host's clock will need to be corrected.

Module 15: Installing Software

yum

Enterprise Linux comes with **rpm**, the RedHat Package Manager, as the primary way to install, manage, upgrade, and remove software. It will work with software either in `.rpm` binary format or with compiled files with an attached plain-text manifest file. It can install files from local storage or a network location. `rpm` is fully capable of performing everything you might ever need to do with software on an EL system, but it can be tedious to use. It requires you to locate the specific software you want to install, it does not deal with dependencies automatically, and it also lacks the ability to automatically update a system.

To make up for the shortfalls of `rpm`, **yum** was written. It is a higher-level package manager that runs on top of `rpm`, making software management much easier. In EL8, `yum` has been replaced by **dnf**, which is a modern reimplementation of `yum`.

The invocation of `dnf` is almost identical to that of `yum`, to the point that in EL8 `yum` is a link to `dnf`, and the `yum` man page redirects to `dnf`. While there are some small differences in functionality, `dnf` can be treated as a faster, less memory intensive `yum`. In this book we will use `yum` in our examples, because it is cross-version compatible and because as of this writing the `bash-completion` hints for `dnf` are not functional.

When using `rpm` you must locate software packages individually; `yum` uses collections of software known as repositories or repos. Your system will come with multiple Internet-based repos configured. There is a prebuilt repo on most installation media. You can even create your own by running **createrepo** on a directory full of `.rpm` files.

If you are running Red Hat you will need a subscription to access the official repositories. You will also need to register your system:
```
# subscription-manager register
# subscription-manager subscribe
```

To obtain a list of available repos use **`# yum repolist`**, with the **enabled** option it will only show the active ones:
```
# yum repolist enabled
repo id             repo name                        status
AppStream           CentOS-8 - AppStream             4,928
BaseOS              CentOS-8 - Base                  2,713
extras              CentOS-8 - Extras                    3
```

This shows the basic information: which repos are configured, and how many packages each contains. For a repo to be active, it must be in **/etc/yum.repos.d/**, have a file extension ending in **.repo**, and contain the line **enable=1**. You can disable a repo by editing it, moving it, or renaming it. The basic format of a .repo is this:

```
[extras]      ## a unique repository id
name=CentOS-$releasever - Extras  ## the pretty name
mirrorlist=http://mirrorlist... <truncated> ## server pool with the repo
#baseurl=http://mirror... <truncated>  ## server with repo
gpgcheck=1    ## verify software signature
enabled=1     ## the repo is allowed to be used
gpgkey=file:///etc/pki/rpm-gpg/RPM-GPG-KEY-centosoffical  ## signature
```

There is an optional repo, the Extended Packages for Enterprise Linux (EPEL) which is not configured by default, but holds many handy tools. To enable this repo:
- On Red Hat: **# yum install https://dl.fedoraproject.org/pub/epel/epel-release-latest-8.noarch.rpm**
    - insert the major version number before .noarch
- On CentOS: **# yum install epel-release**
- On Amazon Linux **# amazon-linux-extras install epel**

You can create your own repos. To use a dvd as an update source for an isolated computer:
- Disable the default repos
- Mount the dvd:
  # mkdir /dvd/ ; mount /dev/cdrom /dvd/
- Create a new file:
  # vi dvd.repo

  ```
  [dvd-repo]
  name=DVD-repo
  baseurl=file:///dvd
  enable=1
  gpgcheck=1
  gpgkey=file:///dvd/RPM-GPG-KEY-CentOS-7
  ```

The system should immediately recognize the newly created repo. If you were using a network resource the **baseurl** would be **http://** or **ftp://**. Note that there are three slashes in a file URL: two for the URL itself+ (**file://**), and one to indicate the root directory **/dvd**.

Not all repos will have a GPG Key, for example, in a test and development environment. In this case set **gpgcheck=0**. This should only be done if you know the source of the unsigned software, and should never be set on production systems.

The primary configuration file for yum is **/etc/yum.conf**, relevant directives include:
- **gpgcheck** / **local_gpgcheck** – these should both be set to **1**, forcing yum to verify signatures on software before installing.
- **group_package_types** – by default **groupinstall** will only install default and mandatory packages. To install all packages in a group, set this to **default, mandatory, optional**.
- **installonly_limit** – install only packages do not automatically have the old version removed when a newer version is installed. The main "install only" package is the kernel, therefore this setting controls how many old kernels are retained.
  Default is **5**, recommended is **2**, which is also the minimum. This allows booting to an older, known good kernel in case of a problem with a kernel upgrade.
- **keepcache** – if **0** or **false** remove downloaded packages after successful installation. Default is varies by distribution and version.

In addition to saving old downloaded packages, yum relies on a series of caches for information such as package listings, descriptions, and which mirrors are fastest. Over time the old packages will build up and the caches will go stale. This will fill /var, and will also make you wait to rebuild caches the next time you run yum. To avoid this it is good practice to create scheduled event at least weekly which will run **# yum clean all** and **# yum makecache**. In EL8 the makecache is automatically accomplished with **dnf-makecache.timer**.

Use of **yum** itself is pretty straightforward. Common invocations and options are:
- **-y** – assume yes
- **-q** – quiet, often used with & to background the process
- **install** *package-name* – installs a given package
- **remove** *package-name* – removes a package and anything that depends on it
- **reinstall** *package-name* – reinstall a package, will not alter configuration files or dependent packages
- **check-upgrade** – show, but don't install available upgrades
- **upgrade** – upgrades all installed software to the current version
  - **-x** *package-name* – excludes package from upgrade
- **upgrade-minimal** – only performs security upgrades
- **search** *string* – looks for *string* in all package names and short descriptions
- **provides** */*program-name* – returns the package that supplied that program
- **info** *package-name* – provides details including status: installed/available
- **repoquery**
  - **-l** – list files in a package
  - **--whatdepends** – show dependent packages
- **list installed** – show all installed software
- **grouplist** – show software groups (related packages for a particular purpose)
- **groupinstall** – install a complete set of related packages

Sometimes a group will not install, even though it shows as available. A workaround for this is
yum -y group mark install "package-name" && yum -y upgrade
This tells yum that the group is installed. When you run the upgrade, it gets the latest version to replace the missing one.

Both yum and dnf support plugins that enhance their functionality. A particularly useful plugin is **versionlock**, which will protect packages from upgrade.

The plugins available will vary between versions and distros, to see which are available to you:
yum search dnf-plugin | xargs yum info | less
For EL7 substitute **yum-plugin**.

packagekit

Often a service called **packagekit** will be installed and enabled. It provides automatic updates. Typically we want more control than is provided by packagekit. It also tends to run at annoying times, locking the installation process, and preventing manual installation of software.

To disable it, we first make sure it isn't doing anything at the moment:
pkill -9 yum

This terminates any currently running installations.

Now stop and mask packagekit and its related offline update service.
systemctl stop packagekit.service
systemctl mask packagekit-offline-update.service
systemctl mask packagekit.service

rpm

As mentioned earlier, **yum** isn't an answer to everything; **rpm** is still sometimes needed. Examples of common usages:
- # **rpm -qf /usr/bin/at** – shows the package that installed the at binary
- # **rpm -qc at** – show configuration files for at
- # **rpm -qd at** – list all documentation for at
- # **rpm -ql at** – list all files installed by the at package
- # **rpm -qlp /dvd/Packages/at-3.1.13...** – list all files in a package
- # **rpm -q --scripts gnome-packagekit** – show pre- and post-installation scripts
- # **rpm -i** or **-U** – install or upgrade
- # **rpm --import** *https://some.url.to/aGPG/key.pub* – install a software signing key, can be done instead of **gpgkey=** in yum configuration
- # **rpm -Va** – Verify all files against the original installation, should be run regularly & the output reviewed

The output of **rpm -Va** will look something like this:
SM5..UGT.   c /etc/plymouth/plymouthd.conf

Anything other than a period in the first block means that something is different from the original installation. The codes are:
- **S** – file Size differs
- **M** – Mode differs (includes permissions and file type)
- **5** – MD5 sum differs
- **D** – Device major/minor number mismatch
- **L** – symLink path mismatch
- **U** – User ownership differs
- **G** – Group ownership differs
- **T** – mTime differs

The **c** before the path means that this is a configuration file and changes to it can be probably be safely ignored, this is usually the case for .xml files as well:
rpm -Va |grep -v -e " c " file | grep -v -e xml > *file*
will keep you from spending too much time looking at irrelevant results.

Mode, User, or Group mismatches, indicated by **M**, **U**, or **G** can be corrected by finding the package that controls the offending file with
rpm -qf *filename*
   then
rpm   --setperms *package-name*
rpm   --setguids *package-name*

In the case of hash mismatches, indicated by a **5**, the package should be reinstalled using
rpm -Uh *package-name*

Linux Installation

Enterprise Linux can be installed from a DVD, USB, or network source. The installation source is available at:
- https://www.centos.org/download/ – Get the DVD ISO for most purposes
- https://access.redhat.com/downloads/ – Login required
- https://getfedora.org/en/server/download/ – If you want to live on the edge a little

After you've downloaded the source, simply burn it to a DVD. To create a bootable USB from a Linux machine ensure that your USB device is unmounted then:
 # dd if=/path/to/boot.iso **of=**/dev/sd-usb **bs=512k**

If you need to create a bootable USB from Windows or Mac, use the FedoraMediaWriter available at https://getfedora.org/en/workstation/download/.

Methods for installation from network sources can vary wildly. The official documentation should be consulted.

The initial boot menu has three options: Install, Test media and install (default), and Troubleshooting. The Troubleshooting menu provides options to Install in basic graphical mode (in case the installer has issues with your graphics card), a Rescue mode for unbootable systems, a memory tester, and an option to just boot from local disk.

You can also press **tab** to break out of this menu and add options to the end of the command line. Press enter to continue installing. In addition to the kernel command line options discussed in Booting, you may also add:
- **inst.dd=**http://someurl.com/weird-drivers.iso – Add drivers from a URL
- **inst.ks=**ftp://localserver/pub/ks.cfg – Use a kickstart script
- **inst.text** – Force a text mode install
- **inst.sshd** – Enable sshd during installation
- **modprobe.blacklist=**ahci,firewire,ohci – disable kernel modules, persistent after installation
- **dracut** options – Uncommon, more info is in the **dracut.cmdline** man page.
- **fips=1** – enable FIPS 140-2 compliance – required

The FIPS (the Federal Information Processing Standard) is a series of standards to which all government, and other regulated secure systems must conform. To enable strict compliance with FIPS 140-2 (cryptographic standards), add `fips=1` to the kernel command line at installation. This ensures that all keys are generated with FIPS algorithms and that FIPS will be enabled on boot. To verify FIPS compliance run `sysctl crypto.fips_enabled`; it should return `1`.

There is a published procedure to implement FIPS on an existing system, but it should not be used as it is more likely to break the system than it is to actually secure it. Also, if you implement FIPS after installation, there is no guarantee that keys generated for the system are made with the proper algorithms and with appropriate entropy sources.

For best results you should add entropy to the system by inputting some random keystrokes or mouse movements (at least 256) during the installation procedure.

Reference – http://csrc.nist.gov/publications/PubsFIPS.html

Both for practicality and for STIG compliance you should create these separate partitions:
- `/`
- `/boot`
- `/tmp`
- `/var`
- `/var/log`
- `/var/log/audit`
- `/home`
- `swap`

Example kickstart files which will do the partitioning for you, and implement a lot of other essential security measures can be found in `/usr/share/scap-security-guide/kickstart/` after installing the `scap-security-guide` package. This can be edited appropriately to meet the needs of your environment and provided using pretty much any URL based protocol (http, ftp, scp, nfs, etc.)

If you are not using a kickstart file, you will then be led through a straightforward installation. Note that many installations will default to a very minimal installation if you do not click on "Software Selection" and add additional packages. Also, if you do not configure networking and set it to "On" your system will not automatically connect to a network.

If available you should also select the Security Profile appropriate to your environment (for instance 'STIG: Server with GUI').

Previous versions of this book explained how to install VMware tools, this is no longer required as EL7/8 will autodetect virtualization and install a guest-managed version.

Module 16: Kernel Modules and Parameters

The core of an operating system is the kernel. It is responsible for direct access to and manipulation of a system's hardware. Typically, the kernel will be as small as is practical. It will have the capability required to boot a system and operate things like memory and processors, with a minimal set of tools for dealing with storage and networking.

Kernel modules provide additional functionality to the kernel. This can include advanced networking, firewall filtering, encryption, and device drivers. When a kernel module is loaded it effectively becomes part of the kernel, and runs with direct access to hardware and with the full privledges of the operating system itself. Unneeded kernel modules should be unloaded as they can bloat the operating system, and increase the potential attack surface.

Kernel modules come in two basic types, static and dynamic. We will only be concerned with dynamic modules in this book.

- **Static** modules are compiled into the kernel.
    - Requires a kernel recompililation to build
    - Requires a system reboot to load
    - Makes the kernel's memory footprint larger
    - Increases boot time
    - Usually chosen when a system cannot boot without the capabilities of the module
- **Dynamic** modules, may be loaded or unloaded as needed.
    - Keeps the kernel small and lean
    - Does not require a reboot to load and use
    - Yields faster boot times and more efficient use of system resources
    - Generally preferred to static modules

lsmod, modinfo, modprobe

To see a list of kernel modules and a summary of their dependencies use **lsmod**, which provides a formatted version of the contents of **/proc/modules**:

```
# lsmod
Module                    Size    Used by
bnx2fc                  110592    0
cnic                     73728    1 bnx2fc
uio                      20480    1 cnic
libfcoe                  81920    1 bnx2fc
libfc                   147456    2 bnx2fc,libfcoe
scsi_transport_fc        69632    2 libfc,bnx2fc
<truncated>
```

```
# cat /proc/modules
bnx2fc 110592 0 - Live 0xffffffffc08a6000
cnic 73728 1 bnx2fc, Live 0xffffffffc088e000
uio 20480 1 cnic, Live 0xffffffffc0844000
libfcoe 81920 1 bnx2fc, Live 0xffffffffc0879000
libfc 147456 2 bnx2fc,libfcoe, Live 0xffffffffc084b000
scsi_transport_fc 69632 2 bnx2fc,libfc, Live 0xffffffffc0832000
<truncated>
```

The best use of **lsmod** is in determining the existence or nonexistence of a particular module. For more specific information about these modules use **modinfo**:

```
# modinfo bnx2fc
filename:       /lib/modules/4.18.0-80.el8.x86_64/kernel/drivers/scsi/bnx2fc/bnx2fc.ko.xz
<truncated>
parm:           debug_logging:Option to enable extended logging,
                Default is 0 - no logging.
                0x01 - SCSI cmd error, cleanup.
                0x02 - Session setup, cleanup, etc.
                0x04 - lport events, link, mtu, etc.
                0x08 - ELS logs.
                0x10 - fcoe L2 fame related logs.
                0xff - LOG all messages. (int)
parm:           devloss_tmo: Change devloss_tmo for the remote ports
attached via bnx2fc. (uint)
<truncated>
```

The bolded output above shows that the **bnx2fc** kernel module has associated *parameters*. Parameters are configurable values that modify the behavior of kernel modules. There are some tools, such as insmod, rmmod, lsmod, which can be used to directly manipulate modules and their parameters. But the preferred tool is **modprobe**, as it can handle multiple module-related tasks in a safer, more controlled fashion.

Using **modprobe** we will load the **bnx2fc** module normally, then set the value of the **debug_logging** parameter to **0x01** (1 in hexadecimal).

```
# modprobe bnx2fc
# modprobe bnx2fc debug_logging=0x01
#
```

That seemed successful. To see what effect that had, we can look in the module's parameters directory:

```
# ls /sys/module/bnx2fc/parameters/
debug_logging   devloss_tmo    log_fka    max_luns    queue_depth

# cat /sys/module/bnx2fc/parameters/debug_logging
0
```

The current value for the **debug_logging** parameter is still **0**.

This is because kernel module parameters cannot be altered while the module is in use. When we ran the command **modprobe bnx2fc debug_logging=0x01**, **modprobe** attempted to *load* the module with that value. Since the **bnx2fc** module was already loaded, **modprobe** ignored the parameter settings and exited with a return code of 0.

To alter this parameter, we must first unload the module. Before we attempt this, we should first check to see if any other modules are dependent on it.

 # lsmod | grep bnx2fc
```
bnx2fc                 110592  0
cnic                    73728  1 bnx2fc
libfcoe                 81920  1 bnx2fc
libfc                  147456  2 bnx2fc,libfcoe
scsi_transport_fc       69632  2 libfc,bnx2fc
```

The above output tells us that while bnx2fc depends on several other modules, it doesn't have any modules that depend on it.

Let's unload the bnx2fc module:

 # modprobe -rv bnx2fc
```
rmmod bnx2fc
rmmod libfcoe
rmmod libfc
rmmod scsi_transport_fc
rmmod cnic
rmmod uio
```

When we instruct modprobe to unload a module. It will:
- not unload a module that is in use by a device or process
- not unload a module that is used as a dependency for another active module
- intelligently unload a module upon which it was dependent, if it is no longer be needed

When we asked modprobe to unload bnx2fc, cnic, uio, and other modules were also removed as no other device, process, or module required them. If any of these modules had been in use or required elsewhere, they would **not** have been unloaded.

Now that the bnx2fc module has been unloaded, we can load it again with desired parameters, and verify the new setting.

 # modprobe bnx2fc debug_logging=0x01

 # cat /sys/module/bnx2fc/parameters/debug_logging
<u>1</u>

If the module is unloaded and loaded again, either manually or by any other process (during boot for example), it will be reloaded with the default values for all parameters.

To make changes persistent, create or modify configuration files in **/etc/modprobe.d/**. Any files placed in this directory will be read by modprobe when loading modules. The file name is not important as long as it ends in **.conf** but the internal structure and values are. The format is:
options *module_name parameter=value*

We're altering the parameters of the bnx2fc module, so we will name our configuration file accordingly:
cd /etc/modprobe.d

echo "options bnx2fc debug_logging=0x02" > bnx2fc.conf

cat bnx2fc.conf
options bnx2fc debug_logging=0x02

When we unload and reload our module, we should see the value of the **debug_logging** parameter change to **2** as described in our configuration file:
modprobe -r bnx2fc
modprobe -v bnx2fc
insmod /lib/modules/4.18.0-
80.el8.x86_64/kernel/drivers/scsi/scsi_transport_fc.ko.xz
<truncated>
insmod /lib/modules/4.18.0-
80.el8.x86_64/kernel/drivers/scsi/bnx2fc/bnx2fc.ko.xz
debug_logging=**0x02**

cat /sys/module/bnx2fc/parameters/debug_logging
2

Blacklisting

In some situations, we may wish to prevent kernel modules from loading. This is done for security, to prevent loading of unstable modules, or avoid driver conflicts. While it is possible to entirely remove some modules from a system, a less drastic option is blacklisting.

Blacklisting allows us to prohibit loading of kernel modules that exist on our system. We can create a file in /etc/modprobe.d/ to disallow loading of a specific module:
echo "blacklist bnx2fc" > blacklist_bnx2fc.conf

cat blacklist_bnx2fc.conf
blacklist bnx2fc

This will prevent **automatic** loading of the bnx2fc module. It will not, however, prevent an administrator from manually loading the module, or prevent the module from being loaded as a dependency for another non-blacklisted module. To keep this module from ever being loaded, add another line to the configuration file:
echo "install bnx2fc /bin/true" >> blacklist_bnx2fc.conf

```
# cat blacklist_bnx2fc.conf
blacklist bnx2fc
install bnx2fc /bin/true
```

The effect of the line above is to redirect any attempt to load the bnx2fc module to **/bin/true**, which will simply exit with code **0**. In other words, it will succeed in doing nothing. You could also use **/bin/false**, which will do nothing, unsuccessfully (with an exit code of 1).

sysctl

To this point, we have been discussing kernel *module* parameters. There are also some parameters of the kernel itself that are exposed to direct manipulation. We can get a list of these using the **sysctl** command:

```
# sysctl -a
abi.vsyscall32 = 1
crypto.fips_enabled = 1
debug.exception-trace = 1
debug.kprobes-optimization = 1
dev.cdrom.autoclose = 1
dev.cdrom.autoeject = 0
dev.cdrom.check_media = 0
dev.cdrom.debug = 0
<truncated>
```

We can alter these in realtime with the **sysctl -w** command, for example:
```
# sysctl -w net.ipv4.ip_forward = 0
```

To alter them persistently, create files with the desired changes in **/etc/sysctl.d**. These files can have any name, so long as they have an extension of **.conf**.

Changes in these files will alter the value for the specified parameter when the kernel is next loaded at boot. We can force a reload of kernel parameters with
```
# sysctl --system
```

Altering these parameters without full knowledge of the effects that will result is **highly inadvisable**. There are a large number of required settings in the STIG, and some software (such as databases) will run better with certain kernel parameter changes. But without a known good reference any changes should be approached with extreme caution, particularly on production systems. More information on kernel parameter settings specified by STIG can be found in the Security module.

Module 17: Backups

tar

One of the oldest programs for backing up and restoring files, `tar` is filesystem and directory structure aware. It backs up files, not bytes. While it can capture a file in an inconsistent state, it will not break the underlying filesystem. Commonly used invocations for `tar` include:
- `tar -czpf  arc.tar  /etc/*.conf` – where `arc.tar` is the destination and `/etc/*.conf` is the source
    - `-c` – create archive
    - `-z` – zip compress the archive
    - `-p` – preserve permissions (happens for root by default)
    - `-f` – archive filename follows, must be the last option
- `tar -tvf arc.tar`
    - `-t` – list contents of archive
    - `-v` – verbosely
- `tar -xf arc.tar -C /alt/path`.
    - `-x` – extract, modern tar will autodetect the compression type
    - `-C` – change directory to `/alt/path`
        - with no further direction `tar` will restore relative to the current directory
    - Individual files can be extracted by path as recorded by `tar`, wildcards acceptable.
- `tar -cvf arc.tar $(find /etc/ -name f*.conf)` – use the output of `find` as the list of files to archive

Other useful options for tar include:
- `-d` – find differences between archive and filesystem
    - will find altered or deleted files, but not added ones
- `-r` – append files to archive
- `-u` – update, append newer files
- `-l` – store hard links as links
- `--dereference`, `--hard-dereference` – store symlinks and hard links as full files
- `--acls` – preserve extended acls, use when creating and extracting
- `--selinux` – preserve SELinux context, use when creating and extracting
- `--xattrs` – preserve both SELinux and acls attributes, use when creating and extracting

rsync

A more modern tool, **rsync** allows copy and archive either locally or between machines. It is content aware, will only transfer the differences between file sets, and can compress during transit for bandwidth savings. It can be used either as a stand-alone command to transfer between two machines; or it can be configured as a service, allowing multiple clients to synchronize files to a centralized server.

To perform transfers rsync uses remote shell protocols such as ssh to perform the transfer. Verify that you can ssh from the source to the destination machines before using rsync. The basic invocation is:

rsync -av */source/dir/ username@target.server:/dest/directory/*

If you omit the trailing **/** on the source, it will create the final directory name at the destination, e.g.: **/dest/directory/dir/**. To reverse the process, simply flip source and destination. A source with no destination will list the files instead of copying.

Common switches for rsync include:
- **-a** – archive, equivalent to **-rlptgoD**, which is to say:
  recurse, copy links; save permissions, timestamps, group, and owner; preserve Device and special files
- **-v** – verbose
- **-z** – compress (during transit, it will decompress at the destination)
- **-h** – present human readable output
- **-e** – use specified transport, must be in quotes: "**ssh -i** */path/key*"
- **-x** – do not exit this filesystem
- **-X** – preserve extended attributes
- **-H** – preserve hardlinks
- **-A** – preserve ACLs
- **-S** – squeeze sparse files (those with long zero blocks)
- **-L** – turn links into files
- **--delete** – remove files not at the source, default is to preserve them at the destination
- **--remove-source-files** – delete source upon success, useful for temporary tarballs
- **--include / --exclude / --filter** – allows detailed specification of files
  - e.g.: # **rsync -av --exclude "*log*" /var** remote.server/backup
  - Filters can get quite involved, consult **FILTER RULES** in the man page

dd

We will briefly look at **dd**, not so much as a backup solution, but because it does other useful things. If used on a working filesystem, it is recommended that the source filesystem either be unmounted and treated as a raw device, or remounted as read-only. If dd is run with a read-write filesystem as a source, corruption may occur.

It can be used to perform a full backup of a device using:
`# dd if=/dev/source of=/dev/dest conv=noerr`

The **noerr** option tells dd to press on even if it has a read error. This performs a byte-wise copy of **/dev/source** to **/dev/dest**, wiping all data on the destination. This can also be used to copy a partition to a file (**of=**/path/file.bak).

Other uses of **dd** include
- converting optical media to .iso image
  `# num=$(isosize -d 2048 /dev/cdrom)` – set $num to the cd's block count
  `# dd if=/dev/cdrom of=some.img bs=2048 count=$num`.
- creating a new file
  `# dd of=/new/file` – type, then **CTL-d** when done.
- repairing master boot records
  `# dd if=/dev/good/drive of=mbr.img bs=446 count=1` – copy boot code
  `# dd if=mbr.img of=/dev/bad/drive bs=446 count=1` – restore to bad drive
  - **bs=446** only copies the boot code
  - **bs=512** copies boot code and partition table
- wiping drives
  `# dd if=/dev/zero of=/dev/sda bs=32M` – zero sda with very large blocks
  - A better way to wipe data is
    `# shred -n 20 -fuz /xfs/file`

ReaR

ReaR (Relax and Recover) is a lightweight disaster recovery program capable either of standalone backup and recovery or as an adjunct recovery system for third-party backups. At its most simple you create a server and backup to it.

The clients will only need **rear** installed. Servers should have **rear**, **genisoimage**, and **syslinux** installed.

The preferred means of communication for rear is rsync. The user running the backup should have read permissions for the full source system, and have full (**rwx**) permissions on the destination folder. That is the only required server-side configuration.

Client configuration is in **/etc/rear/local.conf**:
```
OUTPUT_URL=rsync://servername/storage-directory
BACKUP=RSYNC
BACKUP_URL=rsync://servername/storage-directory
BACKUP_PROG_EXCLUDE=("${BACKUP_PROG_EXCLUDE[@]}" '/media' '/var/tmp' '/var/crash')
```

To initiate a backup simply run **# rear mkbackup -v**. The first backup may take some time, but because rsync only copies differences, later backups will run faster. To only make a backup use **mkbackuponly**; **mkrescue** only creates a rescue disk. ReaR does sometimes leave files in /tmp, it's a good idea to **# rm -Rf /tmp/rear.*** afterwards.

Additional configuration can be found at **/usr/share/rear/conf/default.conf**.

For restoration, simply download the .iso from the server. Burn and boot from the .iso. You will be prompted several times for the root password of the backup server, certificates will not suffice. If you are restoring to a VMware virtual machine move the .iso to the host:
 # scp /path/**rear-**XX**.iso root@**esx**:/vmfs/volumes/**datastore/**rear-**XX**.iso**

Module 18: Security

We've addressed much of the implementation of the STIG and security best practices in the appropriate modules, and much can be accomplished using `oscap` and `ansible` as shown below, but some relevant points to keep in mind include:
- Password protect the BIOS if possible.
- Disable alternate boot methods such as cdrom and USB.
- Use LUKS encryption when practical. It is required on mobile systems.
- If you don't know that you'll need it, don't install it.
- If you don't need graphics all the time, set the default to `multi-user.target`.
    - For the most part a server should not have graphics installed.
- Disable, mask and uninstall services, sockets, groups, and packages if they are unneeded.
- Consider restricting login hours using the `pam_time` module:
    - In `/etc/pam.d/login` add `account    required    pam_time.so`
    - Create rules in `/etc/security/time.conf`
- Always login as an unprivileged user and use `sudo`.
- Force read-only for removable media.
    - Create a file `/etc/udev/rules.d/80-ro-media.rules` add the following `SUBSYSTEM=="block",ATTRS{removable}=="1",RUN{program}="/sbin/blockdev --setro %N"`
- If remote access is required, consider using an IPsec VPN tunnel using libreswan.

Additionally, you should reference: https://access.redhat.com/documentation/en-US/Red_Hat_Enterprise_Linux/7/html/Security_Guide/index.html

Remove any non-essential software. If you want a list of software without parent dependencies:
`package-cleanup --leaves --all`.
To run `package-cleanup` you must install `dnf-utils`.

When removing language packages, they will be listed in the format `Arabic Support [ab]`, and will tab complete as `Arabic\ Support\ \[ab\]`, but must be named in the format `arabic-support` to be successfully removed by yum.

Common programs to consider removing:
- `abrt` – automatic bug reporting
- `alsa*` – command line for sound
- `autofs` – automatically mounts filesystems
- `avahi-daemon` – provides Zeroconf networking
- `bind*` – DNS server
- `bluetooth` – nobody needs this on a server
- `cdparanoia, vorbis-tools, brasero, icedax` – media stuff
- `colord` – manages color profiles for graphics
- `cups` / `lpd` / `hplip` / `foomatic` / `redhat-lsb-printing` – provides printer support
- `dhcp` – the dhcp server
- `dovecot` – imap & pop3 server
- `firstboot` – not needed after install
- `fprintd` – fingerprint scanner support
- `gpm` – mouse for console
- `hidd` – bluetooth mouse and keyboard support
- `httpd` – web server
- `irqbalance` – balances between processors, not needed on single socket machines
- `iscsi-*` – iscsi protocol support
- `krb5-appl-clients` – Kerberos versions of ftp, rcp, rlogin, rsh and telnet.
- `libvirtd` – virtualization daemon
- `mdmonitor` – software raid
- `microcode_ctl` – transforms and deploys CPU microcode
- `ModemManager` – for wireless modems
- `net-snmp` – SNMP server
- `nfs, nfslock, rpcgssd, rpcbind, rpc.mountd, rpcidmapd, rpcsvccgssd, netfs`
- `oddjob` – provides privileged access to unprivileged processes, never use
- `openldap-servers` – for authentication
- `portreserve` – pre-allocated ports for services
- `rhnsd` – Red Hat proprietary update agent
- `samba` – file sharing
- `squid` – web proxy
- `wireless-tools` – not on a server
- `xinetd, telnet, rsh, rlogin, ypbind` – defunct network protocols, never use

aide

After configuration of a new system, you should install **aide**, the Advanced Intrusion Detection Environment. **aide** detects file tampering by scanning all files and folders while in a known good state, producing a baseline from that scan, and comparing that baseline to the current state.

The configuration file is **/etc/aide.conf**. **aide** uses multiple means to compare files. Folders and files which are expected to be changed in the normal course of business should be excluded using one of these directives:
! /dirname prevents scanning of the directory entirely, or
/dirname CONTENT_EX, excludes content, but monitors permissions, SELinux context, etc.

This should be done if you encounter too many false positives using the defaults. Remotely mounted filesystems should be excluded, instead they should be scanned by the hosting device. After configuration changes, the integrity of the configuration file should be checked with
 # aide -D.

Before using aide, you must create an initial database with **aide -i**. This scans the entire computer and produces a database **/var/lib/aide/aide.db.new.gz**. A copy of this database should be retained as a baseline, in case a forensic investigation occurs. If possible it should be stored on read-only media, off-line and off-site. To use this database as your baseline copy it to **/var/lib/aide/aide.db.gz**, the name of the working database.

To check against the working database, **aide -C**. The output is stored in **/var/log/aide/aide.log**. Examine this for unexpected changes, which should be investigated.

Checking integrity does not update the database, this must be done manually. Update and archive the database after documented changes (software installation or patches) using
 # aide -u.

Best practice says that aide should be run at least weekly and the results archived. A wrapper script that copies the results to a centralized server would be appropriate.

When setting up checks for multiple machines, it is advisable to offset the start times. This is particularly important in a virtualized environment, as aide does a full scan of the system each time it is run, and can place a very large load on shared storage.

Prelinking is a deprecated feature designed to speed performance by altering the linkage sets within executable binaries. It was found to yield minimal benefit, and under certain circumstances causes system corruption, including full bricking. Beginning with EL7 **prelink** is not installed by default. But it may be installed on EL6, or if a system administrator followed an out-of-date performance tuning document.

Because prelinking changes files it will cause false positives when using **aide** and **rpm -V**. This effectively renders any system integrity checks useless.

If **prelink** has been installed, disable it by creating a file **/etc/sysconfig/prelink**, with the line **PRELINKING=no**. You can then undo the changes it made to binaries by running **/usr/sbin/prelink -ua**. When this has completed, **yum remove prelink**.

Enterprise Linux versions 7 & 8

oscap, scap-workbench

OpenSCAP (`oscap`) is an open source security content automation protocol toolkit approved by DISA and NIST as an 'Authenticated Configuration and Vulnerability Scanner'. It also can perform remediation based on its findings. This works quite well: on a default installation of EL7 with "STIG compliant server with GUI" selected as the installed security profile, the number of findings went from 106 down to 19 in minutes. Installing `scap-workbench` will install all required packages. Alternatively you can `group install "Security Tools"` if `group_package_types=mandatory,default,optional` is set in `yum.conf`, or select them during initial server build.

Ideally `oscap` should be run from a GUI as the command line is complex and poorly documented. A "simple" command line to scan and remediate EL7 as run from `/usr/share/xml/scap/ssg/content` looks like this:
```
# oscap xccdf eval --remediate --profile /stig-rhel7-server-upstream \
--cpe /ssg-rhel7-cpe-dictionary.xml /ssg-centos7-xccdf.xml
```

The command line can get as interesting as:
```
# oscap xccdf eval --datastream-id \
  scap_org.open-scap_datastream_from_xccdf_ssg-rhel7-xccdf-1.2.xml \
--xccdf-id scap_org.open-scap_cref_ssg-rhel7-xccdf-1.2.xml           \
--profile xccdf_org.ssgproject.content_profile_C2S                   \
--oval-results --results /tmp/tmp.74oUO0gtVd/results-xccdf.xml       \
--results-arf /tmp/tmp.74oUO0gtVd/results-arf.xml                    \
--report /tmp/tmp.74oUO0gtVd/report.html                             \
--progress /usr/share/xml/scap/ssg/content/ssg-centos7-ds.xml
```

That block of text was generated by `scap-workbench`, the graphical tool. It can be invoked off the action menu or by running it from a graphical terminal (as root). While not as powerful and versatile as running `oscap` directly from the command line, `scap-workbench` is very straightforward. Some features of scap-workbench:

- Local or remote scanning and remediation (via ssh)
- Multiple profiles to meet industry and government standards including:
    - United States Government Configuration Baseline (NIAP OSPP v4.0, USGCB, STIG)
    - U.S. Government Commercial Cloud Services (C2S)
    - CNSSI 1253 Control Baseline
    - Criminal Justice Information Services (CJIS) Security Policy
    - Payment Card Industry – Data Security Standard (PCI-DSS) v3
    - DISA STIG
- Ability to customize profiles
- Export of custom profiles to rpm format, allowing remediation of isolated systems

The STIG SCAP content for Red Hat 7/8 has been approved by NIST. It is available at `https://nvd.nist.gov/ncp/repository`. Pre-release (working) content is available at `https://github.com/ComplianceAsCode/`. Local content is installed and will be updated with the `scap-security-guide` package.

This content should be treated as 'trust, but verify' as simply using it does not constitute a full validation. Much more information is available at `https://www.open-scap.org`, which also has one of the most readable versions of the STIG at `https://static.openscap.org`.

There is no STIG content for CentOS as CentOS is not commercially supported and therefore by definition can not be STIG compliant. It was decided to no longer provide content as it might be construed as a STIG certification of CentOS. The content for Red Hat can be converted by renaming the `.xml` files and substituting the proper strings using `sed`, but that is an exercise beyond the scope of this book.

ansible

Ansible is a centralized configuration and automation platform capable of controlling not just EL family Linux hosts, but everything from routers and switches, to Azure and AWS cloud services. Full documentation is at `http://docs.ansible.com`, the source for ansible is available at `https://github.com/ansible`. Ansible is now a subsidiary of Red Hat.

A simple ansible command looks like this:
`# ansible -m shell -a 'free' all`.

In the above example `all` is a target host list is defined in `/etc/ansible/hosts`, grouped below a header contained in `[brackets]`. You will need key-based ssh to each host listed. Use `-u` to run as an alternate user.

Where `-m` loads the module `shell`, `-a` passes the argument `'free'` to `shell`, and `all` is the target host list. This will run the command `free`, via the `shell` on `all` listed target hosts. This command could also have been run as
`# ansible all -a 'free'`.

The modules control a certain action or type of command. A full list of modules can be obtained with `# ansible-doc -l`. For documentation on the shell module: `# ansible-doc shell`. Another useful module is `service`, the following line restarts httpd on `all`:
`# ansible all -m service -a "name=httpd  state=restarted"`.

While you can call commands directly, the strength of `ansible` comes from its ability to run `playbooks`, which call tasks and can produce fully automated workflows. The Ansible-Lockdown group has produced a STIG compliance playbook, which will perform much of the STIG-requisite configuration for you. It is primarily this task that we will focus on.

To obtain the STIG playbook for EL7, in an empty directory (such as `/gitpath/`):
`# git clone --recursive https://github.com/ansible/ansible-lockdown.git`

To run the STIG playbook, create a host list and run:
`# ansible-playbook -l` *hosts* `/gitpath/ansible-lockdown/stig.yml`.

Ansible also has a GUI-based control station called Ansible Tower. A free limited-feature version can be run for up to 10 hosts. Red Hat has open sourced a version of Tower, called `awx`, which does not have these limitations. Releases of `awx` will be developmental, much as Fedora is related to RHEL. It is anticipated that there will eventually be a stable release version, following the CentOS model. Installation is lengthy, involved, and varies between distributions and environments. If you are managing a large number of computers it may well be worth the effort. Consult the documentation.

clam

Many people will tell you Linux systems do not need an anti-virus/anti-malware solution. With the ever increasing pace of malware development, this is wrong and dangerous. It is also required by STIG. There are two acceptable alternatives for provision of virus scan capability: McAfee VirusScan and `clamav`. `clamav` is FOSS and included in the EPEL repo.

- Install the following:
    - `clamav, clamav-data, clamav-devel, clamav-file system, clamav-lib, clamav-scanner, clamav-server, clamav-update`

- If not already done, in `/etc/clamd.conf`
    - Comment out `Example`
    - Uncomment `LocalSocket`
    - Uncomment or add
        - `ExcludePath ^/proc/`
        - `ExcludePath ^/sys/`
        - `ExcludePath ^/sys/`
    - `CrossFilesystems no`

- If not already done, in `/etc/freshclam.conf`
    - Comment out `Example`

- Run `# freshclam` to update the AV database.

- Start and enable the `clamd` service
  You will receive a warning that Bytecode was disabled, this is ok

- Run the following at appropriate intervals:
    - `/bin/freshclam`

    - `/usr/bin/nice -n 15 /bin/clamscan --quiet \`
      `/ -roI /var/log/clamscan.log`

Securing the network stack

There are a number of steps to get networking to STIG. The firewall should be on, enabled and the active zone set to DROP, as noted above. Some time should be spent evaluating networking needs and building rules to restrict unneeded and unwanted traffic. For instance, restricting inbound ssh connections to those originating from your management network, or restricting an internal web server to only respond to internal traffic.

The following line should be added to `/etc/sysconfig/network`
`IPV6_AUTOCONF=no`

Then there are the kernel parameters that need to be adjusted. You can change the running state with `sysctl -w`, but it is easiest to simply add all the lines to `/etc/sysctl.d/99-sysctl.conf` and reboot or run `# sysctl --system` when all modifications are complete. These are the lines to be added

```
net.ipv6.conf.default.accept_source_route = 0
net.ipv6.conf.all.accept_source_route = 0
net.ipv6.conf.all.accept_redirects = 0
net.ipv6.conf.default.accept_ra = 0
net.ipv6.conf.all.accept_ra = 0
net.ipv6.conf.default.accept_redirects = 0
net.ipv4.conf.default.accept_source_route = 0
net.ipv4.icmp_ignore_bogus_error_responses = 1
net.ipv4.conf.default.rp_filter = 1
net.ipv4.conf.all.secure_redirects = 0
net.ipv4.conf.all.accept_source_route = 0
net.ipv4.tcp_syncookies = 1
net.ipv4.conf.all.accept_redirects = 0
net.ipv4.conf.all.log_martians = 1
net.ipv4.conf.all.rp_filter = 1
net.ipv4.icmp_echo_ignore_broadcasts = 1
net.ipv4.conf.default.secure_redirects = 0
net.ipv4.conf.default.log_martians = 1
net.ipv4.ip_forward = 0
net.ipv4.conf.all.send_redirects = 0
net.ipv4.conf.default.send_redirects = 0
```

Unused network protocols should be prevented from loading by creating a file in `/etc/modprobe.d` which contains the following:

```
install atm /bin/true
install firewire-core /bin/true
install tipc /bin/true
install sctp /bin/true
install can /bin/true
install bluetooth /bin/true
```

A review of all installed kernel modules should also be done, and any unwanted ones added here.

Command Summary

Module 1: Introduction
- `ls` – list files
    - `-l` – long
    - `-a` – all
    - `-d` – directory
    - `-Z` – selinux
    - `-i` – inode information
- `cd` – change directory
    - `.` – this directory
    - `..` – the parent directory
    - `~` – the home directory
    - `-` – the previous directory
- `pwd` – print working directory
- `cat` – print a file
    - `-n` – number lines
    - `-b` – number non-blank lines
- `wc` – count lines, words, and characters
    - `-l` – count lines only
- `less` – view output one page at a time
    - `q` – quit
    - `/string` / `?string` – search forward, backward for string (`n` / `N` repeats)
    - `gg` / `G` – top / bottom
    - `F` – follow (`CTL-c` to stop)
- `alias` – remap a command (add to `~/.bashrc` to make permanent)
- **redirection**:
    - `a | b` – send output from command `a` to command `b`
    - `a > x` – overwrite file `x` with output of command `a`
    - `a >> x` – append output of `a` to file `x`
    - `a | xargs b` – send output from command `a` as arguments to `b`
    - `b $( a )` – expand command `a` as arguments to `b`
- **command separation:**
    - `;` – separate commands on a line
    - `a && b` – run `b` if `a` succeeds
    - `a || b` – run `b` if `a` fails
    - `&` – run a command in the background
    - `\` – continue command on next line

- **streams:**
    - `0` – `STDIN`
    - `1` – `STDOUT`
    - `2` – `STDERR`
    - `2> /dev/null` – suppress errors
    - `2>&1> /dev/null` – suppress all output
- CTL shortcuts:
    - `CTL-a` / `CTL-e` – start / end of line
    - `CTL-c` – stop a running command or input
    - `CTL-d` – send End Of File (logs out if sent to a bare prompt)
    - `CTL-L` – clear the screen
    - `CTL-r` – reverse search for commands
- `history` – display previous commands
    - `!###` – run command ### from history
- `!!` – last command
- `!$` -- last argument
- `$?` – last exit code
- `exit`, `logout`, `CTL-d` – ways to end a shell
- `--help` – standard short help option
- `man` – manual pages
    - `-k` *string* – find man pages about *string*
    - `mandb` – update man page database
- `info` – documentation

Module 2: Files and Directories
- `file` – determine file type
- `stat` – display file status (metadata)
- `which` – locate first command in `$PATH`
- `whereis` – search for a command and related files
- `locate` – find files based on an index database
    - `updatedb` – update the locate database

- **find**
    - **-maxdepth** / **-mindepth** – directory depth of search
    - **-type** – of file
    - **-name** – literal name
    - **-iname** – case insensitive name
    - **-nouser** – unowned
    - **-o** – OR (default is AND)
    - **-perm** – permissions (**/** = match any)
    - **-exec** `command` **{}\;** – run command on the results
    - **-atime**, **-ctime**, **-mtime** – access, change, modify time
        - **-1** = last 24 hours
        - **1** = 24-48 hours
        - **+1** = more than 48 hours
    - **-newer** – compare time to a file
        - **-newermt** YYYY-MM-DD – newer modify time
        - **-not -newerct** YYYY-MM-DD – older change time
    - **-ls** / **-delete** – list or delete the results
- **head** – display the top of a file
    - **-n** – number of lines to display
- **tail** – display end of a file
    - **-f** – follow
- **touch** – change file timestamps, create empty file
- **echo** – display something

- **mkdir** – make directory
    - **-m** – mode (permissions)
    - **-p** – create path if not extant
- **rmdir** – remove directory
- **rm** – remove file
    - **-r** – recursively
    - **-f** – force
- **cp** – copy
- **mv** – move, rename
- **dmesg** – print kernel ring buffer (boot messages)
- **tee** – split output to STDOUT and a file
- **column** – put lists into columns
- **sort**
    - **-n** – numerically
    - **-r** – reverse
    - **-u** – unique
- **tr** – translate characters
- **uniq** – find unique lines
- **diff** – compare two files

Module 3: vi
- **Normal** – command mode; `ESC`
    - `u` – undo
    - `ctrl-r` – redo
    - `yy` – yanks (copy)
    - `dd` – delete / cut
    - `p` – paste
    - `:` commands:
        - `w` – write
        - `q` – quit
        - `a` – all
        - `!` – force
        - `!` *cmd* – run command
        - `e` – edit from last write
        - `n` / `N` – next / previous file
        - `split` / `vsplit`
        - `r` – read
        - `r !` *cmd* – read command into file
        - `abbr` – abbreviate
        - `set number` – turn on line numbering, `!` turns it off
- **Visual** – select mode; `v`, `V`, `CTL-v`
    - `y` – copy
    - `d` – delete
    - `p` – paste
- **Insert** – typing mode; `i`, `o`, `A`

Module 4: Users and Groups
- `useradd`
    - `-G` – additional groups
    - `-u` / `-g` – UID / GID
    - `-s` – shell
    - `-Z` – SELinux
- `passwd`
    - `-l` / `-u` – lock / unlock
    - `-S` – status
- `usermod`
    - `-aG` – add to Groups
- `userdel`
    - `-r` – remove home directory
- `vipw`, `vigr`, `visudo` – editors for special files
- `groupadd`
- `groupmod`
- `groupdel`
- `groupmems`
    - `-g` – groupname, mandatory
    - `-a` / `-d` – add /delete
    - `-l` – list
- `id` – show real and effective UID
- `su` – change current UID
    - `su -` – use destination environment
- `sudo` – change effective UID to root
- `who` – is currently logged on
- `w` – who plus stats and current command
- `uptime`
- `lastlog` – last logins
- `last` – successful logins
- `lastb` – bad logins
- `loginctl` – control the login manager
    - `list-users` – list current logins
    - `user-status` *user* – show info about *user* session
    - `show-user` *user* – show info about *user*
    - `terminate-user` *username* – end all processes for user
    - `kill-user --signal` *XX username* – send a signal to all processes of a user
    - `list-sessions` – show active sessions
    - `session-status` *session-id* – show details, including log snippets, of a session
    - `terminate-session` *session-id* – end all processes in a session
    - `kill-session` *session-id* – send a signal to all processes of a session
    - `enable-linger` *username* – allow a user to run processes without logging in

Module 5: Permissions and Ownership
- **chown** *user:group* – change ownership
- **chmod** – change permissions
    - **r** = 4
    - **w** = 2
    - **x** = 1
    - **SUID** = 4 (**s**)
    - **SGID** = 2 (**s**)
    - **Sticky** = 1 (**t**)
    - **u**, **g**, **o**, **a** – user, group, other, all
- **umask** – permissions to unset on file / directory creation
- **getfacl** – get file ACL
- **setfacl** – set file ACL
    - **-m** – modify an ACL
    - **-x** – remove an ACL entry
    - **-b** – remove all ACLs for file
    - **-R** – apply ACL recursively through subdirectories
    - **[d]**:**u**|**g**|**o**|**m**:*UID*|*GID*::*perms*
        - **d** – default
        - **u**, **g**, **o** – user, group, other
        - **m** – mask
        - **UID**,**GID**
        - **perms** – rwx permissions

Module 6: Regular Expressions

- **character sets**
    - `[a-z]` – any single lowercase alpha character
    - `[A-Z]` – single uppercase alpha character
    - `[abc]` – a, b, or c.
    - `[0-9]` – any single digit
    - `[^a2]` – any character NOT **a** or a **2**
    - `.` – any single character other than line break
    - `[.]` – a literal period
    - `[a|b]` – **a** OR **b**
    - `^/$` – beginning / end of line

- **modifiers** – Match the preceding…
    - `?` – 0 or 1 times
    - `*` – 0 or more times
    - `+` – 1 or more times
    - `{N}` – exactly N times
    - `{N,}` – N or more times
    - `{N,M}` – between N and M times

- **backreferences**
    - `( )`   Encloses the pattern to store matches from
    - `\N`   Return the match from the Nth (1-9) stored backreference

- `grep`
    - `-v` – invert the match (return ONLY lines where pattern was NOT matched
    - `-o` – match entire line (rather than within the line)
    - `-b` – respect word boundaries
    - `-i` – case insensitive
    - `-E` – extended grep
    - `+ ? | {} ()` – literals in basic grep, metacharacters in extended (`-E`)
    - `--color` – highlight the matched string

- `sed`
    - `-n` – prevent normal output printing
    - `-i` – perform an in-place edit
    - `-r` – extended regular expression mode
    - `-e` – multiple expressions in a line
    - `-f` – run a sed script. `sed -f` *script original changed*
    - `p` – print
    - `s` – substitute
    - `d` – delete
    - `g` – global
        - `sed 's/`*pattern*`/`*replacement*`/g'` *filename*

- `awk '{` *commands* `}'` *filename*.
    - Commands
        - `print` – print matches
        - `sub()` – substitute, once per line
        - `gsub()` – global substitute
    - `-F` – set delimiter
    - `-f` – run a script
    - /*pattern*/   match a pattern (occurs before commands portion)

    - Variables
        - `$0`   – entire current record
        - `$n`   – where **n** is a number; field by sequence e.g. **$1,$2**
        - `NF`   – number of fields in current record
        - `NR`   – number of current record
        - `FNR` – if multiple input files, record number of current file
        - `FS/RS` – input field separator/record separator
        - `OFS/ORS` – output field separator/record separator
        - `FILENAME` – the name of the input file; undefined in BEGIN block
        -
    - Scripting Constructs
        - `BEGIN`   Run first, used to make header or set variables.
        - `BODY`   Where the bulk of the script resides.
        - `END`   Run last, used to create a footer.

Module 7: Booting
- `grub2-mkconfig -o` /path/`grub.cfg` – generate the GRUB configuration file
- `grub2-setpassword` – set a grub password
- `systemctl` – control systemd
    - `status` – shows general status and state
    - `show` – lists all properties
    - `list-units` – show units in memory
    - `start/stop/restart` – control the running state
    - `reload` – force the service to re-read configuration files (.conf, not unit files)
    - `daemon-reload` – re-read unit files and re-run the systemd generator for dependencies
    - `enable/disable` – turn on/off service auto-start
    - `enable --now` – equivalent to `enable` and `start`
    - `mask/unmask` – completely prevent a service from starting
    - `is-enabled` – query enable status
    - `verify` – check syntax on unit files
    - `cat` – print assembled unit files for a service
    - `isolate` – change running state to a designated target (`multi-user`, `graphical`)
    - `get-default` / `set-default` – control default target
    - `halt` / `reboot` / `poweroff` – control power state
    - `list-depends` – show dependencies
    - `set-property` – change parameters of running units
- `systemd-analyze` – analyze systemd
    - `unit-paths` – show directories read by systemd
    - `verify` – check unit file syntax
    - `calendar` – evaluate time specification
- `runlevel` – view previous and current runlevel
    - `N` – none (booted)
    - `1` / `S` – single-user, `rescue.target`
    - `3` – `multi-user.target`
    - `5` – `graphical.target`

Module 8: Processes and Services

- `ps` – show running processes
    - `-e` – everything
    - `-f` – full listing
    - `-u` – user
    - `-o` – modify output, takes arguments separated by commas: `%cpu, %mem, args, cgname, cgroup, comm, pid, gid, uid, nice, user`
    - `-Z` – selinux
- `kill` – pass a signal
    - `-9` – `KILL`
    - `-20` – `SPT` (pause)
    - `-18` – `CONT` (resume)
- `pgrep` / `pkill` – process grep / pgrep and signal processes
    - `-u` – user
    - `-l` – long (shows command line)
    - `-n` – newest
    - `-v` – **invert** selection
- `killall` – signal multiple processes
    - `-u` – user
    - `-i` – interactive (prompt)
    - `-v` – verbose, **not** invert
- `CTL-z` – pause a process
    - `fg`/`bg` – resume foreground / background
    - `jobs` – show paused or backgrounded processes
    - `disown`
        - `-a` – all
        - `-h` – leave in table, do not terminate on exit
- `top` – view running processes
    - `h` – Display a help screen
    - `i` – toggle idle processes
    - `f` – Select fields to display
    - `F` – Select sort field
    - `M` – Sort by memory usage.
    - `P` – Sort by CPU usage.
    - `V` – Show parent process relationships
    - `u` – Filter by user.
    - `r` – Renice a process.
    - `k` – Kill a process.
    - `q` – quit top

- `uptime` – show system status
- `free` / `vmstat` – display memory
- `nice` – set an initial process priority
    - `-n` – value (-20 to 19)
- `renice` – change a running process priority

- `systemd-cgls` – show control groups
- `systemd-cgtop` – show control group resource usage
- `systemd-delta` – show changes to systemd configuration files
- `systemd-run` – start a new transient scope, slice, service or timer

- limit user resources in `/etc/security/limits.conf`
    - `ulimit` – adjust limits on the fly

Module 9: Filesystems

- `xfs_db` – examine an xfs filesystem
- `ln` *original link* – link file
    - `-s` – symbolic
- `lsblk` – list block devices
- `parted` – partition table manipulation
    - `print free`
- `fdisk` – partition table manipulation
    - `-l` – list
    - `m` – menu
    - `n` – new
    - `p` – print current
    - `w` – write
    - `q` – quit
- `fallocate` – allocate space to a file
    - `-l` – set length (`KB`, `MB`, `GB`…)
- `partprobe` – inform kernel of changes
- `mkfs.*` – make filesystem
    - `-L` – label
- `mount` */device /dir*
    - `-a` – mount all automatically
    - `-o` – options
        - `defaults` – alias for `async,auto,dev,exec,nouser,rw,suid`
        - `async` – allow the asynchronous input/output operations
        - `auto` – mount automatically using `mount -a`
        - `noauto` – no automatic mount
        - `dev` – interpret character or block special devices on the filesystem
        - `exec` – allow the execution of binaries
        - `noexec` – no execution of binaries
        - `nouser` – disallow non-root to mount and unmount
        - `rw` / `ro` – read/write / read-only
        - `suid` – allow set-user/group bits to take effect.
        - `remount` – remount the filesystem in case it is already mounted.
        - `noatime` – do not update access times
- `umount` – unmount
- `blkid` – show block device attributes
- `fstab` – format:
  [device] [directory] [type] [options] [dump(0,1)] [fsck(0,1,2)]
- `mkswap` – create a swap filesystem
- `fdisk` – interactive partition table maniputlation

- `swapon`/`swapoff` – control swap devices and files
    - `-s` – show swap
    - `-a` – all
    - `-L` – label
    - `-v` – verbose
- `mkswap` – create swap area
    - `-L` – label
- `df` – show disk usage
    - `-h` – human readable
- `systemd-escape` – translate strings for use in systemd unit names
    - `-p` – path formatting

- `pvcreate` – create a PV
- `pvdisplay` – display detailed information about a PV
- `pvremove` – remove (destroy) a PV
- `pvresize` – resize PV to reflect size of underlying device
- `pvs` – display information about PVs on a system
- `pvscan` – scan devices for LVM (PV) data; update cache

- `vgcreate` – create a VG
- `vgdisplay` – display detailed info about VG(s)
- `vgextend` – add PV(s) to VG
- `vgreduce` – remove PV(s) from VG (CAUTION!)
- `vgremove` – destroy a VG
- `vgs` – display information about VGs
- `vgscan` – scan devices for LVM (VG) data; update cache

- `lvcreate` – create an LV
- `lvdisplay` – display detailed information about an LV
- `lvextend` – add physical extents to an LV
- `lvreduce` – remove physical extents from an LV
- `lvremove` – destroy an LV
- `lvresize` – shrink or grow an LV (-r autoresize resident FS)
- `lvs` – display information about LVs
- `lvscan` – scan devices for LVM (LV) data; update cache

- `cryptsetup`
    - `luksFormat` – create a LUKS device
    - `luksOpen` – open LUKS for reading
    - `luksClose` – close LUKS access
    - add mapping and keys in `/etc/crypttab`

Module 10: Scheduling Events
- `cron` – schedule precisely
    - `-l` – list
    - `-e` – edit
    - `-u` – user
    - Format:
      [minute] [hour] [day] [month] [day of week] [/path/cmd]
- `anacron` – schedule roughly
    - create link from job to **/etc/cron.**`interval`
- `at` – schedule events once
    - `atq` – list jobs
    - `atrm` – remove jobs
    - `-c` – show job script
    - `batch` – schedule when cpu usage is below threshold
        - set with `at -l` or in **/etc/sysconfig/atd**

Module 11: Networking
- `nmcli` – command line for Network Manager
- `nmtui` – text menus for Network Manager
- `ip` – view network information
    - `addr`, `route`, `link`, `neigh`
- `hostnamectl set-hostname` – set hostname
- `firewall-cmd` / `firewall-offline-cmd` – configure firewall
    - `--permanent`, `--runtime-to-permanent`
    - `--reload`
    - `--list-all`
    - `--zone=`*zonename*
        - `--set-target=DROP`
        - `--add-service=`*servicename*
        - `--add-source=`*address*/*mask*
        - `--add-port=###/`*tcp*
        - `--add-protocol=`*protoname*
    - `--get-default-zone` / `--set-default-zone`
- `ss` – socket status
    - `-m` – memory usage
    - `-o` – time
    - `state` – established, syn-sent, syn-recv, connected
    - `src/dst` – source or destination address
    - `sport/dport` – source / destination port (`:443`)
- test connectivity: `ping`, `arping`, `traceroute`, `tracepath`
- resolve hostnames and IP addresses: `dig`, `nslookup`, `host`, (and EL8 only) `resolvectl`

Module 12: Remote Access

- `sshd` – configured in `/etc/ssh/sshd_config`
- `ssh` *user@host*
  - -i – identity file (key)
- `ssh-keygen` – make key
- `ssh-copy-id` – copy key to remote host
- `scp` *localfile user@host:/path/file* – copy localfile to remote host
- `sftp` – ftp client over ssh
- `cockpit` – web interface, uses port `9090`
- `vsftpd` – configured in `vsftpd.conf`
  - `lftpd` – ftp client
- `httpd` – configured in `httpd.conf`
  - `apachectl` – used instead of systemctl to start and stop apache
  - `curl`, `wget`, `lynx`, `elinks` – clients for url-based targets
- `nfs` – part of nfs-utils package
  - edit `/etc/exports` format:
    [local share] [hostname or network] [options]
  - options include:
    - `rw` – read/write
    - `sec=` – security flavors (`sys`, `krb5`, `krb5i`, `krb5p`)
    - `sync` – do not reply until write
    - `fsid=0` – sets the "root" of the virtual filesystem in NFSv4
    - `anonuid` – set the system UID to be assigned to anonymous users
    - `no_root_squash` – do not map UID 0 requests to `anonymous`
- `exportfs` – re-read /etc/exports
  - `-a` – all
  - `-u` – unexport
- `x2go` – remote GUI sharing via ssh
- `vnc` – another GUI sharing tool, less secure

Module 13: SELinux

- **`getenforce`** / **`setenforce`** – view/change SELinux status
- **`sesearch`** – policy query
    - **`-b`** – boolean
    - **`--`***`rule`* – **`allow`**, **`type`**, **`neverallow`**, **`audit`**, **`dontaudit`**, **`all`**
    - **`-s`** – source
    - **`-t`** – target
    - **`-c`** – class (file, dir, socket)
    - **`-p`** – permission type (read, write, create)
- **`semanage`** – policycoreutils-python-utils package
    - **`login`**
    - **`user`**
    - **`port`**
    - **`permissive`**
    - **`boolean`**
    - **`fcontext`** – file context
    - **`-l`** – list
    - **`-d`** – delete
    - **`-a`** – add
    - **`-e`** – set equal (requires source and target)
    - **`"/web(/.*)?"`** – wildcard a directory
- **`ausearch`** – query audit logs
    - **`-c`** – command name
    - **`-i`** – interpret numbers to names
    - **`-m`** – message type
    - **`-ts`** – time start
    - **`-ua`** – match username or User ID
- **`restorecon`** – restore SELinux context on a file/directory
    - **`-R`** – recurse
    - **`-v`** – verbose
- **`seinfo`** – setools-console package
    - **`-a`** – attribute (no space)
    - **`-x`** – print a list
- **`sealert`** – setroubleshoot-server package
- **`getsebool`** / **`setsebool`** – view/change selinux boolean
    - **`-P`** – persistent
- **`audit2allow`**
    - **`-o`** – output file
- **`semodule`** – manage SELinux policy modules
    - **`-i`** – install
    - **`-d`** – disable

Module 14: Logs
- `rsyslog.conf` severities
    - 0 `emerg`
    - 1 `alert`
    - 2 `crit`
    - 3 `err`
    - 4 `warning`
    - 5 `notice`.
    - 6 `info`
    - 7 `debug`
    - `.none`
- `logrotate.conf`
- `logger -p` – generate syslog message with priority
- `journalctl` – parse the `journald` logs
    - `-f` – follow
    - `-u` *unitname* – filter by unit
    - `-r` – reverse, show newest at the top
    - `-S` / `-U` – since / until, uses systemd.time specification
- `auditd` – configured with rules added to `/etc/audit/rules.d`
- `augenrules` – convert rules in `rules.d` to permanent config in `audit.rules`
- `service auditd` – control audit service: `start`, `stop`, `restart`, `state`
- `auditctl` – control / view running audit rules
    - `-l` – list rules
    - `-w` – watch
    - `-p` – permissions
    - `-k` – key field recorded in the log
    - `-a` – audit an event
    - `-F` – match a field
    - `-S` – systemcall
- `aureport` / `ausearch` – parse the audit logs
- `timedatectl` – manage clock time
    - `show` / `status`
    - `list-timezones`
    - `set-timezone`
    - `set-time "YYYY-MM-DD HH:MM:SS"`
    - `set-ntp true`
- `crony.conf` – ntp configuration, restart `chronyd.service`
- `chronyc` – control chronyd
    - `sources` / `source status` / `tracking` – check status
- `clockdiff` – compare time using ICMP
- `hwclock -w` – write software clock to hardware

Module 15: Installing Software

- `yum`
    - `repolist` – shows repos in `/etc/yum.repos.d/`
    - `repoquery`
    - `list installed`
    - `search`
    - `info`
    - `provides` – what package provides a binary
    - `clean all` – clear caches
    - `makecache`
    - `install`
    - `remove`
    - `update`
    - `group` commands – `info`, `list`, `install`, `remove`, `update`
    - `--install-root` – use a different directory as `/`
- `createrepo` – build repository metadata
- `subscription-manager` – used to register Red Hat installations
- `rpm`
    - `--import` – import GPG key
    - `-Va` – verify all
    - `-q` – query
        - `f` – file (shows parent package)
        - `c` – configuration files
        - `l` – list all installed by package
    - `-i` – install
    - `-U` – upgrade

Module 16: Kernel Modules and Parameters

- `lsmod` – list kernel modules
- `modinfo` – provide information about a module
- `modprobe` – add / remove modules from the kernel
    - reads files (options and blacklists) from `/etc/modprobe.d/`
    - `-l` – list
    - `-r` – remove
    - `-c` – show configuration
- `sysctl` – alter kernel parameters
    - `-a` – display all
    - `-w` – write active parameter
    - persistent settings in `sysctl.conf`
    - `--system` – read and apply setting from configuration files

Module 17: Backups
- `tar` – archiving
    - `-c` – create
    - `-z` – zip
    - `-p` – preserve permissions
    - `-t` – list contents of archive
    - `-v` – verbose
    - `-x` – extract
    - `-C` – change directory
    - `-d` – find differences between archive and filesystem
    - `-f` – archive filename follows, must be last
    - `--xattrs` – preserve both SELinux and acls attributes, use when creating and extracting
- `rsync` – remote syncronization
    - `-a` – archive, equivalent to `-rlptgoD`: recurse, copy links; save permissions, timestamps, group, and owner; also preserve Device and special files.
    - `-e` – use specified transport, such as `"ssh -i /path/key"`
    - `-X` – preserve extended attributes
    - `-A` – preserve ACLs
    - `-S` – squeeze sparse files (those with long zero blocks)
    - `-L` – turn links into files
    - `--delete` – remove files not at the source, default is to preserve them at the destination
    - `--remove-source-files` – delete source upon success, useful for temporary tarballs
    - `--include` / `--exclude` / `--filter` – allows detailed specification of files
- `dd if=`*infile* `of=`*outfile* – copy data
    - `conv=noerror` – ignore read errors
    - `bs=` – block size
    - `count=` – number
- `shred` – securely delete
- `rear mkbackup` – relax and recover

Module 18: Security
- `aide` – exclude active files in `aide.conf`
    - `-D` – check configuration
    - `-i` – create initial database
        - remove `.new` from the name
    - `-C` – compare (outputs to `/var/log/aide/aide.log`)
    - `-u` – update the database
- `oscap` – security scanning and compliance tool
- `ansible` – remote management and compliance tool
- `git` – stupid content tracker
    - `clone` – a repository to a local director

Labs

Lab resources are available at: https://github.com/janustechacademy/EL7

Lab 1: Initial Configuration

1. Log into your lab machine.
2. Using redirection (>, >>, |) create a file named `IP-info` which contains the output of the following commands: `ip a`, `ip route`, `ip neigh`.
3. From the contents of `IP-info` create a new file named `192-info`. It should only have lines containing the string `192`.
4. Examine the man pages for: `cp`, `mv`, `ln`, and `history`.
5. Create a file called `TZ-man` which contains a list of all the man pages relating to timezone. Did it work? If not, fix it.
6. Clear your history list by deleting all entries.
7. Copy `IP-info` to `IP-old`; rename `192-info` to `192-old`. Do this on one line.
8. Insert your history at the bottom of `192-old`.
9. Make a directory (`mkdir`) called `192-zzz`
    a. `cat 192-*` – this will return the contents of `192-old`, and an error message because cat can't read a directory.
        i. Create a file `err-192` that contains only the error from this command.
    b. Run the command again, displaying only the error.

Lab 2: Files and Directories

Finding Things

For the following exercises, unless otherwise specified, you may use any commands you choose to determine the answers. These might be helpful: `locate`, `whereis`, `which`, and `find`.

1. Find the location of the `cp` command.
2. Find the location of the man pages for the `mv` command.
3. Find all instances of a file called `findme.script`.
    a. How many did you find?
    b. How many instances of this script are in root's `$PATH`?
    c. Which instance of `findme.script` runs when root calls `findme.script` without a path?
4. Create a file in `/lab/02-Files/` called `mxyzptlk`. Use `locate` to locate it. Did it work? If not, fix it.

Finding Things with find

In this section, use the **find** command to answer the questions. Putting **2>/dev/null** after a query will suppress errors from the **/proc** file system.

5. The **/etc** directory contains directories and files that begin with **rc** and end with **.d**. Find only the directories.
6. Find any unowned files on your system.
7. Find any files with the SUID bit set which ARE ALSO writable by others.
8. Find any files which haven't been accessed in more than 20 years (they do exist!).
9. Use a single line command to locate and **optionally** remove the **/lab/02-Files/killme** directory and all its contents. Do be careful.
10. Find any file in **/boot** greater than 20 megabytes in size.

Manipulating Files and Directories

In this section, we will create, manipulate, and destroy files and directories. You may use any commands you like to achieve these goals.

11. Create a directory in **/lab/02-Files/** called **new**.
12. Change directories to **new**.
13. Create a file named **file1**. Put the phrase "this is file 1" inside of it.
14. Copy **file1** and call the copy **file3**.
15. Rename **file3** to **file2**.
16. Create an empty file called **file3**
17. Create a directory in **/lab/02-Files/new** called **subfiles**
18. Use a single command to copy all files in the **/lab/02-Files/new** directory into **subfiles**.
19. Move **file1** up one level using dot notation.
20. Without using **vi**, read **file1** and append its contents to **file3**.

Lab 3: vi

vi /lab/03-vi/edit-me, follow the directions in the file.

When complete you can check your work:
```
# diff edit-me edit-me.finished | grep "<"
```

Enterprise Linux versions 7 & 8

Lab 4: Users and Groups

1. Configure your computer such that users are created with:
   a. default password expiration of one month from now
   b. immediate inactivation on password expiration
   c. password aging fields and logon failure delay meets standards
   d. Do not set minimum password length or quality requirements at this point.
2. Enable **wheel** in **sudoers**.
3. Configure **/etc/pam.d/su** to restrict use of **su -** to members of **wheel**.
4. Create the following users as specified.
   Unless otherwise stated, all should have a primary group of their own.
   All users should have a password set.
   Usernames should be **all lower case**.
   a. Adam and Brenda – regular users
   b. Don and Emma – can use **sudo**, members of group **dev**.
   c. Frank – cannot login interactively, with a comment noting that fact.
   d. Grace – **UID = 3001**, member of **dev**, **helpdesk**, and **wheel**
   e. Harry – **UID = 3002**, member of **recruiting**,
      home directory **/lab/05-Permissions/recruiting**
   f. Jane and Mary – members of **recruiting** and **restricted-users**
   g. Nick – member of **helpdesk**.
5. Try to log in as Frank.
6. Change Brenda's shell to **vi**. Change to her environment.
   a. Attempt to read the date into a file – what caused the failure?
7. Check your work by viewing the relevant files in **/etc/**.

Lab 5: Ownership, Permissions, and Access

Preparation:
>Ensure that **grace** is a member of **helpdesk**, but NOT **recruiting**.
>Ensure that **harry** is a member of **recruiting**, but NOT **helpdesk**.

Setting Ownership and Basic Permissions

1. As root, create the following directories: `/lab/05-Permissions/recruiting`, `/lab/05-Permissions/helpdesk`
2. Assign ownership of **recruiting** to user **harry** and group **recruiting**.
3. Assign ownership of **helpdesk** to user **grace** and group **helpdesk**.
4. As **harry**, set the permissions of **recruiting** to **770**.
5. As **harry**, set the access mode of **recruiting** so that new files in that directory will automatically be owned by the **recruiting** group.
6. As **grace**, set the permissions of **helpdesk** to `rwxrwx---`.
7. As **grace**, set the access mode of **helpdesk** so that new files in that directory will automatically be owned to the **helpdesk** group.
8. As **grace**, attempt to access the **recruiting** directory. This should fail.
9. As **harry**, attempt to access the **helpdesk** directory. This should fail.

Extended ACLs – The order in which you do these tasks matters, as some ACL commands may overwrite previous entries. Review the exercise first, and plan your ACLs before applying them.

10. Create a file in **recruiting** called **rfile**. It should contain the line, "this is rfile."
11. Create a file in **helpdesk** called **hfile**. It should contain the line, "this is hfile."
12. Set an extended ACL on recruiting that will allow members of the **helpdesk** group to list the contents of the directory and read the files inside of it.
13. Grant full control of any files created in this directory to **grace**.
14. Others should have no access.
15. Set an extended ACL on helpdesk that will allow members of the **recruiting** group to list the contents of the directory and read the files inside of it.
16. Grant full control of any files created in this directory to **harry**.
17. Others should have no access.
18. Ensure that these ACLs are applied recursively to the existing files in the directories.

Testing SUID

19. Verify that all executables in `/lab/05-Permissions` are `SUID/SGID root:root`
20. `# su - adam`
21. `# cd /lab/05-Permissions`.
22. Run **who**, **id**, and **whoami**. Note the results.
23. Run those three commands once again, this time with a `./` preceding each.
24. Add `.` to the beginning of Adam's path. Run the commands one last time, this time without the leading `./`

Lab 6: Regular Expressions

You will find the files for this exercise in /lab/06-regex.

1. Copy something.com.zone to else.com.zone.
2. Copy something.named.conf to else.named.conf.
3. Take a moment to read over these two files and familiarize yourself with their contents.
4. Display any lines in else.com.zone which contain IP addresses.
5. Place the result in else.ip.
6. Display any lines in else.com.zone which contain hostnames.
7. Place the result in else.host.
8. Repeat these tasks for the else.named.conf file.
9. Append the results to else.ip and else.host.
10. Your network has been renumbered from 192.168.10.0/24 to 10.10.10.0/24.
    Use sed to make the appropriate changes IP addresses in the else.com.zone and else.named.conf files.
11. You have a new domain. Your old domain something.com is being replaced with else.com.
    Use awk to make the appropriate changes in both files.
    a. This includes both hostnames and filename references.
    b. DO NOT change any references to domains other than something.com.
    c. Do not alter any portion of a hostname OTHER THAN the something.com domain.

Take a moment to review your work. Compare the new files to the originals. Did you miss anything? Did you accidentally change anything you shouldn't have? If you did, resist the urge to hand correct this with vi. Try to use sed or awk to fix mistakes.

If you finished early, and need something to do, try this:

12. Copy /etc/passwd to /lab/06-regex/passfile
13. Use sed to remove all lines in passfile that start with a and save the file in place.
14. Use diff to compare passfile and /etc/password.
15. Display passfile, sorted alphabetically, saving a copy to alphapass in one line.
16. Display alphapass to your screen, but replace all the colons with linebreaks.
17. Repeat the last step, but eliminate duplicate lines.
18. Repeat the last step, but only show lines that start with a slash.

Lab 7: Booting

1. Make a copy of **/etc/default/grub**
    a. Alter the copy to:
    b. Have a timeout of 15
    c. Not hide the menu
    d. Have a new boot entry called Other which
        i. Displays all boot messages
        ii. Has SELinux disabled
2. When done have an instructor verify your changes.
3. Commit your changes to **grub.cfg**

Lab 8: Processes and Services

Preparation:

Open at least three connections to your server. You may even want more.

Run **top** in one session…you will want to keep **top** open throughout this lab.

All scripts are in **/lab/08-Processes**; alter permissions as needed.

Read through the instructions before executing any given step.

Verify who you are before running **memmy**. If run as **root**, it will break your box.

1. Pause top; open **vi**, and **man top** – in the same window.
2. Toggle between them using **jobs** and **fg**.

3. Run **chew**, this will execute **bc** (a calculator) – using quite a bit of cpu. Note its PID.
4. Using the signal passing function of **top**, pause and resume the **bc** process.
5. Background the **bc** process from the command line that originated it.
6. **disown** it and log out. Did it continue running?

7. Start **spread**, this will run the **bc** backgrounded at varying nicenesses.
8. Create a file with the PIDs of the **bc** process in it
9. Pause all of them except the nicest.
    a. If you get really stuck on this there are hints in **/lab/08-Process/killer**.
10. Resume the 5 least nice.
11. Clean up all the **bc** processes before proceeding.

Enterprise Linux versions 7 & 8

12. Start a **watch** for processes named sleep. In a separate window watch for processes belonging to Jane.
13. Run **nappy** as root, Jane, and Mary. This starts multiple **sleeps**.
14. Run **spread** as Jane.
15. What is different when Jane runs **spread**?
16. Kill all of Jane's **sleep** processes, without affecting any others.
17. Kill all of Mary's processes.
18. Clean up the **bc** and **sleep** processes before proceeding.

19. Using **limits.conf**, give Mary a hard limit of 1 minute cpu. Set hard limits on Nick for nproc = 5000, nice and priority =15.
20. As Mary, run **chew**. Observe what occurs when processor time hits 60 seconds.
21. As Nick, run **spread**. Notice the priorities.
22. As Nick run **forkbomb**.
    a. Make sure you don't do this as root!
23. Clean up all of Nick and Mary's processes.

24. Start a **vmstat -a -S M 5**. This will display memory information in MiB.
25. Run **swapoff -a**, watch the swap file drain. Confirm that swap was disabled using **# swapon --summary**.
26. In a new window prepare to issue **pkill grep**, do not press enter yet.
27. As Mary, run **memmy**.
28. Observe the change in memory usage.
29. As soon as Out of memory errors begin **pkill grep** .
30. Near the end of **/var/log/messages**, search for **oom-killer**.
    a. Read down from there.
31. Re-enable swap.
32. Run **memmy** again as Mary. Observe the differences.
33. Create a .slice for Grace, limiting memory usage to .5 G and CPU to 50%.
34. Run **memmy** and **chewy** as Grace. Observe the differences.
35. To ensure that no rogue processes are left over, **# reboot**.

Lab 9: File Systems

Throughout this lab, you will be making extensive changes to disk structures. Please remember to check your work and ensure that the kernel is aware of your changes. If it is not, provoke rescans of your SCSI bus using the methods supplied in the course manual.

Partitioning with `fdisk` or `parted`

1. You should have an empty hard drive attached to your system. Identify it.
2. On your free disk, create 3 partitions of 1 GB each.
3. Ensure that the partition table is updated to reflect your work.
4. File System creation and mounting
5. Put an `xfs` filesystem on your first empty partition.
6. Create a mountpoint called `/mount1`.
7. Mount the filesystem to `/mount1`.
8. Check it.
9. Unmount the filesystem
10. Configure `/etc/fstab` to automatically mount your new filesystem at boot or by mountpoint. Use default options.
11. Mount your new filesystem with: `# mount /mount1`.
12. Check your work.

LVM

13. Create a physical volume from your second partition.
14. Create a volume group containing only that physical volume.
15. Create a logical volume that uses 100 percent of the free space in that volume group.
16. Create an xfs filesystem on that logical volume.
17. Create a mount point `/mount2` and mount the filesystem to it.
18. Unmount it.
19. Create a `.mount` unit for this filesystem.
20. Mount it. Unmount it.
21. Create an `.automount` unit for this filesystem and enable it.
22. Enter the `/mount2` directory and check the status of your mount unit.
23. Pretend the filesystem is full. Use the 3rd free partition to extend the volume group, logical volume, and filesystem.

Hard Links

1. Create a file in `/lab/07-Filesystems/` named `original`, with content: "This is the original file."
2. Create a hard link to the file in the same directory. Call the link `copy`.
3. Get a list of inodes for all files in `/lab/07-Filesystems`. What are the inode numbers for original and copy? Record the inode of original.
4. Read the contents of `copy`. What does it say?
5. Add a line to copy that says, "edited from copy."
6. Read the contents of `original` to the screen. What does it say?
7. What is the link count for `original`? What is it for `copy`?
8. Delete `original`.

Enterprise Linux versions 7 & 8

9. What is the link count for **copy**?

Symbolic Links

10. Create a symbolic link to **copy** in the same directory. Call the link **original**.
11. What are the inodes of the files? What does a long listing tell you about **original**?
12. Move **original** to **/mount1/original**.
13. Add a line to **original** that reads, "edited from symbolic original".
14. Read **copy**. What does it say?
15. What is the link count for **copy**?
16. Delete **copy**. Attempt to read **/mount1/original**. What happened?
17. Create a file in **07-Filesystems** called **copy**.
18. Add a line to it that reads, "this is not the same file."
19. Attempt to read **/mount1/original**. What happened?
20. Delete **/mount1/original**.
21. Read **copy**. Did deleting **/mount1/original** have an effect on **/lab/copy**?
22. Make a hard link from **/lab/07-Filesystems/copy** to **/lab/07-Filesystems/original**.
23. Delete **/lab/07-Filesystems/copy**. What are the contents of **original**? What is the inode and link count? Does the inode for **original** match the one recorded earlier in this lab?

Lab 10 : Scheduling Events

All tasks for this lab are in **/lab/09-Events**

1. Schedule the following using **at**:
    a. **at.task1** five minutes from now
    b. **at.task2** a few minutes after midnight tonight
    c. **at.task3** an hour from now and Friday afternoon
    d. **at.task4** next Tuesday at 11 am
2. View the jobs.
3. Remove the job which would run **at.task3** Friday afternoon.
4. Schedule the following with **cron**:
    a. **cron.job1** weekly beginning ten minutes from now
    b. **cron.job2** at 2130 on odd numbered dates during the week
5. Schedule these with systemd timers
    a. **cron.job3** at 15 minutes after boot, and every twelve hours after that
    b. **cron.job4** at 1130 on weekdays
6. Use **anacron** and a symbolic link to run **cron.job5** weekly
7. Lower the **batch** threshold to 0.01
8. Run **chewy** from the previous lab
9. **batch** a job that will wall "Done with this lab!"
10. End the **bc** processes started by **chewy**

Lab 11: Networking

Configure and test static networking

1. Confirm that the NetworkManager service is uninstalled.
2. Configure your hostnames and IP addresses to match your student sheet.
3. Ping the another student's machines by FQDN and by single name.

Use network tools

4. Find the name server (NS) and mail exchanger (MX) names and addresses for redhat.com, and doe.gov.
5. Using `ss`, start a `watch` on all tcp ports.
   a. ssh to localhost, then ping yourself. Notice the difference in results.
6. Run `ss` by itself (without `watch`), modifying the results to exclude listening ports and connections from `::1`, and include process information.

Configure the firewall

7. Create an at job to disable the firewall 20 minutes from now. If you haven't locked yourself out, remove and renew the job every now and then. If you do lock yourself out, it will let you back in when it runs.
   Note: the most common method of locking yourself out is by creating a default DROP with no other rules configured.
8. Configure your default zone to have a policy of DROP.
9. Allow `https` on TCP port 443 inbound from anywhere, for NEW, ESTABLISHED, and RELATED connections.
10. Block `http` on TCP port 80 inbound from anywhere.
11. Restrict `ssh` access to an appropriate network.
12. Test these rules using `nmap` from your other machine.

Lab 12: Remote Access

1. Secure `sshd`, provide a login banner.
2. Work with one of your neighbors to `ssh` without password as Grace and as root from one machine to the other.
3. Use `scp` to copy the a file you generated earlier to /labs/16-Remote on your neighbors machine.
4. Restrict Adam to `sftp` only.
5. Create a chrooted sftp home directory for him.
6. Move a copy of your local `/etc/hosts` to Adam's home directory on your neighbor's machine.
7. Create a file showing all nonroot logins which have occurred on your computer called `nonroot.txt`. Make it available via `http`.
8. Get a copy of your classmate's `nonroot.txt`, without using a graphical browser.

Lab 13: SELinux

We'll be working with Apache and SELinux in this lab. The httpd daemon should already be installed, and the configuration files on your machines should already be altered to allow the labs to function as written. You should only need to make changes of an SELinux nature to accomplish the stated goals.

1. Ensure **httpd** is not running, and that the firewall is off.
2. Change to the **/etc/httpd/conf** directory and copy **httpd.back** to **httpd.conf**.
3. Create a directory, **/web** with permissions of **755**
4. In **/web** create **index.html**, with permissions of **744** and content "Successfully viewed the file in /web."
5. Start **httpd**.
6. Attempt to access this address: **http://*server-name*/**
7. What happened? Did you get the results you were expecting?
8. Place SELinux into Permissive Mode. Try again. Did the issue resolve?
9. Examine log files related to this issue.
10. Correct the issue
11. Turn your firewall back on, shut down **httpd**, and check that SELinux is enforcing.

There are no labs for Modules 14 & 15.

Lab 16: Kernel Modules and Parameters

1. In your terminal, display a list of currently loaded kernel modules.
2. Locate **bnx2fc**.
3. Display more detailed information about **bnx2fc**. What does the description tell you about it? Does it have any associated parameters?
4. What is the default value of **bnx2fc**'s debug_logging parameter? Is that the currently loaded value? Verify this.
5. Attempt to alter the **debug_logging** parameter of **bnx2fc** to **0x01** without unloading the module first. Did this succeed? Why or why not?
6. Are there any other modules that depend on **bnx2fc**?

Loading and Unloading Kernel Modules

7. Unload **bnx2fc**. Did any other modules unload with it? Why or why not?
8. Attempt to load **bnx2fc** with the **debug_logging** set to **0x01**. Did this succeed?
9. Unload the module again.
10. Configure **bnx2fc** to load with a **debug_logging** value of **0x02** when next loaded.
11. Load it. Did the changes take? Why or why not?

Blacklisting Modules

1. Unload **bnx2fc**.
2. Blacklist the module. Ensure that this module will not be loaded either manually or automatically.
3. Test it.

Lab 17: Backups

1. Create compressed archives of **/lab** called **lab.tar** and **/etc** called **etc.tar**, preserving all attributes
2. Restore the **lab.tar** to a new directory **/new-labs/**
3. Create an archive of all files changed in **/etc** and **/lab** in the last two days. Place it in **/lab/18-disaster/**.
4. Delete **/lab/03-vi/editme.finished**
5. Add a file **/lab/03-vi/editme.added**
6. Compare the **lab.tar** with the current filesystem using **tar**.
7. **rsync** all **.conf** files from **/etc/** to **/new-labs/saved-confs** on your neighbor's machine.
8. Delete **/etc/sane.d/** on your machine.
9. Add a comment to **/etc/asound.conf**
10. Restore **sane.d** without overwriting your changes to **asound.conf**

Lab 18: Security

1. Install and configure **aide**.
2. Write a script to be run daily which archives the results of aide on a neighbor's machine.
3. Audit your installed software and services. Write a series of removal recommendations in **/lab/19-Security/software-cleanup**.
    a. Don't forget to check dependencies, don't remove things that would break functionality.
    b. Outline further steps you would take to secure this machine.
    c. Be prepared to justify your results

Lab 20 – Final

You have just inherited a new computer. It has been severely misconfigured, and may have been compromised.

Your new box is currently only reachable by telnet, and is drawing a DHCP address. Your instructor will provide you its current address, as well as the static addresses and hostname that it should be given.

Current logins are `student` and `root`, both with password `ujm<KI*(98`

The `student` account can use `sudo`, `root` is currently locked out.

You will have the use of one of the computers you used during the class, access to the Internet, the course materials, and any notes you have made during the course.

You must secure the computer. You will be given a subset of the STIG as the standard for security.

Some features and functionalities must also be added.

All security and functionality should work without intervention after a reboot.

It is recommended that you review all tasks and the Security Standards before beginning.

1. Configure your IP addresses, DNS, and hostname.
2. Establish secure communication with your box, and remove telnet.
    a. Secure ssh appropriately.
    b. Restrict ssh to your local network.
    c. Create a login banner saying:
       "I've read & consent to terms in IS user agreement."
3. Enable the web management interface.

4. The boot sequence should be protected from unauthorized meddling.
    a. set the boot password to `BootMe`
    b. The kernel command line should ensure that fips is on, auditing begins appropriately, and SELinux is enforcing.

5. The firewall and SELinux must run automatically.
    a. The firewall should silently drop packets without responding.
    b. SELinux must be enforcing.

6. Create two partitions of approximately 400 MB each on the second drive.
    a. One of these partitions should be used as the base directory for web services.
    b. This file system should
        i. be mounted at `/new-web`
        ii. be labeled `web`
        iii. be mounted by label rather than device name.
    c. Create an index.html with the output of hostnamectl and your ip address information.
        i. index.html should only be viewable from your subnet.

7. Create these users:
    a. Kate – member of group `staff` and `developers`
    b. Mike – member of group `developers`, account expires at the end of the year
    c. Nick – member of `developers` and `helpdesk`, UID = 4001
    d. Paul – UID = 4002, shell = `vim`
8. Dave has been terminated. His account should be dealt with.

9. In the second new partition create a shared directory `/code` for the developers.
    a. Allow all members of developers, except Nick, read/write access to code.
    b. Nick should have read access only.
    c. Users should not be able to delete files owned by another user.
    d. Any new files or directories created in code should
        i. be owned by the creator and by the developer group
    e. have appropriate permissions

10. Allow only Kate and Mike the ability to use sudo.
11. Configure bidirectional key-based login between your class computer to your new box for Kate.

12. Create a new 200 MB swap file on the second hard drive using a logical volume. Add it permanently to the current swap space.

13. Configure `aide` to run every day at 11 PM.
    Limit it to no more than one-half of a core of CPU and 250 Megabytes of RAM.

14. Configure `yum` to remove all metadata and caches, and create a new cache weekly.
    a. If the computer is powered off, the task must run when it is next powered on.

15. The system must be no more than 30 days out of date.
    a. If a new kernel is available, it should be installed as the default
    b. Two old kernels must remain available and bootable

16. Set the timezone and configure `ntp` to use an NIST server or another server as directed.

17. Configure your new machine to send log files to your class machine.

18. Configure auditing to STIG standards.
19. Disable ping to your machine.

20. Configure the kernel parameters appropriate to secure networking.

21. Verify that only root has user id `0`

22. Disable CTL-ALT-DEL

23. Configure the machine to default to multi-user, not graphical mode.

24. Find and remove any unowned files.

25. Remove the `abrt` package.

26. Create a daily task which will archive all local configuration files to `/backup` on your class machine. It should run as a non-root user, with no interaction.

Made in the USA
Monee, IL
26 December 2020